500 Year Journey

Corey Piper's book *500 Year Journey* is seriously phenomenal. It blew me away. I loved it from beginning to end. Don't miss out! Get it, learn, and enjoy how God worked in history to bring his Son into our world in human flesh.

—**Scott Putnam,** president and CEO of Apex Technology Management

With a youthful love of adventure and an historian's eye for examination and detail, Corey Piper in his new book *500 Year Journey* takes us on a fascinating trek from Daniel to Jesus and makes a compelling case for the exact day and year of the birth of the Messiah. And it's not in December! More than anything, his care and affection for the Savior and that you understand why this matters shines like the Star of Bethlehem itself. Piper has given me reason to return to his volume time and again.

—**Douglas Van Dorn,** MDiv, pastor, podcaster, and author of many books, including *The Angel of the LORD: A Biblical, Historical, and Theological Study*

Corey Piper's topic in *500 Year Journey* is the chronological complexity of determining the date of Jesus's birth—not just the calendar date, but the year in which he was born. His anchors are the timelines for the reigns of Caesar Augustus and Herod the Great. When, during the reigns of those two most important political leaders, was Jesus born? I won't give away the ending to the story, but I invite you to read the fascinating paths that Corey has pursued to arrive confidently at an answer to the historical problem. There is extensive research here and clear analysis as to what it all means and how the pieces fit together. As a historian myself, I've been surprised by the intricate and conflicting nature of the ancient sources. Some are trustworthy, and some clearly made mistakes. Corey explains in simple layman's terms how to evaluate the sources and arrive at a careful conclusion. I recommend his book for anyone who has wondered about the dates of Jesus's birth. It is more than an academic problem. And the solution shows God's providential care and careful ordering of all the details of the Incarnation. Corey Piper has done an admirable job, and the results will be of great service to the church and all followers of Jesus of Nazareth, the prophesied Messiah who fulfilled what the prophets had predicted.

—**Rob Shearer,** author, historian, teacher, and the director at the Francis Schaeffer Study Center

Was December 25 the actual day that Jesus was born? Does it even really matter if we know the exact date? Corey Piper is a historian and cares deeply about the details. In *500 Year Journey* he writes with passion and clarity on when he believes the Messiah was born and why it should matter to us. When you complete *500 Year Journey*, you will have a greater appreciation and more complete view of the Christmas story.

—**Nick Martineau,** pastor of Hope Community Church, Wichita, KS

For some, tackling the precise date of the birth of Christ would seem a quest only fools dare tread. Yet, Piper has no interest in a fool's errand. Through a stunning blend of scholarly rigor, theological reflection, and typological themes, *500 Year Journey* takes us on an expedition half a millennium in the making. Some may be unconvinced of Piper's conclusions, but he has constructed the most detailed and plausible solution to date. A thought-provoking contribution for the convinced and critics alike.

—**Matt Boswell,** lead pastor of Redemption Church, Duvall, Washington

In his new book *500 Year Journey*, Corey Piper takes us on his personal journey of discovery through the labyrinth of theories, traditions, and claims about the birth of Jesus Christ as he unravels the Gordian knot surrounding when Jesus was actually born. In the process, he shows us the political intrigue and religious shock that his birth brought about. God incarnate coming to us as a helpless infant in humble surroundings. The historical realities are far richer and dramatic than the diluted and inaccurate nativity scenes that come to us at Christmas. Even the heavens danced at Christ's birth—just one of the most fascinating and awe-inspiring truths that Piper found. This will be a book you will return to often.

—**Matthew A. Boardwell,** pastor, church planter, and missionary
with WorldVenture; also writer of three Bible study guides
(Galatians, Joshua, and Judges/Ruth)

My friend Corey Piper has written a book that beckons the reader to keep turning the pages. Twenty centuries of theologians and Bible scholars have researched the details surrounding the Incarnation of Jesus Christ, including the actual date of his birth. While many books have been written, Corey has added his *500 Year Journey* to the mix. His book displays impeccable research on the subject, and I believe it deserves an honest evaluation. You will find that *500 Year Journey* is written with careful thought given to Christian doctrine and history, and that it is written with passionate purpose. Follow Corey on his journey to find the truth about Jesus's amazing birth.

—**Ray Pew,** retired Bible teacher at Central Christian Academy, Wichita, Kansas; graduate of Trinity Seminary, Newburg, Indiana

How the Magi Knew When Christ Would Be Born

500 YEAR JOURNEY

From Babylon to Bethlehem

COREY PIPER

NASHVILLE

NEW YORK • LONDON • MELBOURNE • VANCOUVER

500 Year Journey
From Babylon to Bethlehem

How the Magi Knew When Christ Would be Born

© 2024 Corey Piper

Published in New York, New York, by Morgan James Publishing. Morgan James is a trademark of Morgan James, LLC. www.MorganJamesPublishing.com

Proudly distributed by Publishers Group West®

Unless indicated otherwise, all Scripture quotations are taken from the New King James Version®, copyright © 1982 by Thomas Nelson. Used by permission. All rights reserved. Scripture quotations marked NLT are taken from the Holy Bible, New Living Translation, copyright © 1996, 2004, 2015 by Tyndale House Foundation. Used by permission of Tyndale House Publishers, a Division of Tyndale House Ministries, Carol Stream, Illinois 60188. All rights reserved. Scripture quotations marked NASB are taken from the New American Standard Bible® (NASB), Copyright © 1960, 1962, 1963, 1968, 1971, 1972, 1973, 1975, 1977, 1995, 2020 by The Lockman Foundation. Used by permission. www.Lockman.org. Scripture quotations marked KJV are taken from the King James Version, public domain.

All emphases in Scripture quotations have been added by the author.

A **FREE** ebook edition is available for you or a friend with the purchase of this print book.

CLEARLY SIGN YOUR NAME ABOVE

Instructions to claim your free ebook edition:
1. Visit MorganJamesBOGO.com
2. Sign your name CLEARLY in the space above
3. Complete the form and submit a photo of this entire page
4. You or your friend can download the ebook to your preferred device

ISBN 9781636980447 paperback
ISBN 9781636980454 ebook
Library of Congress Control Number:
2022945077

Cover & Interior Design by:
Christopher Kirk
www.GFSstudio.com

Morgan James is a proud partner of Habitat for Humanity Peninsula and Greater Williamsburg. Partners in building since 2006.

Get involved today! Visit: www.morgan-james-publishing.com/giving-back

To my uncle Art, the wisest man I have ever known, and my aunt Bonnie, whose compassion and love for the Savior never fails.

Their lives are the shining light that led me to the manger.

Contents

Illustrations

Drawing

Earthly Maps

Genealogy Charts

Photographs

Star Maps

Tables

Timelines

Foreword

Like most people, I grew up thinking that December 25 was Christmas, and Christmas was a holiday that celebrated Jesus's birthday. In other words, sometime in the past, Jesus was born on December 25.

But in what year? No one ever said, at least not to me. And that didn't seem important to anyone. After all, what mattered most was that Jesus was God's Son become a man. And this happened in a faraway land now known as Israel.

I knew about some of the details surrounding Jesus's birth because my parents had me read either Matthew's or Luke's account of it in the days leading up to Christmas. My mom and dad were Christians, and they wanted their children to know that Christmas was much more than presents, lighted trees, tasty desserts, and fine meals. Christmas was sacred, even though it had been secularized.

But when I read the Gospel accounts of Jesus's earthly beginning, I did not find a birth date. I read about a census, a Caesar, a king, a governor, a journey, a virgin, a husband-to-be, some shepherds and angels, and some strange folk called magi—however, I never ran across a birth date. *Oh well*, I thought, *other people must have figured this out and the whole world celebrates December 25 as Jesus's birthday, so it must be right.*

Then, a few years after becoming a Christian, I decided to do graduate work in seminary. I chose Dallas Theological Seminary. One of my professors in the New

Testament was a man named Harold Hoehner. He was funny, bright, demanding, and well-versed in biblical studies, including in the subject of chronology. When it came to the life of Jesus, he said, matter-of-factly, that Jesus was *not* born on December 25, and the year was not AD 1. Well, that was the first time I had heard anyone mention a year, but not born on December 25? Really? Why didn't anyone else seem to know that? As it turned out, what Hoehner said was common knowledge among Bible scholars. They did not think that December 25 marked Jesus's birthday, nor did they think that AD 1 was his birth year.

Then what was the right date? That's where the matter became incredibly complicated. As I soon learned, different ancient peoples had different ways of reckoning time. The Egyptian calendar differed from the Persian one. The Jewish calendar was different from the Roman one. Some peoples had years of 360 days, others 354 days, and the Romans under Julius Caesar went to a 15-month year of 445 days. Later this approach was changed to a year of 365.25 days, which was later changed to a 365-day year.[1] How, then, could anyone figure out when exactly Jesus was born with so many different ways to approach time?

As it turns out, Dr. Hoehner was one scholar who did the work, and he put his reasoning and conclusion in his book *Chronological Aspects of the Life of Christ*. According to Hoehner, Jesus was born in the winter of 4 or 5 BC, probably in December or January. Hoehner could not be more precise than that.[2]

To me, that sounded as if December 25 was at least in the ballpark, even somewhere close to the pitcher's mound, assuming you picture that as just one step from the target base, that of hitter. That was good enough for me. And it was a date I worked with for years. Still, I wondered if someone could show even greater precision than this.

On occasion, I ventured into the confusing chronologies of the ancient world to see what I could discover, confirm, or disconfirm, and I grew to have greater confidence in my abilities but still not enough information and clarity to come to a better conclusion than Hoehner had. Along the way, though, I solved other chronological problems. And when it came to Jesus's birthday, I settled for the amazing truths I discovered about the drama that led up to and surrounded his birth. Suffice it to say that most of the nativity stories told at

Christmas time to young children and even adults were trite in comparison to what ancient historical accounts recorded.

Then, Corey Piper, a long-time friend, fellow lover of history, and former coworker, told me about research he had been doing on the birthday of Jesus. He told me about his exegetical work in Scripture, his studies in Josephus, his astronomical research, and a host of other sources he had consulted. He also said that he believed he would soon be able to pinpoint Jesus's actual birthday. I was stunned and still a bit skeptical, and I encouraged him to keep up his pursuit, which he did. The result of his painstaking, dedicated labor is now sitting in your hands. What Corey has done is blazed new ground by paying closer attention to the ancient trail left for us in Scripture and outside of it, even as far above us as the movement of the heavens.

I will not reveal the conclusion he has reached about the day, month, and year of Jesus's birth. He will tell you that in good time. In *500 Year Journey*, he shares his personal trek of discovery—a journey that took him through ancient cultures and histories as well as calendars strange to most of us. It also led him to ancient corrupt government officials, well-intentioned Christians who made poor judgments, prophets and prophecies, as well as stargazers informed by a man of God. Overall, what comes through most, at least to me, is the sovereignty of God over human history and nature. The Lord of all gave human beings enough revelation and insight to know when the Messiah would arrive and where. But they had to pay attention, and for a very long time. Those who did were rewarded with witnessing perhaps the greatest miracle of all—the arrival of God's Son in human flesh.

Take the journey with my friend. Relive what Mary, Joseph, the shepherds, and the magi experienced—not the trite stories often told at Christmas but the politically and religiously charged and dramatic events that led to and surrounded Jesus's actual entrance into human history as one of us. You will be amazed, and you may, as I did, lift up your voice in praise of the God who "so loved the world, that He gave His only Son" (John 3:16 NASB).

William D. Watkins
Theologian, philosopher, apologist, writer, and editor

Trials of the Trail

I admit that it would be wrong to dismiss offhand a claim that has been consistently held by so many people; by doing such a thing I risk letting my love of saying something new distort all my conclusions. But because it seems to me that reason itself argues against the accepted opinion, the truth ought to carry more weight than the authority of a scholar.
—*Petrus Cunaeus (1586–1638)*

I stood on the rim of the Grand Canyon at the South Kaibab trailhead, and I had no idea what kind of agony I was about to encounter. I was well prepared and young and an experienced outdoorsman, so I thought I knew what I was getting myself into. But this would be a whole new level of agony. I had hunted in eastern Oregon with my family, and I had hiked across the Olympic National Park in the state of Washington. I was also a landscaper for a company in Sedona, Arizona. But after carrying a sixty-pound pack nine miles down the Grand Canyon to the river and then six more miles to Cottonwood camp, the final gentle rise seemed like Mt. Everest.

I learned a valuable lesson that day: until the Canyon has kicked you in the teeth, made you bleed, and broken your knees, you haven't experienced it. The Canyon is one thing to view from the rim; it's another to view it while crawling in the dirt. And it's altogether another thing to get up the next morning and hike out of the Canyon.

That is what it has been like writing this book. I started this journey optimistically. I stood on the rim and I thought I would document what others had discovered about the birth of Christ and come to a consensus conclusion. I knew there were some disagreements among scholars on when Christ was born, but I felt I could sort out the issues and bring them to a defining point of clarity and certainty. What I soon discovered, however, was how controversial every step along the trail would be, how utterly divergent many opinions were. Some scholars thought they had figured out when Jesus was born, but they were proven wrong by others, and then the others were proven wrong, and on and on my journey went. The trail was winding with multiple switchbacks and numerous ups and downs. I found that I wasn't even close to prepared for how much effort would be involved in sorting through all the controversies. Every idea, every theory, and every conclusion has been a hard-fought battle. While I have strived to smooth out the trail in places, it's still a challenging hike in places.

So let's be real. This is definitely not your typical Christmas book that seeks to give you warm fuzzies. Everything—I mean everything—you have heard about when Christ was born is going to be on trial, but please don't blame that on me. It is the nature of the Canyon, and it has been this way for millennia. We will have to look out for rattlesnakes, fend off dehydration, descend rockslides, and walk along trails at the edge of a cliff where one wrong twitch could plunge us a thousand feet down into the river. This trail is going to be difficult and backbreaking. And I am asking you to join me. Willingly. The Canyon is a commitment from start to finish.

But the journey will be fun and rewarding too. And it will end with what I believe is the actual birth date of Jesus Christ, and it is *not* December 25. And the year is *not* AD 1.

My backbreaking first hike in the majestic Grand Canyon also taught me another lesson: the hardest journey is the most meaningful one. I have known people who visited the Canyon once and weren't all that impressed with it. They had heard all of these marvelous things about it, but when they finally got there, looked over a railing, and saw the expansive views, they said, "Eh. No big deal. I don't know what all the fuss is about. It's just a big hole in the ground." They then got back in their car and drove away. Their problem was that they never truly experienced the Canyon. A casual tourist will never appreciate the joy of taking a nap on the green moss next to Ribbon Falls Cove, exhausted. Or the wonder of seeing a lizard swallow another lizard. They will never know the refreshing relief of removing their pack and dousing their head with cool water from a creek in 120-degree weather, or the sense of accomplishment when looking back down Devil's Corkscrew and saying, "I just did that." Nor will they ever know the long-term pleasure of having crawled into a campsite on their knees. There are rewards that only pain can bring, and I wish people knew that the Canyon is more than a nice view—and that the birth of Christ is more than a mere date on a calendar.

It is so much more.

I wish I could make this journey easy for you and guide you to the Magical Conclusion Overlook where you would be able to see the truth from the safety of your car. But even if that were possible, that would never replace the experience of loading up your pack, lacing up your hiking boots, and experiencing the Canyon with me. So I ask you to join me on this journey to untangle the mess that has been made of one of the most transformative events in human history: the birth of Jesus Christ, the Son of the living God.

But before we begin—consider it getting your pack ready—I need to explain my unique approach to finding Jesus's birth date. I used to think that I had to figure out what the magi had discovered in their astrological studies in order to solve the riddle. If I could find the beckoning star, I could find the right date. But that turned out to be more elusive than the proverbial needle in a haystack. It seems as if there are as many different theories about what the magi saw as there are stars in the heavens! The magi certainly saw something that convinced them that the King of the Jews had been born, but what exactly did they see?

After years of effort, it finally dawned on me that my whole approach was backwards: instead of looking at the stars first, I needed to solve the historical, chronological puzzle first and *then* look at the stars. Once I could confidently locate Christ's birth in history—if that were even possible—I could then look at the stars and see if there was anything interesting enough going on up there that would have caused the magi to rejoice. And there is! In fact, it is so incredible that the traditional nativity scene will become like looking at a child's toy in comparison. A mere conjunction is so boring. The truth is more elaborate and interesting than the medieval Orloj astronomical clock in Prague, Czechoslovakia.[3] It is beyond magnificent!

What I came to realize is that the date of Christ's birth can only fit during one moment in history, and it did not fit there accidentally. God intended it to fit. He designed the whole thing. He synchronized world events with the vast clock of the universe, all in order to announce the arrival of his Son. It's more than a date; it's a miracle!

Our journey together will traverse over 500 years of history, and it will span the distance between Babylon and Bethlehem. We will explore the ancient world, Old Testament prophecies, and the movements of the stars. And all of this exploration will focus on answering one central question: When was Jesus of Nazareth actually born? The Western church settled on December 25, but why did they choose that date? And if wrong, can we ever know when the Son of God entered into the womb of Mary and then came out into the world as a living, breathing, kicking, crying human infant?

You may also be wondering, "Why does Jesus's birth date matter?" Does it change anything? It seems like a rather boring topic. Oh ye who merely glances over the edge of the Grand Canyon and says, "Eh." I wish I could say something practical like "It will cure your marriage ills" or "It will provide you with ten steps to becoming a successful leader," but all I can encourage you to do is join me on the journey, get to end of the book, and see what happens to your soul. You might "rejoice with exceeding great joy" like the magi did, and one cannot underestimate the power of awe. A wise rabbi once said:

> *Awe is more than an emotion; it is a way of understanding, an insight into a meaning greater than ourselves. The beginning of awe is wonder, and the beginning of wisdom is awe. Awe is an intuition for the dignity of all things, a realization that things not only are what*

they are, but also stand . . . for something supreme. Awe . . . enables
us to perceive in the world intimations of the divine, to sense in small
things the beginning of infinite significance.[4]

The date of Christ's birth matters, but you may not appreciate why unless we hike this journey together. Sometimes awe will only come after experiencing the trials of the trail, so let me be your guide to one of the most amazing moments in world history.

To arrive at our destination, though, we need to first map out our path. We will begin by revisiting the key events surrounding the birth of Christ and reacquaint ourselves with the key characters and hear their stories anew. You might be surprised by how many assumptions we accept as absolute truth, so we dare not take for granted that what we have heard and read or watched on screen or on stage are accurate. And this fresh perspective will be our compass through the many twists and turns of the trail that will lead us to the amazing historical context of the greatest event to ever occur since the creation of the world.

So lace up your boots, cinch up your pack, and let's get going on this 500-year journey!

STAGE I

Laying Out the Plan

1

A New Hope

Inasmuch as many have taken in hand to set in order a narrative of those things
which have been fulfilled among us, just as those who from the beginning
were eyewitnesses and ministers of the word delivered them to us, it seemed
good to me also, having had perfect understanding of all things from the
very first, to write to you an orderly account, most excellent Theophilus,
that you may know the certainty of those things in which you were instructed.
—Luke 1:1–4

Imagine hearing the gospel for the first time. Imagine a world where the news that a man who had been crucified on a cross by the Romans as a criminal had risen from the dead, proving that he was the Son of God. The stories further claim that he could cure the decadent, immoral, violent nature of self-centered humanity, and—most unlikely of all—he would return one day to judge the world in righteousness.

That is quite the message! Kind of unbelievable, especially considering it was referring to an unknown Jew from a backwater province of the ancient empire of Rome. And yet there seemed to be something to it because these followers of the Way, as it was called, were being transformed. They were forsaking the gods, refusing to participate in pagan temple worship, rejecting sexual immorality of any kind, and forming communities where they would help each other out by giving each other money and food in times of famine and need. And they did all of this *voluntarily*! As strange as the message may have seemed—a guy rising bodily from the dead—the people who believed it appeared to be changing. They became more compassionate, hardworking, content, and peaceful. They weren't angrily organizing riots; they were quietly organizing prayer groups in homes and worshiping the risen Messiah. And they couldn't get enough of those stories.

As with most movements, people want to learn about the central leader's origin story. They want to know where he was born, and what he was like as a kid. Who had been his friends? What did his parents think of him? Also, anyone who had met him became the coolest kid on the block. I still brag about the time my mom shook the hand of the famous actor John Wayne (she said his hand felt like rough leather) because even though I wasn't there, I somehow feel connected to the Duke. I can feel those rough, strong hands just from my mom's description. When my dad was a young boy, he met Helen Keller—a blind, deaf, and mute diplomat, writer, and speaker. He told of the time when Keller had felt his face, which he remembered for the rest of his life. His story about this incident has led me to imagine what it would have been like to feel her fingers going over my own face. I personally have met Roy Rogers and Dale Evans, and now whenever I watch one of their movies, I feel like they are old friends.

Now imagine having been healed by Jesus back in the first century. You didn't just hear him teach or catch a glimpse of him as you stood on your toes at the edge of a crowd. You were touched by him and your malady was taken away. You became whole. You would be in the upper stratosphere of awesomeness in the early church. You would tell your story and that story would spread like wildfire.

Sadly, though, considering the weakness of human nature, some people might get jealous and would want a little of that popular attention directed toward themselves. Maybe, just maybe, such a person might take one of the stories they had heard someone else tell and make it their own or even make up one altogether. Many people would automatically believe you because, after all, who would lie about an encounter with Jesus?

My in-laws once met a woman who claimed she was a Holocaust survivor. She had written a book, and we went to one of her book signings. We were all so impressed with her that she even came to our house, and we sat around and visited with her. We were awestruck that we were talking with a Holocaust survivor in our home! Sometime later, a police officer became skeptical of her story and discovered that she had literally made up everything about her life. She was a complete fraud and had to flee the state in order to escape being arrested. What used to be a wonderful memory became a gross feeling of embarrassment. How gullible we had been! She had manipulated us. How could anyone lie about being a Holocaust survivor? We found that disgusting.

Likewise, human nature being what it is, the ancient physician and Gospel writer Luke knew he had to document and confirm the truth about Jesus because various inaccuracies and even lies were spreading. Indeed, the apostle Paul had to make a point of signing his letters with his own hand so his readers could distinguish his real letters from the false ones in circulation (2 Thessalonians 3:17). Some people were misrepresenting what Paul taught in order to increase their own fame. So it is reasonable to believe that the spread of false stories about encounters with Christ and what the gospel meant were just as much a part of early Christian culture as false views of Christ have been throughout history. People today try to misrepresent who Christians are and what we believe, and some will even pretend to be one of us in order to spread doubt, discord, and dissension. They are wolves in sheep's clothing, and it would be naive for us to think that there weren't those kinds of people around at the time of the early church.

The way some people talk about that time period, they make it sound like Christian culture was pure, flawless, bold, and purely altruistic, filled with the wonder and newness of the resurrection and with everybody getting along splendidly. But that is not how it was at all. Yes, there were moments of great unity and blessedness at the very beginning of the church, but all it takes is a cursory reading of the New Testament to realize that much of the early church was facing huge doctrinal and ethical challenges within just a few years. There were degrees of healthiness, of course. But there's ample evidence that the church in Corinth, for example, was anything but healthy. Paul even wrote the church and said, "It is actually reported that there is sexual immorality among you, and such sexual immorality as is not even named among the Gentiles—that a man has his father's wife!" (1 Corinthians 5:1). There's nothing good about that. It is easy to prove that Paul and the other New Testament writers wrote their letters *because* they saw problems and strove to solve them. Yes, their letters affirmed and praised the healthy and godly aspect of many churches, but this was as much to encourage them to stay faithful to the true gospel as it was to guide them away from falling into error. The apostles were painfully aware that the early church faced spiritual dangers, and this is why, I believe, Luke wants to write "an orderly account" to Theophilus of Jesus's life. He wants to document and confirm the real stories in order to distinguish them from the increasing number of lies and errors that were being spread among the churches.

Luke was uniquely qualified as a Greek doctor and traveling companion of Paul (Colossians 4:14) to carefully record exactly what happened and to build a rock-solid foundation of truth. The church's apostolic leaders wanted the truth told, not errors and myths. As the apostle Peter wrote: "For we did not follow cunningly devised fables when we made known to you the power and coming of our Lord Jesus Christ, but were eyewitnesses of His majesty" (2 Peter 1:16). And the apostle John said:

> *That which was from the beginning, which we have heard, which we have seen with our eyes, which we have looked upon, and our hands have handled, concerning the Word of life—the life was manifested, and we have seen, and bear witness, and declare to you that eternal life which was with the Father and was manifested to us. (1 John 1:1–2)*

Christianity is not founded on esoteric philosophies or mystical visions of the divine, but on the real life, tough, gritty, leathery, unidealized truth.

Jesus walked in the dust and the grime of our world. He was blasted with the wind, chilled by the cold, and scorched by the heat just as much as we are. And he was dragged through the blood, gore, and hardships of human experience. He suffered as one of us because he became one of us.

Luke was taking on a daunting task, for even during the life of Jesus people misunderstood exactly who he was. In Luke 9:18–19, Jesus took a poll of his disciples, asking them, "Who do the crowds say that I am?" They answered, "John the Baptist, but some say Elijah; and others say that one of the old prophets has risen again." In other words, people didn't fully understand who they were dealing with even while Jesus was among them doing miracles and teaching parables. People didn't "get" him. That is why Luke had to go beyond mere public opinion and give us firsthand accounts of the people who had seen, heard, touched, and personally interacted with the Messiah while their stories could be corroborated. He wanted to convince Theophilus—and by extension, the rest of us—that Jesus had performed the miracles claimed of him and that he was God in the flesh.

Luke also had the advantage of having an insider's connection to the apostles because of his association with Paul. Luke's specific conversion story is not recorded, but it is believed that he was from Antioch.[5] Luke begins to appear as a frequent companion of his from about "the time of Paul's Macedonian vision (Acts 16:9–10) until his martyrdom" (2 Timothy 4:11),[6] even though Paul's ministry in Antioch had begun years earlier (Acts 11), and Luke may have been converted at that time. A doctor would have also been useful to have around considering the physical abuse Paul suffered while on his journeys (2 Corinthians 11:22–33).

This connection with Paul, then, helps us make sense of how Luke would have had access to all the eyewitnesses. Paul's ministry frequently took him to Jerusalem and Antioch, and he was a recognized missionary and leader in the church within just a few years of the church's start at the time of Pentecost (Acts 2; 9:1–29; Galatians 1:13–2:10). Years later at the council of Jerusalem (Acts 15) when the debate about gentile converts and circumcision was resolved, Paul stood tall in defense of the gospel, and it wasn't much after this that he confronted Peter in Antioch for hypocrisy (Galatians 2:11–21).

Since Paul's ministry took him to the geographical origins of Christianity, this may have been when Luke was able to interview the people Jesus had healed and served. Luke would have interviewed Peter about the healing of his mother-in-law. He would have heard the stories of how Simon Peter, his brother Andrew, and the brothers James and John first met Jesus on the Lake of Gennesaret (Luke 5). He would have interviewed the leper who had been healed, and the paralytic who had been lowered through a roof by his friends. Luke would have met Matthew and talked to people who had heard Jesus preach the beatitudes. He would have met the centurion and the son of the widow of Nain who Christ chose to raise from the dead out of compassion for her loss. Luke specifically chose the stories he could confirm. He was meticulous and careful as he sought to present the strongest evidence linked to real people and real events. That is why Luke mentions the census by Augustus (which will be discussed in detail in chapter 6), and that Herod was king when Christ was born (chapter 7). These are the markers by which the birth of Jesus could be placed into its historical context for his audience.

That is also why Luke starts with the most powerful eyewitness of all: Mary, the mother of Jesus. Imagine sitting down with her, hearing her tell the story about her son Jesus and the rest of the family in her own words. I'm sure she must have told the story countless times, but Luke knew he needed to document it. All of it. Mary was still alive during Paul and Luke's ministry. No one knows exactly how long she lived, but tradition has it that John took her to Ephesus with him after Peter and Paul were martyred in AD 64. That would mean it is plausible that she would have been in Jerusalem with John during the 50s when Paul and John were there (Galatians 2:9).[7] And if Luke had been traveling with Paul at that time, he would have been there too. If Luke wasn't in Jerusalem, then he would have been able to interview Mary in Ephesus, where church tradition says John took her later in life, and where she lived her final days. If you remember, Jesus, while on the cross, specifically designated the apostle John to take care of his mother:

> *Now there stood by the cross of Jesus His mother, and His mother's sister, Mary the wife of Clopas, and Mary Magdalene. When Jesus therefore saw His mother, and the disciple whom He loved standing by, He said to His mother, "Woman, behold your son!" Then He said to the disciple, "Behold your mother!" And from that hour that disciple took her to his own home. (John 19:25–27)*

Mary, therefore, remained with John for the rest of her life, and since Luke knew John, it makes sense that he knew Mary too. Isn't it amazing to realize that when we read the first two chapters of Luke, we can be confident that Luke got many of his details from Mary herself, including the whole story of Zacharias and Elizabeth and the birth of their son, John, the forerunner of Jesus? As archaeologist and New Testament scholar William Ramsey eloquently observes:

> *The beautifully told story of Luke 1, 2, is an episode of family history of the most private character. The facts could be known only to a very small number of persons. If Luke had the slightest trace of historical instinct, he must have satisfied himself that the narrative which he gives rested on the evidence of one of the few persons to whom the facts could be known. It is not in keeping with the ancient style that he should formally name his authority; but he does not leave it doubtful whose authority he believed himself to have. "His mother kept all these sayings hid in her heart;" "Mary kept all these sayings, pondering them in her heart;" (Luke 2:19 and 51) those two sentences would be sufficient. The historian who wrote like that believed that he had the authority of the Mother herself.*[8]

Let's turn now to Mary's account.

2

The Last Priest

There was in the days of Herod, the king of Judea, a certain priest
named Zacharias, of the division of Abijah. His wife was
of the daughters of Aaron, and her name was Elizabeth.
—*Luke 1:5*

With Zacharias and Elizabeth, we have presented to us the godliest elderly couple you could ever hope to meet. Zacharias was a priest, which meant he was a descendant of Moses's brother Aaron, and so was his wife, Elizabeth. When Luke records their story, he is establishing the credentials of their future son, John the Baptist, and highlighting his role as the transitionary prophet between the old covenant and the new. Later when John says about Jesus, "He must increase, but I must decrease" (John 3:30), he refers to his role as the one who had baptized Jesus, and who now steps back for the Messiah to rise before the public.

Luke further writes of Zacharias and Elizabeth: "they were both righteous before God, walking in all the commandments and ordinances of the Lord blameless" (Luke 1:6). This is a lofty compliment. It was reserved for some of the most notable Old Testament personages such as Job: "[He] was blameless and upright, and one who feared God and shunned evil" (Job 1:1), and of

Noah: "Noah was a just man, perfect in his generations. Noah walked with God" (Genesis 6:9). However, it is also the foremost call of God on all of us: "Observe and obey all these words which I command you, that it may go well with you and your children after you forever, when you do what is good and right in the sight of the LORD your God" (Deuteronomy 12:28).

Yet, in spite of the devotion to God that Elizabeth and Zacharias had, they had not been blessed with any children of their own. If they were indeed so righteous, why hadn't God granted them children? The fruit of the womb was a reward for following the Lord:

> *Blessed is everyone who fears the Lord,*
> *Who walks in His ways.*
> *When you eat the labor of your hands,*
> *You shall be happy, and it shall be well with you.*
> *Your wife shall be like a fruitful vine*
> *In the very heart of your house,*
> *Your children like olive plants*
> *All around your table. (Psalm 128:1–3)*

If you have ever felt that kind of hole in your heart, you are not alone. My wife, Beth, and I had such a dilemma. I was a widowed dad[9] and already had a daughter whom Beth welcomed into her life when we got married, but we wanted more children. However, there were some medical issues, which a specialist helped us through. Within a few months, Beth became pregnant.

After our daughter was born, we decided that we wanted one more child, but this time we couldn't get pregnant. We knew we were getting to the edge of the childbearing age, but we also knew we shouldn't give up. It wasn't until the year my dad died that Beth finally got pregnant again, and we completely give God credit for blessing us in that time of grief (we even wonder, jokingly, if dad didn't give us a good word before the Lord).[10] This time we had a son, and I continue to hold him dearly as he turns seven years old.

I feel amazed and blessed by all of my children. Each one is a miracle, but I still remember the dark days when we were longing for a child and we had no guarantee that God would bless us that way. Such was the patience of Zacharias and Elizabeth.

As with all of God's promises, he always keeps them. We may not know when he will or the exact manner he will, but he *always* keeps his word. The author of Hebrews reminds us of this. After retelling some stories of the faith of God's people, he wrote: "These all died in faith [Abraham, Sarah, etc.], *not having received the promises*, but having seen them afar off were assured of them, embraced them and confessed that they were strangers and pilgrims on the earth" (Hebrews 11:13). Faith does not demand that God give an answer *now*. Faith believes that his answer will come in its own time, and God is not constrained by the limits of our lives.

Zacharias

The descendants of Levi—who was the third son of Jacob and Leah (Genesis 29:34)—eventually became the tribe which was exclusively tasked with taking care of all things in regard to the tabernacle and eventually the temple in the service of the Lord and his law. Three of Levi's more famous descendants were Miriam, Aaron, and Moses. However, the priesthood was not officially appointed to the Levites until Aaron. That's when God told Moses: "Now take Aaron your brother, and his sons with him, from among the children of Israel, that he may minister to Me as priest, Aaron and Aaron's sons: Nadab, Abihu, Eleazar, and Ithamar" (Exodus 28:1–2).

Later, the rest of the Levites were set apart from all the other tribes to the general service of the Most High: "you shall appoint the Levites over the tabernacle of the Testimony, over all its furnishings, and over all things that belong to it; they shall carry the tabernacle and all its furnishings; they shall attend to it and camp around the tabernacle" (Numbers 1:50).

By the time of David's reign as king of Israel, which was about 500 years after the Exodus and the conquering of the Promised Land, it had become difficult to keep all the descendants of Aaron involved in performing the daily offerings. There had been a lot of babies born in 500 years. The tabernacle was permanently set up in Jerusalem (the temple had not been built yet), and one of the responsibilities was to offer a sacrifice and burn incense every morning and every evening of every day in front of the tabernacle—tasks that fell exclusively to the descendants of Aaron (Exodus 29:38–44).

Therefore David, with the help of Zadok and other priests, decided to divide the descendants of the sons of Aaron into their respective families and make a schedule, randomly choosing which family would serve and when. First Chronicles lays out the schedule: "Now the first lot fell to Jehoiarib, the second to Jedaiah, the third to Harim, the fourth to Seorim, the fifth to Malchijah, the sixth to Mijamin, the seventh to Hakkoz, the eighth to *Abijah*," and on the list went up to twenty-four individuals (1 Chronicles 24:7–18). Zacharias was a descendant of Aaron through his son Eleazar and then through Abijah. When Luke tells us about Zacharias that "according to the custom of the priesthood, his lot fell to burn incense when he went into the temple of the Lord" (Luke 1:9), he is referring to this schedule that was set up in the time of David. Rabbinic sources give strong evidence that "The system [begun under David] remained unchanged even till Josephus's time."[11] Keep in mind that this was a twice-a-day offering every day of the year that came with very detailed instructions given to them in Exodus 30:1–10.

What the priests had to do is described in even greater detail in the Babylonian Talmud: "*He who gained the lot for the incense*, took the spoon; and the spoon resembled a great measure of gold containing three cabs. And the pan was heaped full of incense; and it had a covering like a kind of weight upon it."[12] Continuing on in the Talmud:

> He who gained the lot for the incense, took the pan from the cup, and gave it to his friend or to his neighbor. When the incense was dispersed in it, he supplied it to him in handfuls, and he instructed him, "Be careful and do not begin too near yourself, lest you be burned." He smoothed it and went out. The offerer could not offer the incense till the Captain said to him, "offer incense."[13]

This is what Zacharias was doing when the messenger of the Lord, Gabriel, appeared to him.

After the incense was properly offered, then the priests involved would come out and stand on the steps of the porch to recite a different liturgy depending on the day of the week. On Sunday, for example, they would intone: "The earth is the Lord's and the fulness thereof; the world, and they that dwell therein."[14] The people would be waiting outside the temple to hear the blessing every morning and every evening. Luke paints the scene for us when he says the "whole multitude" was outside praying (Luke 1:10). Devout Jews would attend these rituals twice daily.

But on this particular day, something extraordinary happened. Zacharias came out to stand with his brethren on the steps, but he couldn't speak. He was supposed to join in with the memorized liturgy, but he couldn't say it. Instead, he gestured wildly, trying to help everyone know that his voice was gone, and that something had happened to him while in the temple (vv. 21–22).

What Luke tells us (which is what Mary had told him, and she got it from Zacharias) was that while Zacharias had been performing the sacred rituals inside the temple, "an angel of the Lord appeared to him, standing on the right side of the altar of incense." The altar of incense was within the inner sanctuary, but it was *not* in the holy of holies.[15] It was just in front of the curtain that separated the holy of holies from the rest of the inner sanctuary. The angel Gabriel appeared to the right of the altar of incense and pronounced to Zacharias that God was going to bless him and his wife with a child who they were to name John, and that child would be a prophet who would pave the way for the Messiah (vv. 13–17). As the apostle John explains about Zacharias's son: "There was a man sent from God, whose name was John. This man came for a witness, to bear witness of the Light, that all through him might believe. He was not that Light, but was sent to bear witness of that Light" (John 1:6–8). John, Zacharias's son to be, would become the embodiment of everything that the law of God and the priesthood stood for: to point to the Messiah.

And yet in spite of this incredible vision, Zacharias responded with doubt: he asked Gabriel to prove his proclamation. Gabriel's answer is awesome: "you will be mute and not able to speak until the day these things take place, because you did not believe my words which will be fulfilled in their own time" (Luke 1:19–20). Essentially, Gabriel told the priest that if you want proof, here's your proof: you won't be able to talk for nine months. How's that for proof?

Zacharias got the message (see vv. 67–79).

Elizabeth

Elizabeth discovered she had become pregnant several weeks after Zacharias returned home. One would think she would have shouted from the rooftops, proclaiming the glory of God and how he had blessed her. Instead she does a very curious thing: "she hid herself five months" (Luke 1:24). At first glance, this would imply that she was depressed, ashamed, or embarrassed over her pregnancy, but none of that was so. Her view of things was quite different. She said, "Thus the Lord has dealt with me, in the days when He looked on me, to take away my reproach among people" (v. 25). She knew people had been judging her for not being able to bear children. Now, however, she was confident that God had finally blessed her—a decisive divine act that would silence wagging, judgmental tongues. That's all good, right? So why hide away for five months?

Maybe she wanted more time to be sure that she really was pregnant. It was unbelievable, after all, and like her husband, maybe a bit of skepticism still lingered. Maybe she needed to feel the kicks in her belly before she fully believed. While this is a possible reason, her comment undermines it. She believed God had opened her womb to new life, for nothing else would remove her reproach among other people.

Perhaps she thought others wouldn't believe she was with child until she was showing signs of pregnancy. Can you imagine getting such news from a woman you knew was in her fifties or sixties? As a first-century Jew, you may have thought that God was withholding his blessing from Elizabeth and Zacharias because of some sin one or both of them had committed (like Job's "friends" many centuries before had believed about him, though he was a righteous man). But now that Elizabeth was pregnant, maybe you would not have been able to conceal your concern for her health. Or maybe a judgmental heart would say to her, "What are you doing? Don't you know how old you are?" Maybe Elizabeth didn't want to risk hearing that from her neighbors. I doubt it, but maybe.

Or perhaps Elizabeth was concerned about having a miscarriage. I have known women who have intentionally withheld announcing that they were pregnant, even to family members, because of the emotional pain of a previous miscarriage. This is a possibility, but her words of praise to God seem to imply that she was confident that she would give birth: "Thus the Lord has dealt with me, in the days when He looked on me, to take away my reproach among people" (v. 25).

So if she didn't go into seclusion because of doubts or fears she had, why did she? I believe that she was so deeply moved by the incredible news of her pregnancy that all she wanted to do was be alone with God. Has something ever happened to you that was so profound, so sacred, so special, that words could not express your experience? Indeed, putting your feelings into words would diminish the sanctity of the event. Whatever happened was important to you on a level so deep that to tell someone risked facing their indifference or lack of understanding or appreciation. It would be too heartbreaking to hear someone say, "Oh, okay," or for them to just express criticism.

We live in a world where we can quickly and easily share every fantastic moment in our lives with everyone on planet Earth through technology and social media. But aren't there some things that are so special you should *not* share them, at least for a season? Aren't there moments so touching, so wonderful, so personal, that only you can treasure them? I believe Elizabeth is the only one who fully understood what this pregnancy meant to her, and her intuitive response was to fall on her face before her Lord privately. It was a sacred experience. She waited to share it with everyone else because her sovereign God had just answered a lifetime of tear-stained prayers. And the answer came in the form of a miracle.

After five months, Elizabeth began to open up to others. For her it became a blessing to talk with her friends and extended family. She had taken the time to worship God in holy seclusion, but now it was time to glorify him in public, and let her friends rejoice with her.

But this was not all. During these five months of praise and worship, God was also preparing Elizabeth for what was about to come, for it was just one month later that Mary, her niece, showed up.

3

Angels We Have Heard on High

*Now in the sixth month the angel Gabriel was sent by God to a city
of Galilee named Nazareth, to a virgin betrothed to a man whose name
was Joseph, of the house of David. The virgin's name was Mary.
And having come in, the angel said to her, "Rejoice, highly favored one,
the Lord is with you; blessed are you among women!"*
—*Luke 1:26–28*

For most of my Christian life, my image of the angel Gabriel has been one of a handsome, glowing man wearing a gold-fringed white robe and sporting some pretty awesome wings. He appears in every Christmas play—rightfully so—but his first announcement about the Messiah wasn't to Mary: it was to Daniel in the Old Testament. Some modern interpretations have him appearing as a man without any wings, although he does slightly glow around the edges. But whichever version of him is true, I haven't paid much attention to Gabriel for most of my life. The way he is portrayed gave me the impression that he is a necessary, albeit incidental, prop. He is responsible for delivering messages, but that's about it.

But after studying Daniel and the birth of Christ for years, it began to dawn on me how important to Gabriel were those messages to Daniel and Mary. He was not only revealing to Daniel and Mary our salvation but also the eventual redemption of all creation—which will include the angelic realm. The angels are eagerly anticipating the arrival of the Messiah as much as we are, albeit for different reasons.[16]

Angels

My grandma Fay collected angels. So many that she had an entire cabinet full, most of them gifts. (What else can a grandson buy for his grandma?) They were beautiful, cute, and charming, but they do not at all represent what angels are truly like. They capture a certain peaceful beauty or child-like innocence that's comforting, but I can't find one passage in Scripture which even remotely represents angels that way. The game *Dungeons and Dragons* does a better job of depicting the angelic realm than Precious Moments figurines do.

In the broadest sense, an angel is a messenger of God. The Hebrew word *mal'āk*[17] means "messenger," and it refers to an angel, prophet, priest, or teacher. Angels are spiritual beings who dwell in the heavenly places; however, they can also appear in human form (Genesis 18–19) in order to deliver messages of hope and judgment.[18] They are God's ministers (Psalm 104:4; Daniel 7:10), and there is a host of them. As Michael Heiser, a scholar in the fields of biblical studies and the ancient Near East, points out, "Since the spirit beings in God's service are called 'stars,' it is no surprise to see them collectively referred to as the 'host of heaven'" (Jer 33:22; Neh 9:6; Dan 4:35)."[19]

The Throne of God

The most well-known image of angels sits atop the ark of the testimony itself. In Exodus 25:10–22, God gave Moses specific instructions for what the ark of the testimony should look like. Of interest to us is the following: "Make one cherub at one end, and the other cherub at the other end; you shall make the cherubim at the two ends of it of one piece with the mercy seat. And the cherubim shall stretch out their wings above, covering the mercy seat with their wings, and they shall face one another; the faces of the cherubim shall be toward the mercy seat" (vv. 19–20).

Drawing: Ark of the Covenant

The mercy seat is the top of the ark which represents the throne of God. Structurally, the ark was just a wooden chest made of acacia wood and covered in gold, but it contained the second set of the Ten Commandments (Deuteronomy 10:1–2) and became the most sacred artifact of Israel.[20] It was placed in the holy of holies within the tabernacle and later the temple, and its presence meant that the presence of God was with Israel. Indeed, the entire temple—its design, dimensions, decorations, and objects—collectively represent the heavens where God dwells surrounded by a multitude of cherubim singing his praises night and day. The temple is the shadow of the substance (Hebrews 8:1–5).

When the prophet Ezekiel has a vision of heaven, he sees cherubim in the throne room of God and describes them as having two wings with "the form of a man's hand under their wings" (Ezekiel 10:8).[21] Moving with the cherubim are wheels filled with fire (vv. 6–7), and he describes cherubim as having four different faces: "the first face was the face of a cherub, the second face the face of a man, the third the face of a lion, and the fourth the face of an eagle" (v. 14). Later Ezekiel says, "Each cherub had two faces, so that the face of a man was toward a palm tree on one side, and the face of a young lion toward a palm tree on the other side" (41:18–19). And the number of cherubim is huge: "Ten thousand times ten thousand stood before Him" (Daniel 7:10). The throne room of God is filled with angelic beings, and the temple was designed to reflect that.

God commanded that "artistic designs of cherubim" should be woven into the veil at the entrance to the holy of holies and used with other fine curtains within the tabernacle (Exodus 36:8). Later, Solomon makes two large cherubim that spread their wings over the entire inner room within the temple (1 Kings 6:23–28). He also carves into the walls of the temple images of cherubim, palm trees, and open flowers. And throughout the history of Israel, God is called "the One who dwells between the cherubim" (2 Kings 19:15; 1 Chronicles 13:6; Psalm 80:1), which is a reference to the mercy seat on top of the ark of the covenant. God does not dwell within the ark; it is his throne (contrary to the depiction in the movie *Indiana Jones and the Raiders of the Lost Ark*).

Heavenly Places

We might better understand *what* angels are if we think about *where* they are. A common metaphor is that angels are stars and that their dwelling place is in the heavens above. I think the metaphor's purpose is to draw our attention upward in a spiritual sense. We are to consider higher things, higher values, higher ethics, something that transcends our own earthbound selves. That is an important concept.

However, the idea of "above" has transformed into a literal image of angels sitting among puffy white clouds playing harps. Many have come to think that angels—and God as well—are high above us *geographically*, when in fact the angelic realm is all around us. To help understand what this means, C. S. Lewis suggests in his science fiction trilogy that angels are physical beings but not in the same sense that we are. God created them, but they exist at a different speed of light than us, one that our eyes and brains cannot normally process:

> *The swiftest thing that touches our senses is light. We do not truly see light, we only see slower things lit by it, so that for us light is on the edge—the last thing we know before things become too swift for us. But the body of an* eldil *[angel] is a movement swift as light; you may say its body is made of light, but not of that which is light for the* eldil. *His "light" is a swifter movement which for us is nothing*

at all; and what we call light is for him a thing like water, a visible thing, a thing he can touch and bathe in—even a dark thing when not illumined by the swifter. And what we call firm things—flesh and earth—seem to him thinner, and harder to see, than our light, and more like clouds, and nearly nothing. To us the eldil *is a thin, half-real body that can go through walls and rocks: to himself he goes through them because he is solid and firm and they are like cloud.*[22]

It is a beautiful explanation, and what I appreciate most about his idea is that it brings angelic beings out of a phantasmagoric delusion and into God's creation. Some of his creatures are not visible to us, like some frequencies of light. This might help explain why when Gabriel appears to Daniel and Mary, their experience is disconcerting and terrifying. The angel's coming is unseen and unheard. Suddenly, he is just *there*.

Fallen Angels

Angels may be immortal, but they can sin. Satan took a third of the angels with him when he rebelled against God (Isaiah 14:12–15; Revelation 12:4), and Paul says, "For we do not wrestle against flesh and blood, but against principalities, against powers, against the rulers of the darkness of this age, against *spiritual hosts of wickedness in the heavenly places*" (Ephesians 6:12). There is a war going on, and Peter informs us that Satan "walks about [the earth] like a roaring lion, seeking whom he may devour" (1 Peter 5:8).

These many descriptive terms about angelic beings are not just figures of speech or some psychological symbolisms used to explain the conflict within our minds and souls. In 2 Kings 6:15–17, Elisha prays for his servant to be able to see what he could see:

And when the servant of the man of God arose early and went out, there was an army [the Syrians], surrounding the city with horses and chariots. And his servant said to him, "Alas, my master! What shall we do?"

So he answered, "Do not fear, for those who are with us are more than those who are with them." And Elisha prayed, and said,

"Lord, I pray, open his eyes that he may see." Then the LORD opened the eyes of the young man, and he saw. And behold, the mountain was full of horses and chariots of fire all around Elisha.

This army that Elisha saw was comprised of angelic warriors sent by God to defend the city of Dothan in northern Israel.

There is a spiritual war going on all around us which is reflected in the conflicts on earth, and we have lost perspective if we think that what is happening on earth isn't influenced by what is happening in the heavenly places. There is an interactive influence angelic beings can wield over individuals, peoples, and nations, for good or for evil, and although some angels may spend time praising God in his throne room, they can also be like soldiers fighting battles with swords while riding around on chariots of fire. That's awesome!

The book of Daniel gives us an incredible insight into the spiritual war going on. In chapter 10, we are introduced to the archangel Michael who comes to the aid of the angel Gabriel who has been trying to give Daniel the interpretation of his disturbing visions. Gabriel's mission was interfered with by the Prince of Persia and the Prince of Greece, angelic beings who oversee these nations. What's going on, and who are these princes?

In Revelation 12, we see Michael leading the good angels against the dragon (Satan), and in Jude 1:9, Michael *the archangel* "contended for the body of Moses."[23] Michael is referred to in Daniel 10:13 as "one of the chief princes," and verse 21 refers to Michael as the prince of Israel.[24] Michael and Gabriel are on the side of God, but these other princes—fallen archangels—are not. Some apocryphal works from this Second Temple period (ca. 517 BC–AD 70) explicitly state that Gabriel is an archangel on par with Michael, but nowhere in the Bible is he called such.[25] Michael is an archangel (a cherubim with the rank of a general), but Gabriel seems to be one of the cherubim who was assigned to reveal God's plan of redemption to mankind.

Servants of Mankind

As amazing, exciting, and magnificent as angels are, the truth is that God made them to be the servants of mankind, not the other way around. The author of

Hebrews asks about angels, "Are they not all ministering spirits sent forth to minister for those who will inherit salvation?" (Hebrews 1:14). The answer is yes. He also points out that "[God] has not put the world to come . . . in subjection to angels" (2:5). Angels have their assigned roles, but they do not rule us or this earth. Ever. They are awesome, but they are not in charge. We are. In Genesis, God made us caretakers of his creation (Genesis 1:26–28), and angels are *our* servants. However, that doesn't mean we are better than the angels. The writer of Hebrews makes this point, quoting from Psalm 8:

> *What is man that You are mindful of him,*
> *Or the son of man that You take care of him?*
> *You have made him a little lower than the angels;*
> *You have crowned him with glory and honor,*
> *And set him over the works of Your hands.*
> *You have put all things under his feet.*

The author of Hebrews starts his book with a powerful argument. In chapter 1 he makes the case that Christ is above the angels in glory and power. He is their Creator, not one of them. Jesus isn't an angel. Then in chapter 2 the author explains that Christ was made "a little lower than the angels" (Hebrews 2:4). He was made a man—less than the angels—*in order to save mankind.* God's created order becomes inverted at the Incarnation. When the Son of God becomes a man, he thereby exalts us to the highest order, saving us and all things in between, and that is why we have been exalted above the angels: because Christ became one of us.

So what happens to the angels? Is there redemption for them? Hebrews 2:16 says, "For indeed He does not give aid to angels, but He does give aid to the seed of Abraham." The redemption we find in Christ is not available to the angels *in the same way*, and since they do not die there is no sacrifice possible for their sin. His blood was shed for us, not for them. In the order of God's creation, they are glorious, magnificent servants of God, but they cannot be redeemed as we can be. They cannot be bought back. If an angel sins, that's it. So when the angels rebelled with Satan, their damnation was established for eternity. Satan's rebellion is described in Ezekiel 28:11–19 by God himself:

You were the seal of perfection,
Full of wisdom and perfect in beauty.
You were in Eden, the garden of God;
Every precious stone was your covering:
The sardius, topaz, and diamond,
Beryl, onyx, and jasper,
Sapphire, turquoise, and emerald with gold.
The workmanship of your timbrels and pipes
Was prepared for you on the day you were created.
You were the anointed cherub who covers;
I established you;
You were on the holy mountain of God;
You walked back and forth in the midst of fiery stones.
You were perfect in your ways from the day you were created,
Till iniquity was found in you.

Satan was an angelic being of the highest order, glorious and exalted, blessed and sinless. But he rebelled because he wanted to rule the earth and subjugate mankind to his will. It is his desired outcome to this day. Milton in *Paradise Lost* presents Satan speaking to his minions:

Fall'n Cherub, to be weak is miserable
Doing or Suffering: but of this be sure,
To do aught good never will be our task,
But ever to do ill our sole delight,
As being the contrary to his high will
Whom we resist. If then his Providence
Out of our evil seek to bring forth good,
Our labour must be to pervert that end,
And out of good still to find means of evil;

Which oft-times may succeed, so as perhaps
Shall grieve him, if I fail not, and disturb
His inmost counsels from their destin'd aim.[26]

Furthermore, a third of the angels rebelled with Satan against God, and they, too, will face judgment on the final day. And they know it.

Jesus encountered a demon in Capernaum in Luke 4:31–37: "And he [the demon-possessed man] cried out with a loud voice, saying, "Let us alone! What have we to do with You, Jesus of Nazareth? *Did You come to destroy us?* I know who You are—the Holy One of God." Even though these spiritual beings knew that the Messiah could destroy them and one day would, they still didn't know exactly how their end would play out.

Angels will not themselves be redeemed, but when Christ returns and judges the world in righteousness, fallen angels will be judged and cast into the lake of fire, thereby terminating the spiritual war and restoring order. There will finally be peace. The battle will be over. Satan will be defeated. Peter tells us that the resurrected Jesus "has gone into heaven and is at the right hand of God, *angels and authorities and powers having been made subject to Him*" (1 Peter 3:22).

When Gabriel later announced the birth of Christ to Mary, we can see that angels are an integral component of God's plan of redemption. Gabriel was a warrior in the service of our Creator, and he was fighting for the ultimate restoration of the heavenly and earthly places. The angelic realm has as much to gain from the arrival of the Messiah as we do. The Messiah is our greatest hope—and Satan's greatest fear.

Taking a Look at the Map

Let us pause for a moment, pull out our map, and see where we are and what comes next. Right now we are hiking along an easy, familiar part of the trail: the events leading up to the birth of Christ. We have been introduced to Luke who recorded Mary's account, and we have met Zacharias, Elizabeth, and Gabriel.

But now we are standing on the edge of a more challenging part of the trail. Gabriel is the one who told Zacharias that he and his wife Elizabeth would soon have a son named John (chapter 2), and it is Gabriel who will announce to Mary that she would conceive of the Holy Spirit (chapter 5). He will also be the one to reassure Joseph that Mary isn't lying to him, and then he will eventually appear to the magi and warn them that King Herod was lying and wanted to use them to kill the Messiah (chapter 11). He will also command Joseph to take his family to Egypt.

But this is not Gabriel's first interaction with the prophecies regarding the Messiah. He is the one who interpreted God's visions for Daniel. Gabriel is a key player in the fulfillment of God's prophecies. So in the next chapter we are going to look more closely at what God revealed to Daniel through the ministry of Gabriel.

Take a drink of water, tighten up your pack straps, and let's keep going.

4

Messiah the Prince

Earlier, during the first year of King Belshazzar's reign in Babylon, Daniel had a dream and saw visions as he lay in his bed. He wrote down the dream, and this is what he saw.
—Daniel 7:1 NLT

D aniel was in his late seventies when he had his first vision during the reign of the Babylonian king Belshazzar (Daniel 7:1), the grandson of Nebuchadnezzar. He had not even been thrown into the lion's den yet.[27] Daniel had been captured when he was a child and taken to Babylon along with other young boys who were going to be indoctrinated into the Babylonian religion, but he stayed faithful to God and his Word and rose to the top of the academic class in the Chaldean capital of Babylon.

When Daniel was nearing the end of his life, God revealed to this faithful man how the divine plans were going to unfold over the next few centuries. We are not given a name for the angel who interprets his first vision, but Daniel 7:15–16 (NASB) says: "As for me, Daniel, my spirit was distressed within me, and the visions in my mind kept alarming me. I approached one of those who were standing by and began requesting of him the exact meaning of all this. So he told me and made known to me the interpretation of these things." A multitude of angels were present (v. 10), so he approached one of them and asked for help to understand what he had seen. I think it is safe to say that Daniel singled out Gabriel because he is the angel who later shows up to interpret the other visions for the prophet. This first vision, though, is a straightforward proclamation that God will set up his kingdom on earth:

> *Then the kingdom and dominion,*
> *And the greatness of the kingdoms under the whole heaven,*
> *Shall be given to the people, the saints of the Most High.*
> *His kingdom is an everlasting kingdom,*
> *And all dominions shall serve and obey Him. (v. 27)*

In the most general terms, God revealed to Daniel that the Jewish Messiah would rule the world someday. He would prevail over his enemies, and he would set up his kingdom forever in heaven and on earth. What an audacious claim! Remember that at the time of Daniel's visions, the Jews were a conquered people. They were exiles and scattered throughout the region. They had no capital and no nation. Their national identity was defined by their faith that they were God's chosen people, but they were being punished for disobeying his law. They weren't living the dream at all. They were in the ultimate "time out," and it was not pleasant or rewarding. There was nothing about them that shouted, "We will rule the world!"

Then Daniel had a second vision in which God gave more precise details about how his plan was going to play out. Daniel sees himself in Shushan, the capital of Persia (modern-day Susa in Iran), and he sees "a ram which had two horns, and the two horns were high; but one was higher than the other, and the higher one came up last" (8:3). He saw so much more, of course, but his visions were so disturbing that he prayed for understanding, and a "man" commanded the angel Gabriel to go and explain the vision to Daniel: "Then it happened, when I, Daniel, had seen the vision and was seeking the meaning, that suddenly there stood before me one having the appearance of a man. And I heard a man's voice between the banks of the Ulai, who called, and said, 'Gabriel, make this man understand the vision'" (vv. 15–16).

The one who had "the appearance of a man" was Christ himself,[28] but it was Gabriel who Christ commanded to tell Daniel the meaning. Gabriel said,

"The ram which you saw, having the two horns—they are the kings of Media and Persia" (v. 20). This part of Daniel's vision would come true within the year when Cyrus the Great of *Persia* conquers Babylon and then graciously and wisely honors Darius the *Mede* (his uncle Cyaxares)[29] with a palace in Babylon.[30] The ram was the Persian empire, and the two horns were Cyrus and Darius, rulers of that empire. But the vision had more to say, and it terrified Daniel:

> *A king shall arise,*
> *Having fierce features,*
> *Who understands sinister schemes.*
> *His power shall be mighty, but not by his own power;*
> *He shall destroy fearfully,*
> *And shall prosper and thrive;*
> *He shall destroy the mighty, and also the holy people. (vv. 23–24)*

Who would this king be who was going to destroy the holy people? Wasn't God going to restore Israel? This was disturbing stuff. Gabriel reassures Daniel that none of these events would happen in his lifetime and that "it refers to many days in the future" (v. 26). Not comforted by these words, Daniel faints and is sick for days (v. 27), during which time he continues to seek God for understanding.

Daniel's third encounter with Gabriel is recorded in Daniel 9 after a lengthy prayer of repentance. The prophet had been studying Scripture and came across a prophecy by Jeremiah:

> *"And this whole land shall be a desolation and an astonishment, and these nations shall serve the king of Babylon seventy years. Then it will come to pass, when seventy years are completed, that I will punish the king of Babylon and that nation, the land of the Chaldeans, for their iniquity," says the LORD; "and I will make it a perpetual desolation." (Jeremiah 25:11–12; cf. Daniel 9:2)*

God reiterated this promise several chapters later in Jeremiah:

For thus says the LORD: After seventy years *are completed at Babylon, I will visit you and perform My good word toward you, and cause you to return to this place. For I know the thoughts that I think toward you, says the LORD, thoughts of peace and not of evil, to give you a future and a hope. (Jeremiah 29:10–11)*

Seventy years. God allowed Egypt to conquer Jerusalem in the first year of Jehoiakim, October 609 BC, as a judgment against Judea, but it wasn't long before Nebuchadnezzar took over all the holdings of Egypt, and in the third year of Jehoiakim, Daniel was taken to Babylon (Daniel 1:1). Cyrus the Great conquered Babylon in October of 539 BC—*seventy years* after the first year of Jehoiakim. What God said would happen, happened exactly.

The first two explanations of Daniel's visions established a broad overview of God's plan, but now Gabriel tells him that God has an exact timetable laid out for when the Messiah would arrive and fully restore Israel:

Seventy weeks are determined
For your people and for your holy city,
To finish the transgression,
To make an end of sins,
To make reconciliation for iniquity,
To bring in everlasting righteousness,
To seal up vision and prophecy,
And to anoint the Most Holy. (Daniel 9:24)

God had kept his promise of 70 years, and now he was promising that *70 weeks* would wrap everything up. But what exactly that means has been a matter of intense debate for millennia.

The Schedule Revealed

Interpreters have been wrestling with the meaning of the 70-weeks prophecy since Daniel's day. It points to the Messiah (see 9:25–26), but it also raises some questions: How many years would it be before the Messiah's coming?

When do the "seventy weeks" start? When do they end? Is this period an uninterrupted flow of time, or are there pauses along the way? We need to answer these questions, and in this chapter we will.

Now, the interpretation of this prophecy gets somewhat technical, but I have prepared charts to help clarify and visually present what I have discovered. I have come to see that this prophecy is crucial to understanding when Christ was born. You should also know that my interpretation of Daniel's 70 weeks is unique, so I'm going to methodically unpack what I think and why. If you bear with me, I think you'll find Daniel's prophecy fascinating and revealing.

The Weeks

To start with, the Hebrew word for week, *šâbûa*, means "a period of seven," either being a period of 7 days or of 7 years.[31] Just like we have 7 days in one week, there are 7 years in one of Daniel's "weeks." The NIV translates the word as "sevens" instead of as "weeks."

In one sense this prophecy seems to be fairly straightforward: A "week" is considered a 7-year time period, so 70 "weeks" (70 multiplied by 7 years) equals 490 years. That is how most people have interpreted it. However, I have come to believe that Daniel's weeks cover a 500-year period, not one lasting just 490 years. Here's why.

God's law says, "And you shall count for yourselves from the day after the Sabbath, from the day that you brought the sheaf of the wave offering: *seven Sabbaths* shall be completed" (Leviticus 23:15). The phrase "seven Sabbaths" means 7 multiplied by 7 literal weeks, which totals forty-nine days. But there is one more command in the next verse: "Count *fifty days* to the day after the seventh Sabbath; then you shall offer a new grain offering to the LORD" (v. 16). So while the period of 7 Sabbaths totals 49 *days* (7 x 7 = 49), one more day is added, the 50th day, and this will become the day of Pentecost. So 49 days becomes 50 days.

In a similar way, Leviticus uses the term "Sabbath" to refer to 7 *years*: "And you shall count *seven sabbaths of years* for yourself, *seven times seven years*; and the time of the seven sabbaths of years shall be to you forty-nine years" (25:8). All good so far: 7 days x 7 days = 49 days; 7 years x 7 years = 49 years. But just as a 50th day is added onto the end of 49 days, a 50th year is added onto the end of 49 years and becomes the year of Jubilee:

> *Then you shall cause the trumpet of the Jubilee to sound on the tenth day of the seventh month; on the Day of Atonement[32] you shall make the trumpet to sound throughout all your land. And you shall consecrate the fiftieth year and proclaim liberty throughout all the land to all its inhabitants. It shall be a Jubilee for you; and each of you shall return to his possession, and each of you shall return to his family. (25:9–10)*

The Year of Jubilee is celebrated *after* the 49 years is completed and is referred to as "the fiftieth year."

What is the Jubilee? It is a societal and economic reset. During that year, debts are forgiven, property redeemed, and slaves freed. Everything about this fiftieth year symbolizes God's salvation. God's people were to purge the sins of injustice and debt. The parallels are striking: Debt represents slavery because people have to work for others in order to pay them back, and God wants us to be free of our debts—free of our sins. The Jewish historian Josephus explains it this way: "He [God] ordained, that they should do the same after *seven times seven years, which in all are fifty years*; and that fiftieth year is called by the Hebrews the Jubilee, wherein debtors are freed from their debts, and slaves are set at liberty."[33] Josephus clearly says that the Jews understood 7 Sabbaths to be a fifty-year time period, not forty-nine years.

These are the reasons I don't believe Daniel's 70 weeks are a span of 490 years. We can't leave out the extra ten Years of Jubilee, which brings the total time period to 500 years.[34]

The Segments

Now let's look at the next part of Daniel's prophecy:

> *Know therefore and understand,*
> *That from the going forth of the command*
> *To restore and build Jerusalem*

Until Messiah the Prince,
There shall be seven weeks and sixty-two weeks. (Daniel 9:25)

In verse 24, God told Daniel that in total "Seventy weeks are determined" (500 years), but in verse 25 he splits the 70 weeks into two segments: "seven weeks *and* sixty-two weeks." That leaves one week, a third segment, remaining, which is mentioned in verse 27: "Then he shall confirm a covenant with many for one week." Why does God break the 70 weeks into three segments?

Gabriel tells Daniel that it will be "seven weeks and sixty-two weeks," but why not just say "sixty-nine weeks"? Almost every Bible commentator I have read assumes that the first two timeframes are consecutive although distinct. For example, Bible teacher H. A. Ironside said: "The 490 years are divided into three series, and do not necessarily run on in direct chronological order. It is true that the sixty-two weeks immediately followed the completion of the seven weeks, but this does not alter the fact that God distinctly separates the sixty-two weeks from the seven that went before."[35]

So the three segments of the 70 weeks looks like this:

Segment 1: Seven Weeks
7 years x 7 years = 49 years.

49 years + 1 Year of Jubilee = **50 years**

Segment 2: Sixty-two Weeks
62 x 7 = 434 years

Add in 8 Years of Jubilee

434 years + 8 Jubilees = **442 years**

Segment 3: One Week
7 years + 1 Jubilee = **8 years**

But are the first 69 weeks (7 weeks + 62 weeks) consecutive? What evidence do we have that they are? Ironside tells us that they are, but that they didn't *necessarily* have to be. What if they were not consecutive? What if there is a time gap between the first 7 weeks and the next 62 weeks? Most prophetic models about the end times already teach that we are living during a gap period between the 69th week and the 70th week. It's called the church age. So, then, it is not a stretch to allow that there may be a gap of time between the 7 weeks *and* the 62 weeks. If so, then we might view the 70 weeks this way:

Seventy Weeks (500 Years)				
7 Weeks	Gap	62 Weeks	Gap	1 Week
50 Years	?	442 Years	?	8 Years

Table 1: 70 Weeks = 500 Years

The final Year of Jubilee will be the 500th year, and it comes *at the end* of the final 7 years. This suggests that the return of Jesus will come at *the end* of the 70 weeks. Total salvation. Complete liberation. Heaven and earth redeemed. His kingdom come. The Messiah on the throne. The Most Holy is anointed. The best and fullest Jubilee ever!

On Your Marks!

So, with this theoretical model in mind—that there are three timed, prophetic segments and at least two gaps of undisclosed lengths of time—let's look at Daniel 9:25 again to see if any clues will help us figure out how all of this fits together and whether my interpretation is correct.

> *Know therefore and understand,*
> *That from the going forth of the command [Cyrus's decree]*
> *To restore and build Jerusalem*
> *Until Messiah the Prince [the birth of Jesus],*[36]
> *There shall be seven weeks and sixty-two weeks;*
> *The street shall be built again, and the wall,*
> *Even in troublesome times.*

As with many prophecies in Scripture, they become much more understandable once they play out in history, and that is certainly the case here with the words that came to Daniel.

History tells us that the Persian King Cyrus conquered Babylon and soon issued a decree to allow the Jews to return to Jerusalem to rebuild their temple. He even ordered for the building funds to be covered by Persia. Because of the significance of this decree and its focus, many Bible scholars see that "the going forth of the command" refers to the decree of Cyrus and that this pronouncement initiates the 70-weeks countdown. Ezra the priest thought so too:

> Now in the first year of Cyrus king of Persia, that the word of the LORD by the mouth of Jeremiah might be fulfilled [see Jeremiah 33:7] the LORD stirred up the spirit of Cyrus king of Persia, so that he made a proclamation throughout all his kingdom, and also put it in writing, saying, "Thus says Cyrus king of Persia: All the kingdoms of the earth the LORD God of heaven has given me. And He has commanded me to build Him a house at Jerusalem which is in Judah." (Ezra 1:1–2)

Some scholars make the case that the command mentioned in Daniel may refer to the decree made by Darius the Great mentioned in Ezra 6:1, or even to the one by Artaxerxes in Nehemiah 2:7–8, but any of these subsequent decrees were merely affirmations of the original decree made by Cyrus. This is confirmed in Ezra 6:14 when he says, "And they [the Jews] built and finished it [the temple], according to the commandment of the God of Israel, and according to the command of Cyrus, Darius, and Artaxerxes king of Persia."[37] Since Cyrus conquered Babylon in October 29 of 539 BC (his decree would most likely have come a few months after his victory), then the fiftieth year of Daniel's first 7 weeks finishes in the autumn of 489 BC. What may be confusing is that we think of a year as beginning in January, but in this case we are counting from autumn to autumn.

The gap starts in the fall of 489 BC, but when does that gap end? Or rather, when does the countdown resume with the 62 sevens? There are two other occurrences mentioned in Daniel's prophecy that need to be considered: the rebuilding of the temple and the reconstruction of the wall that surrounded and

The First Seven Weeks (50 years)

Weeks								7 x 7 = 49 + 1 Year of Jubilee = 50 / Autumn to Autumn
1	1	2	3	4	5	6	7	
2	8	9	10	11	12	13	14	
3	15	16	17	18	19	20	21	
4	22	23	24	25	26	27	28	
5	29	30	31	32	33	34	35	
6	36	37	38	39	40	41	42	
7	43	44	45	46	47	48	49	50

First Gap

Table 2: The First 7 Weeks = 50 Years

protected Jerusalem. Could either of these events begin the 62-week count-down? Recall Daniel's revelation:

> ***There shall be seven weeks and sixty-two weeks;***
> *The street shall be built again, and the wall,*
> ***Even in troublesome times. (Daniel 9:25)***

The "street" is a reference to the entire temple complex, not to merely a city avenue or the city in general. "Street" or "square," as some translations use, is a reference to an open forum, but it must be a reference to the forum of the temple complex. Ezra 10:9 uses the same phrasing but with an added clarification: "So all the men of Judah and Benjamin gathered themselves together unto Jerusalem within three days. It was the ninth month, on the twentieth day of the month; and all the people sat in the *street of the house of God*, trembling because of this matter,

Weeks	The First Seven Weeks (with Dates)							
1	539	538	537	536	535	534	533	
2	532	531	530	529	528	527	526	7 x 7 = 49 + 1 Year of Jubilee = 50 Autumn to Autumn
3	525	524	523	522	521	520	519	
4	518	517	516	515	514	513	512	
5	511	510	509	508	507	506	505	
6	504	503	502	501	400	499	498	
7	497	496	495	494	493	492	491	490 – 489

First Gap (Begins Autumn of 489)

Table 3: The First 7 Weeks (with dates)

and for the great rain" (KJV; see also 2 Chronicles 29:4–5).[38] So when Daniel's prophecy says "the street shall be built again," it infers that the temple will be rebuilt. Indeed, that is how the first Jews who returned to Jerusalem understood it. After Cyrus's decree, many thousands of Jews returned to Jerusalem to rebuild the temple even though they didn't complete it for another twenty-two years. It wasn't finished until the sixth year of Darius the Great in 517 BC (Ezra 6:15).

Notice that this 517 date is not even halfway through the first segment of Daniel's 70 weeks, so it couldn't be the event which restarts the second segment nor does it end it. However, it does bring our attention to an interesting observation: 517 BC just "happens" to be 70 years after Solomon's Temple was destroyed in 587 BC by Nebuchadnezzar (2 Chronicles 36:17–21). We already saw that Jeremiah's prophetic 70 years began in the first year of king Jehoiakim (October 609) and was fulfilled when Cyrus conquered Babylon (October 539).

And yet here it appears we have a second fulfillment of the 70-year prophecy (587–517 BC). Could there be *two* 70-year periods prophesied by Jeremiah?

> *Then they [Nebuchadnezzar's army] burned the house of God, broke down the wall of Jerusalem, burned all its palaces with fire, and destroyed all its precious possessions. And those who escaped from the sword he carried away to Babylon, where they became servants to him and his sons until the rule of the kingdom of Persia, to fulfill the word of the LORD by the mouth of Jeremiah, until the land had enjoyed her Sabbaths. As long as she lay desolate she kept Sabbath,* to fulfill seventy years. *(2 Chronicles 36:19–21)*

In this passage, the chroniclers begin the 70 years when Nebuchadnezzar destroys the temple in 587. But Cyrus conquers Babylon only fifty-one years later in 537. As noted earlier, most prophecies are not fully understood until they are fulfilled, and since the Second Temple was finished *exactly* 70 years after the first one was destroyed, that makes sense of the phrase "As long as she [Jerusalem] lay desolate she kept Sabbath." Jerusalem had a Sabbath rest of 70 years because that is how long the temple did not exist. So which 70-year period does Jeremiah's prophecy apply to?

Perhaps both! There are 70 years from Jehoiakim to Cyrus, and 70 years from the razing of Solomon's Temple to the raising of the Second Temple. Quite stunning, really, and these dates are objectively confirmed by the historical record. Assyriologist Gérard Gertoux confirms that there was the

> "70-year Babylonian domination (609 BCE) which ended with the seizure of Babylon by Cyrus (539 BCE)." [There was then the] "destruction of the Temple dated 10/V/18 of Nebuchadnezzar (Jr 52:12, 13) according to the Babylonian reckoning (October 587 BCE). This 'devastation of the temple' would last 70 years (Dn. 9:2)...[until the] end of the 70-year desolation period and of the exile (517 BC)." [39]

Here's how we can graphically depict the fulfillment of Jeremiah's 70 years:

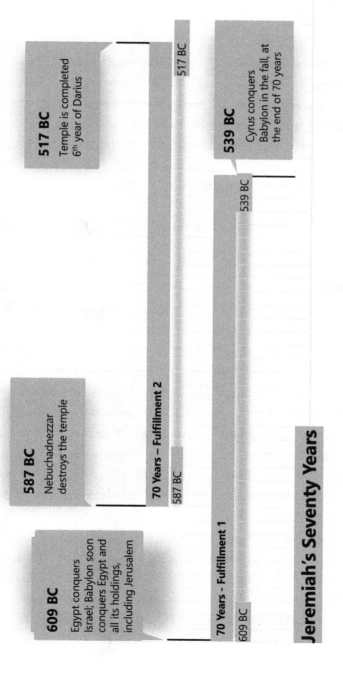

609 BC

Egypt conquers Israel; Babylon soon conquers Egypt and all its holdings, including Jerusalem

587 BC

Nebuchadnezzar destroys the temple

517 BC

Temple is completed 6th year of Darius

539 BC

Cyrus conquers Babylon in the fall, at the end of 70 years

70 Years – Fulfillment 1

70 Years – Fulfillment 2

609 BC

587 BC

517 BC

539 BC

Jeremiah's Seventy Years

Timeline 1: Jeremiah's 70 Years

Between Daniel and Jeremiah, we find two 70-year prophecies. I consider them a double confirmation, like a double rainbow, showing that God is in control of these historical events.

But what does Jeremiah's 70 years have to do with Daniel's 70 weeks? God is about to display his immense power. He doesn't just give us an "almost" or a "close enough to" type of prophecy. He is precise. He is over the top specific with his mathematical precision and leaves no doubt that the date of our Messiah's birth had been planned out 500 years before it ever happened. What I am suggesting is that God supernaturally orchestrated his plan so that the movements of the celestial spheres and the activities of humankind on earth would sync up perfectly on the day Christ was born.

Return to Daniel's Prophecy

The First Gap

The Second Temple was completed in 517 BC, but that was about all that was going on in Israel at the time and for quite a few more years. On the world stage, however, there was a great deal happening.

In the thirty-third year of Darius the Great in 490 (the 50th year of the first 7 weeks ends in the fall of 489), the Persians attacked the Greeks and fought the famous battle of Marathon. The Persians lost, and Darius the Great wanted nothing more than to return to kill all of the Greeks, but he died a few years later.

Xerxes, then, took up his father's cause. In the sixth year of his reign in the spring of 480, Xerxes attacked the Greeks and defeated the Spartans in the epic battle of Thermopylae, a battle depicted in the film *300*. The Persians then burned the Greek city-state of Athens but were later defeated in the Battle of Salamis—a battle at sea that weakened Persia's chances of ever again defeating the Greeks. Xerxes returned to Persia with his tail between his legs, but one of his generals stayed behind to fight, hoping still to win. This time the Spartans defeated the Persians in the battle of Plataea in 479, effectively ending the war. Xerxes reigned for only a few more years until he died on August 24, 475. His son Artaxerxes then took over, and he is most likely the Persian king mentioned in the book of Esther.

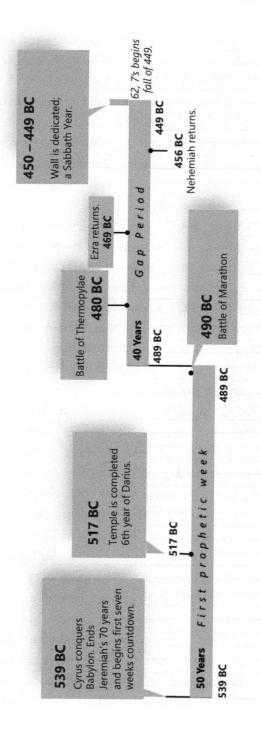

539 BC

Cyrus conquers Babylon. Ends Jeremiah's 70 years and begins first seven weeks countdown.

517 BC

Temple is completed 6th year of Darius.

450 – 449 BC

Wall is dedicated; a Sabbath Year.

62, 7's begins fall of 449.

449 BC

456 BC

Nehemiah returns.

Ezra returns.

469 BC

Battle of Thermopylae

480 BC

40 Years

489 BC

Gap Period

490 BC

Battle of Marathon

489 BC

First prophetic week

517 BC

50 Years

539 BC

Timeline 2: The Persian Period

During this era and after the temple was built, Israel became a lost little snowflake in a blizzard of world events. Complacency set in, and the returned exiles went back to business as usual, accumulating debt, charging outrageous interest rates to their fellow Jews, and starting families with unbelieving locals (Nehemiah 5:1–12; 13:23). They seemed to be content with leaving the walls of Jerusalem in piles of rubble, and a spiritual laziness consumed them. To inspire the Jews to complete the temple, God raised up two prophets, Haggai and Zechariah (Ezra 5:1). But in order to complete the wall around the city, God raised up Ezra and Nehemiah.

Ezra—a descendant of Aaron—is the priest who arranged the Old Testament into the form we have today. He left Babylon and returned to Jerusalem in the seventh year of Artaxerxes, 469 BC,[40] which was thirty-seven years after the completion of the temple. Nehemiah, however, didn't leave Shushan, the capital of Persia, for Jerusalem until the twentieth year of Artaxerxes in 456. Nehemiah was the cup bearer for Artaxerxes, and his heart broke when he heard reports of how decrepit Jerusalem still was. The Jews had neglected the rebuilding of Jerusalem after the temple had been built, and he had to do something about it. So he petitioned God, and the Lord opened the way for Nehemiah to request and receive King Artaxerxes's help (Nehemiah 1:1–2:8).

Once he gained permission from Artaxerxes and Esther (Nehemiah 2:6), he traveled to Jerusalem and governed the city for twelve years (457–444 BC). It's unclear exactly how long it took, but sometime during his governorship he completed the wall around Jerusalem, even though it was likely just a shadow of its former glory. Some scholars say that it took him only a few months to finish the wall,[41] but with all the letter writing that took place between Persia and Jerusalem (which are over seven hundred miles apart) when enemies of Nehemiah opposed the wall's construction, it seems unlikely that the wall was completed in fifty-two days. It took Ezra five months just to make the journey between Babylon and Jerusalem (Ezra 7:9),[42] and although I'm sure letters could be sent more quickly, Josephus gives us a more realistic timeframe and says that it took three years to finish the wall. However long it took, it is notoriously difficult to get all the ancient dates and royal reigns sorted out to find the answer because of different calendar systems and how different cultures kept track of the passage of time. This era is a muddled mess that is heavily debated among scholars. In my many years of research in this period of history, I've come to the conclusions laid out in the timelines below.[43]

The First Seven Weeks = 50 Years			
Fall 539 BC	Cyrus conquers Babylon; Cyrus' decree – ends 70 years of captivity.	22 years	Segment 1 Begins
517 BC	The Second Temple		Seven Weeks =
	Years of complacency		50 Years
490 BC	Battle of Marathon	28 years	
490 – 489 BC	Year of Jubilee – not celebrated		

Timeline 3: The First 7 Weeks: Cyrus to Marathon

The First Gap Period: Fall of 489 – 449 BC			
Fall 489 BC	Beginning of first gap (Fall of 489)	(487 - Darius the Great dies) (487-475) Xerxes (475-425) Artaxerxes	First Gap
480 BC	Battle of Thermopylae		Period
469 BC	Ezra arrives in Jerusalem (Ezra 7:8-9)		40 Years
456 BC	Nehemiah goes to Jerusalem (Nehemiah 2:1)	Governs for 12 years	
450 - 449 BC	Wall dedicated / Sabbath Year	Nehemiah's 7th year	

Timeline 4: First Gap Period

My hypothesis is that after Nehemiah arrived in Jerusalem, it took six years[44] to complete the basic structure of the city wall and to get the final gate hung in place (Nehemiah 6:15). Then the people and their leaders dedicated the wall, but Nehemiah still had to work on the wall faithfully and continuously for the rest of his governorship (5:14–16). One shouldn't envision that this new wall became a grand impenetrable barrier protecting Jerusalem from all enemies. Excavations from that time period show a wall that is not all that impressive and probably in need of perpetual upkeep, but it would nevertheless have had a symbolic effect on the psychological and spiritual well-being of the city's citizens.[45] Jerusalem was independent again (to a certain degree), and now Nehemiah was able to reinstate obedience to the law and the Sabbath Year (10:28–33),[46] thus making the seventh year of his reign in 450 the marker (as my theory states) for celebrating the "completion" of the wall and bringing the Jews back into compliance with God's law:

> *Six years you shall sow your land and gather in its produce, but the seventh year you shall let it rest and lie fallow, that the poor of your people may eat; and what they leave, the beasts of the field may eat. In like manner you shall do with your vineyard and your olive grove. (Exodus 23:10–11)*

I also theorize that it was this dedication that initiated the second stage of Daniel's prophecy—the 62 weeks—after the Sabbath Year ended in the fall of 449 BC. This dedication set the tone for the Jews for the next 442 consecutive years from the dedication of the wall to the birth of the Messiah. If the wall was dedicated in 450 BC with the Sabbath Year lasting until the fall of 449, that would put the birth of Christ in 7 BC.

We need to do more historical digging to confirm my theory, but let's pause for a moment and take a deep breath: We need to keep in mind that scholars have put Christ's birth anywhere between 7 BC and 1 BC. Ezra and Nehemiah are notoriously difficult to decipher in regard to an exact chronology, but I believe that part of the problem has been caused by not including the year of Jubilee in Daniel's prophecy and not taking into account a gap period between Daniel's 7 weeks and the 62 weeks. We could consider this first gap period a pause in the prophetic years so that other world events could play out, like the Greek and Persian war. If we take those two factors into consideration, then the math puts us into the middle of the reign of Nehemiah. Could the Jews have dedicated the wall at the end of his governorship or earlier, or could some of these dates be a bit off? Yes on both counts, but think about how well the dates fit. It's stunning! If we reverse engineer the chronology and can determine when Christ was born for sure without having to rely on knowing exactly when Nehemiah completed the wall, we can then figure out when he did finish the wall by counting back 442 years.

What this means is that Daniel's 62 weeks was completed when Christ was born, not when he was crucified. To say that Daniel's prophecy points to his baptism or crucifixion, as some people claim, doesn't take into account that Daniel calls the Christ "prince," not "king." He is not officially anointed as king until his baptism, and he won't come as the *ruling* king until his return. But he is Messiah the Prince at his birth.[47]

See how absolutely stunning Daniel's prophecies are? They were made approximately 500 years before they were fulfilled, and we have landed in the timeframe of the possible dates of the birth of the Messiah. I know I still need to produce more evidence to demonstrate that my theory hits the bullseye, so let's see whether more of the historical record and further scriptural evidence will confirm it.

Take a Refreshing Break

I think we need to pause at a creek, take off our packs, and dowse ourselves with water. Maybe even set up camp for the night. It's been a hard journey so far with lots of twists, turns, and, yes, some beautiful vistas. So before we move into part 2 of the book, let's take a breather and review where we've been so far.

We have seen that Luke committed himself to the task of recording the birth of Christ as experienced by Mary, the mother of Jesus. In Luke's Gospel he also goes into great detail about the parents of John the Baptist—Zacharias and Elizabeth. But then we left Luke's narrative for a couple of chapters to introduce two other major players in the birth narrative: the angel Gabriel and the prophet Daniel. As we will see in part 2, Gabriel is the one who gets to announce to Mary the conception of the Messiah, but the beginning of his role in the birth-of-Christ saga began during the life of Daniel. Gabriel was the one who got to tell Daniel the 70-weeks prophecy which laid out the timeframe for when the Messiah would come. God revealed his plan to Daniel via Gabriel, making the angel not only present at the vision but also later at the provision. He was at the portent and the advent, and the coming of the Messiah is as important to the angelic realm as it is for humanity. As we will see in the next stage of our journey, God's plan effectively unfolds in the heavenly domain and the earthly domain, fulfilling his plan of salvation according to his own sovereign will.

STAGE II

The True King

5

Anatomy of a King

Joseph also went up from Galilee, out of the city of Nazareth, into Judea, to the city of David, which is called Bethlehem, because he was of the house and lineage of David, to be registered with Mary, his betrothed wife, who was with child.

—Luke 2:4–5

We all hold assumptions near and dear to our hearts. Some we have held for so long that we don't even notice them anymore. Yet, anything we experience or learn which strengthens those invisible foundations is, at least to us, true and true for all. Our assumptions *are* us. They are the foundation of everything we value. They make sense of our world and bring order to chaos. We may have moments in our lives when we are open to change and even wanting to change, but once our foundation has been poured, it may take an asteroid strike to convince us that we are wrong. However, such a personal change does not always need to be so dramatic. A soul-altering transformation can come with an infant's cry in the morning, as it did with Pharaoh's daughter just before she found Moses in the reeds. Or it may come as a whisper, gently, like a soft wind at twilight as when God overshadowed Mary and chose her to be the mother of the Messiah.

A Man of Honor

After Mary told Joseph the news of her pregnancy and the manner in which she had conceived, he didn't take the news very well. Imagine the emotions involved at such a moment. Anger, embarrassment, shame, confusion. I'm certain Joseph never suspected Mary would behave this way. It was completely outside of her character, and he must have been devastated.

Joseph was a carpenter by trade, which meant he was a builder. When I envision Joseph, I think of my grandfather: a brilliant, innovative problem-solver who was tough as a rock. He was a dairy farmer, and he made his start in the era when they used real milk cans—you know, the ones that people put on their porches now as decorations. The heavy ones. The ones that he could lift up with one arm onto a conveyor belt when it was full of milk. Back-handed. That guy. The strong, smart, hard-working, versatile, matter-of-fact tough man who anyone could count on for anything at any time. Even though he was a man of faith, on the surface one wouldn't consider him to be the most religious of men. He did go to church, but he would fall asleep during the service. Who could blame him? Every day of the week he had been up at 5 a.m. to call in the cows, milk them, and clean the barn and all his equipment. Then on Sunday he also had to clean himself up and get to church on time. Yes, he might drift off during the sermon, but at least he was there. I'm not trying to imply he was a perfect man, but he was faithful. And tough.

His one spiritual conversation with me perfectly captures his personality. I was visiting during a summer break when I was in high school. He and I were sitting in the living room, and Billy Graham was on television. Grandpa was in his recliner, and I was on the couch. All he said to me was, "Do you believe in all this?" After I said yes, he said, "Good." And that was that. Some might be critical of his approach, but it was a meaningful moment for me, and it was all that needed to be said. The exchange was efficient, clean, and to the point.

For me, that is what I imagine Joseph to have been like. There isn't a lot written about him because, well, there isn't much to say. God chose a stable, practical, hard-working man of character to be Jesus's earthly dad. He didn't choose an indulgent, self-aggrandizing, backbiting elitist. He wanted Joseph—an honest man—and that's that. No drama.

It is this kind of rock-solid temperament that explains Joseph's reaction after he heard the life-changing news that Mary was pregnant. He wanted to put her away quietly because he wanted to deal fairly with her based on his understanding of things. I firmly believe that if he had been the one who had gotten her pregnant, he would have owned up to it. I don't doubt that for a second. He wouldn't have run away, nor would he have pretended to be someone he wasn't. He would have continued with the marriage and taken responsibility for his actions. If he had really been the father, he wouldn't have tried to put her away discretely.

But he wasn't the father, and his character dictated that he should not embarrass her. That is why he decided to annul their contract. That was that. It made sense. This may seem coldhearted, but a prearranged marriage was a legal agreement, and he believed that it had been breached. This doesn't mean their relationship had been devoid of affection or respect, but neither was it devoid of truth and honor. His initial response reveals that he was a man who was not a silly-minded, star-crossed lover. He may very well have been in love with Mary but not with the emotional obsessiveness that some associate with love. He also wasn't going to make a big, dramatic scene by broadcasting her indiscretion across the ancient equivalent of Facebook and Twitter—Gossiping—and the busybodies it attracts. That would have been weak, pathetic, and vindictive. Only people of low character do that. Joseph was none of that.

And yet, he wasn't going to continue with the marriage either. He obviously didn't believe the "conceived of the Holy Spirit" explanation, but what did he think happened? Did he think she was lying? Probably not. She was too sweet for that. More than likely he thought that she was just innocent enough to not understand the birds and the bees, and that she had filled in a fictional explanation. It was sad that she expected him to believe her, yet even so he felt it was wiser to let her go and move on with his life.

But despite how honorable he thought he was behaving, he was completely wrong. Mary wasn't crazy, nor was she a fool or a misdirected waif. She was telling the truth, and letting her go was the last thing God wanted him to do. Indeed, it was so important for Joseph *not* to leave that God sent Gabriel to reassure him that Mary wasn't lying. Imagine this practical man getting that message: "She's pregnant because of a miracle, not because of a man. She's telling you the truth. Marry Mary!" Joseph's original decision was the respectable one to make under normal circumstances, but God had chosen Mary to be the mother of the Messiah, and God had chosen Joseph to be his earthly father. This pair were of the most ordinary people in town.

Adoption or Foster Care?

Adoption has a special place in my heart because my older sister was adopted. (I was a surprise a couple of years later.) Our brother, Perry, was the first-born, but several years after he was born, the doctor told my parents that they wouldn't be able to have anymore children. This grieved them, and so they decided to go the route of adoption. My dad would tell the story to the end of his days about the time when the doctor brought my sister to their doorstep in mid-December: "She was all bundled up and had the cutest little red-button nose." He would cry whenever he told the story because a spiritual and emotional bond had formed that was as strong as any blood ties.

My brother-in-law and his wife also adopted a little girl, but their experience was far different than the one my parents had back in the sixties. In my parents' day, the adoption process was straightforward and quick, but today it is an expensive, long, drawn-out process that can take years. One of the things I learned is that the parental rights of the biological parents must be terminated before the new parents can legally adopt the child.[48] This was the case when my parents adopted too. When the adoptive parents finally stand before the judge in court, it leads to a sacred moment like that of a birth: the arrival of a new soul into one's family.

Despite the beauty of adoption, however, I'm not certain that when Joseph agreed to continue with the marriage that he was also adopting Jesus in the full legal sense of the word. Yes, Joseph accepted the role to be Jesus's father, but God did not give up his parental rights. A better analogy, I believe, is that Joseph became a foster parent. Here's the distinction:

> **Adoption***: In short, adoption places children in families permanently, and those adopted children become legal and emotional members of the family, just the same as if the adoptees were the biological children of the parent or parents.*

Fostering: *Foster care can lead to adoption, but at its root, fostering is a temporary placement,* with the hope that the child will be reunified with his or her biological parent or parents.[49]

Unlike in adoption, Joseph raised Jesus until he was reunified with his heavenly Father. It was a temporary arrangement. Recall when Jesus was twelve years old and he stayed in Jerusalem and was engaging religious leaders in the temple (Luke 2:41–52). Luke records that Joseph and Mary had not realized that their son was missing during the return trip home. So they went back to Jerusalem to find him. After three days, they found him at the temple listening to and asking questions of the Jewish teachers there. Properly annoyed, Mary chastised young Jesus and said, "Your father and I have sought You anxiously."

However, Jesus seemed to be a bit shocked that they even bothered to come back for him. "Why did you seek Me? Did you not know that I must be about My Father's business?" (v. 49). It sounds rude, but Jesus thought it was time for his ministry to start, and he was merely assuming that they understood a basic truth: "Joseph, you are not my dad. God is."

Nevertheless, in spite of Jesus's eagerness to get on with his ministry, he had to return home with them because it wasn't yet time. Their role as his guardians was not over. That didn't come until years later when his cousin John baptized him and the Holy Spirit descended on him like a dove. A voice from heaven—God the Father—then declared, "This is My beloved Son, in whom I am well pleased" (Matthew 3:17). Joseph performed his role well and faithfully raised Jesus, but he had never been anyone other than Jesus's temporary caretaker.

However, far from diminishing Joseph, I believe this elevates him. Think of what Joseph had to do: he could have morally and ethically put Mary away, but he changed his mind and took Mary to be his wife. When he did that, he was willingly accepting that his neighbors would never consider him an honorable man again. If he had struggled to believe her story, wouldn't his neighbors struggle too? Also, even though he knew that Jesus would never be *his* son, he willingly treated him as if he were. He knew what he was agreeing to, and this tough-minded, practical man obeyed without a complaint, without any reservations, and without any applause.

What this ordinary man did was nothing short of magnificent.

A Woman of Faith

Mary was a young woman when she found out the news that she was pregnant. It seems odd to us today, and even wrong, but women were marriageable by the age of fourteen. The *Jewish Encyclopedia* explains:

> *It is thus considered the duty of every Israelite to marry as early in life as possible. Eighteen years is the age set by the Rabbis (Ab. v. 24). . . . [Although] Some urge that children should marry as soon as they reach the age of puberty, i.e., the fourteenth year (Sanh. 76b).*[50]

Even not so long ago, in 1932, my very own grandmother got married when she was fifteen. She gave birth to my mother when she was eighteen, and my grandmother was one of the godliest women I have known in my life. She read her Bible every day, taught Sunday school, was a faithful, devoted wife, and had a fiery spirit that didn't put up with any guff, and yet she was the kindest woman one could ever meet. The first half of the twentieth century was a different era too, when responsibility and hard work came early and the culture didn't superficially suppress behaving as mature, responsible adults, even to the point of taking care of a household, getting married, and working hard to provide for one's own.

The initial challenge Mary had to face, though, was not her pregnancy, but that since Joseph was considering not marrying her, she not only had to deal with the potential of raising the child on her own without a husband—for who would have her now?—she would also have to face the shame of losing her reputation within the community. From her perspective, she must have felt alone and abandoned.

Nevertheless, Mary responded to the news of her pregnancy with faith and grace. Fortunately, she had extended family to turn to. Gabriel said to her, "Elizabeth your relative has also conceived a son in her old age; and this is now the sixth month for her who was called barren" (Luke 1:36). So since Joseph was intending to "put her away," essentially divorcing her, Mary decided to visit her relative in the hill country of Judea. This had two distinct advantages over remaining with her parents: (1) She could get away to the country and process what happened to her; and (2) she could get away from the inevitable small-town rumors that were bound to swirl around her pregnancy. She needed some time for personal reflection.

Elizabeth plays an important role in Mary's life, not only because the two women were related, but also because they were connected in the purposes of God. It is unclear exactly what their relationship was, but I like to believe that Elizabeth was Mary's aunt. We know very little about Mary's family. Her father may have been Heli (if Luke's genealogy is indeed the one which traces her lineage), and we know she had a sister named Mary (John 19:25). However, the Bible says nothing about her mother.[51] One reason I would like to believe that Elizabeth is her aunt is that I have an aunt like that. She is a second mother to me (especially now that my own mother is with the Lord), and so it makes sense that Mary seeks out the most nurturing soul she can think of to help her in this time of trial. Some scholars believe Elizabeth was a cousin, but I surmise she was more likely her aunt because of her age. A cousin would be closer in age to Mary, and therefore it seems more likely that Elizabeth was the older sister of Mary's mother. The bonus of visiting her is that Mary would also get to help Elizabeth during the last few months of her pregnancy.

The other advantage was that, during those three months that Mary was away, Joseph had time to sort through his own emotions. Scripture says Gabriel came to him "after he had considered this [putting Mary away]" (Matthew 1:20), but it doesn't say how long he had to think about things. Gabriel may have visited him before she left, but after combing through both Gospel accounts, it seems more likely to me that God allowed Joseph some space to think about things while Mary was gone. He was intending to put her away quietly, so she went to stay with Elizabeth, and then during that time God sent Gabriel to Joseph.

Either way is perfectly plausible, but I like the second scenario more because God does allow us space sometimes to sort through our emotions and thoughts, especially regarding big decisions or life-altering moments. Soon after becoming a Christian, I had a huge decision to make and had to spend at least three intensive weeks of immersive prayer experiencing emotional and spiritual combat over what I should do. I'm certain Joseph needed time to reflect on his decision to end his relationship with Mary. Even with potentially three months for him to process things, though, Gabriel still needed to be sent to reassure him that God had performed a miracle. God sent Gabriel to put Joseph back on the right path, and Joseph finally believed and committed to marrying Mary. Whatever the chronology may be, the essential point is that he wrestled with his decision, and then the couple chose not to sleep with each other until after Jesus was born (Matthew 1:24–25). They both were on the same page now and recognized the sacredness of what God had called them to. We need to acknowledge how honorably this ordinary couple behaved.[52]

Disbelieving Neighbors

But this is not a fairy-tale ending either. Joseph and Mary's neighbors didn't start singing and dancing in the streets with joy over the coming Messiah. In fact, the citizens of Nazareth never did accept the story that Joseph was not the biological father. They apparently considered it a lie for his entire life. Can you imagine the whispers behind their backs? Later in Matthew's Gospel, we get a glimpse into what small-town Nazareth thought of the whole virgin birth story:

> When He [Jesus] had come to His own country, He taught them in their synagogue, so that they were astonished and said, "Where did this Man get this wisdom and these mighty works? Is this not the carpenter's son? Is not His mother called Mary? And His brothers James, Joses, Simon, and Judas? And His sisters, are they not all with us? Where then did this Man get all these things?" So they were offended at Him.
>
> But Jesus said to them, "A prophet is not without honor except in his own country and in his own house." Now He did not do many mighty works there because of their unbelief. (Matthew 13:54–58)

First, observe that Jesus had four brothers and several sisters. Isn't that an amazing thought? After the birth of Jesus, Joseph and Mary moved on to a God-ordained married life and had more children. To me this is awesome! It neither makes Mary impure nor Joseph a lecher (how dare he violate the Virgin Mary!). Instead, it makes Joseph and Mary normal. It means that after Jesus was born, they enjoyed a married life together exactly as God had designed: "Behold, children are a heritage from the LORD, the fruit of the womb is a reward" (Psalm 127:3). Holiness in marriage doesn't mean celibacy; it means sex: "The husband should fulfill his wife's sexual needs, and the wife should fulfill her husband's needs" (1 Corinthians 7:3 NLT). God made marriage this way. First Corinthians 7:28 says, "But even if you do marry, you have not sinned; and if a virgin marries, she has not sinned." It isn't a sin to have sex within the context of marriage. In fact, it would be an act of unrighteousness to *not* have sex with one's spouse. Paul says, "Do not deprive each other of sexual relations, unless you both agree to refrain from sexual intimacy for a limited time so you can give yourselves more completely to prayer. Afterward, you should come together again so that Satan won't be able to tempt you because of your lack of self-control" (v. 5 NLT).

But back to the citizens of Nazareth. What's interesting is that the folks who knew Jesus while he was growing up were not only shocked but also *offended* at who he had become. His claim to be the Messiah made no sense to them at all. How could the Savior of the world—the hope of Israel—ever grow up in such an ordinary town and come from such an ordinary (low-class) family? Instead of honoring him and saying, "Wow! I knew him when he was yay high," they refused to see him as anything more than just a regular guy. This attitude implies that Jesus's youth was not extraordinary but ordinary. He did not go around performing miracles or doing anything else that would have set him apart from everyone else. Of course, he didn't sin (Hebrews 4:15), but nothing he did was overtly divine. While some writings outside of the New Testament contain stories about Jesus as a child doing miraculous things, like raising a bird from the dead or making living things from clay, his fellow Nazarenes never noticed such activities in his life. It was only after his adult baptism by John that Jesus began performing supernatural deeds. So how could such a normal boy from a working-class couple have grown up to know the Scriptures so well and be able to do the mighty works of God?

Jesus explains the Nazarene attitude by saying, "A prophet is without honor in his own country and *in his own house*." Apparently, Jesus's immediate family didn't accept the idea that their brother was the Savior of the world either. This, I think, illustrates the normality of their family: they were dysfunctional just like all families are. They had disagreements, and they apparently didn't get along at times. It also explains why Jesus handed off the responsibility for taking care of his mother to his favorite disciple, John, instead of to a family member while he was on the cross. None of his brothers were believers, and Jesus wanted a believer to take care of his mom. That indicates some rough family dynamics. Anyway, it does appear that at least Jesus's brother James eventually believed, but that must not have happened until after the resurrection.[53]

Another possible reason the Nazarenes could not bring themselves to believe that Jesus was the Messiah is that the Messiah was supposed to be a son of David. Yes, Joseph and Mary had the correct pedigree, but they certainly did not fit the royal image at all. Shouldn't the Messiah be from a wealthy, politically connected family that lived in Jerusalem? Shouldn't he be from the ruling classes of the Sanhedrin? Joseph and Mary were as far from that image as possible. Jesus was the son of a carpenter (as it was supposed), and he was from the insignificant town of Nazareth. Are you kidding? It seemed absurd to believe he was a king, let alone the Messiah. Ridiculous! And yet he was the One who all of biblical history had been hoping for and expecting.

A Son of David

The Nazarenes were right about one thing: the Messiah must be a son of David. In 2 Samuel 7:12–13, the prophet Nathan tells David: "When your days are fulfilled and you rest with your fathers, I will set up your seed after you, who will come from your body, and I will establish his kingdom. He shall build a house for My name, and I will establish the throne of his kingdom forever." Solomon clearly fulfills the first part of this prophecy after he takes over and builds the temple. Obviously, the legacy of David's eternal dynasty would have to play itself out over time. However, there is a curious statement made in the next verse that I find intriguing. I will quote the entire passage again so you can hear it in context:

> *When your days are fulfilled and you rest with your fathers, I will set up your seed after you, who will come from your body, and I will establish his kingdom. He shall build a house for My name, and I will establish the throne of his kingdom forever.* I will be his Father, and he shall be My son. *(2 Samuel 7:12–14)*

Did you see that? "I will be his Father, and he shall be My son." How could that be? This is indeed a mystery. Fortunately, Jesus took the time to explain exactly what this means in a conversation he had with the Pharisees:

> *While the Pharisees were gathered together, Jesus asked them, saying, "What do you think about the Christ? Whose Son is He?"*
> *They said to Him, "The Son of David."*
> *He said to them, "How then does David in the Spirit call Him 'Lord,' saying: "The LORD said to my Lord, 'Sit at My right hand, till I make Your enemies Your footstool'"? If David then calls Him 'Lord,' how is He his Son?"*
> *And no one was able to answer Him a word, nor from that day on did anyone dare question Him anymore. (Matthew 22:41–45)*

Mark records the same conversation, but he ends it with "And the common people heard Him gladly" (Mark 12:37).

So what does this mean? Why do the Pharisees shut up and the common people cheer? Isn't Jesus supposed to be the son of David? Others call him that frequently throughout the New Testament, and even he calls himself that, but it seems like here he is distancing himself from the whole notion. Let me reassure you that he is not. Rather, Jesus is revealing a deeper truth that goes beyond him merely being a son of David: he must also be the

Son of God. But how does that work? There is only one explanation: the virgin conception and birth. The Messiah would have to be born of a woman according to the flesh, thereby being a human descendant of David. God the Son would have to enter our weak and fallen frame—the human tabernacle—and become one of us: "Inasmuch then as the children have partaken of flesh and blood, He Himself likewise shared in the same, that through death He might destroy him who had the power of death, that is, the devil, and release those who through fear of death were all their lifetime subject to bondage" (Hebrews 2:14–15).

He took on our flesh and blood and made himself subject to death. God the Son dwelt in a human body. He bore our shame and our weaknesses and yet lived a sinless life. He was tempted as we are, and yet he never sinned (Hebrews 4:15). Christ was obedient for us, but in order to do that he had to live as one of us. Paul says, "For it pleased the Father that in Him [the Son] all the fullness should dwell" (Colossians 1:19). He also says in Galatians 4:4–5, "But when the fullness of the time had come, God sent forth His Son, *born of a woman*, born under the law, to redeem those who were under the law, that we might receive the adoption as sons." Joseph may not have been able to adopt Jesus, but Jesus was able to adopt him. And that is why David can say in the Spirit, without any contradiction whatsoever, that his son—the Messiah—is also his Lord.

The Son of God

Perhaps you have never noticed, but the genealogies regarding Jesus that appear in the Gospels of Matthew and Luke appear to be in disagreement with each other. Matthew says that a man named Jacob is Joseph's father (Matthew 1:16), but Luke says his name is Heli (Luke 3:23). What is going on? How could they mess that up? There are quite a few other unmatched names after David, but before David the two genealogies match up perfectly. Why? The most common explanation (with which I agree) is that one account gives us Mary's genealogy, and the other account gives us Joseph's. Both Jacob and Heli are Joseph's dad in the sense that one of them is his father-in-law. There are other, more elaborate explanations to explore if you are interested, but I am an Occam's razor kind of guy so the aforementioned explanation is sufficient.

However, it is a bit more difficult to discern whether Luke or Matthew has given us Mary's ancestry. Is Mary's father Heli or is it Jacob? There seems to be a fifty-fifty split among scholars. Both sides make strong arguments, but I believe that Luke is the one who traces Mary's lineage. As we saw in the first chapter, Luke derives his account directly from Mary, so it makes sense that he would have written down her family's lineage. However, I think the proponents of Matthew make a strong argument in his favor by pointing out that he includes four other women in the line of Jesus: Tamar, Rahab, Ruth, and Bathsheba. With his inclusion of these four prominent females (all of whom were not Jewish, by the way) in the line of David, he may have been hoping to persuade his brethren to accept Mary too. Whichever side one chooses, I don't think it ultimately matters whether it was Matthew or Luke. It is enough to know that one of them traces the lineage of Mary.

But there is another Gospel which is often overlooked in the context of the birth of Christ: the Gospel of John. Matthew and Luke give us the visual, historical narrative that proves Jesus Christ isn't just a figment of human imagination or a psychological archetype of some deeply seated, mythical messiah complex. Jesus was born to real people and in a real place, within a political/historical context, and raised in a real family. But John skips all that and gets right to the essence of Jesus: "In the beginning was the Word, and the Word was with God, *and the Word was God. . . .* And *the Word became flesh* and dwelt among us, and we beheld His glory, the glory as of the only begotten of the Father, full of grace and truth" (John 1:1, 14). Can't get more to the point than that. Jesus is God's Son. In John's first letter, he manages to say it more explicitly: "we have seen, and bear witness, and declare to you that eternal life which was with the Father and was manifested to us . . . and truly our fellowship is with the Father and with His Son Jesus Christ. . . . . Whoever confesses that Jesus is the Son of God, God abides in him, and he in God" (1 John 1:2–3; 3:15).

The apostle John unequivocally declares that God the Son became flesh and dwelt among us. Combine that with Matthew and Luke's accounts and we can now see more clearly the glory surrounding Christ's birth. Jesus is the Son of man *and* the Son of God.

Mapping Out the Course

As we have seen, the holy family was ordinary, but their first son was not. Jesus's conception was supernatural, but his gestation and birth were natural. His family life was normal, and his hometown small and out of the way of the busy hubs of power. God quietly, gently—almost without being noticed—introduced the Messiah to our world.

But the world was swirling in a whirlwind of activity around this humble family. Rome was ruled by Caesar Augustus who was at the height of his power and was called the son of God (the name Augustus means "son of God"), and Israel was ruled by King Herod—a usurper to the throne of Israel who was not well liked by the Jews or anyone else really. It was a tumultuous and energetic time.

In the midst of these world events—and in some ways because of them—Jesus was born in an obscure village in a subjugated Roman province to a simple, faithful, ordinary couple. With a whisper, God began the process of deconstructing the world system, and even though the world had not yet realized what was happening, soon the true King would take the title "son of God" from Augustus and wrest the title "king of the Jews" from Herod. Jerusalem, Rome, and the rest of the world, from the most powerful to the poorest, would learn about this obscure Nazarene and come to see his great power and humility, his supreme authority and amazing sacrifice—God incarnate here for them and for us.

6

God Emperor of Rome

*And it came to pass in those days that a decree went out
from Caesar Augustus that all the world should be registered.*
—*Luke 2:1*

Jesus Christ was born when Rome was the center of the world. It was the center politically, religiously, economically, and militarily. Rome was also in its golden age of literature. Historians and poets like Livy, Virgil, and Ovid (to name a few) dominated the world of ideas, and through all these means Rome had made herself into the preeminent political and cultural force on earth. Rome was power, and no one wielded her unmatched influence over people and world events more effectively than her first and arguably greatest emperor, Caesar Augustus.

Gaius Octavius (Augustus's given name) was born in 63 BC, 691 years after the founding of Rome (AUC).[54] And his birth was allegedly on the Palatine Hill where Rome began. The Roman biographer Suetonius writes: "Augustus was born in the consulship of Marcus Tullius Cicero and Caius Antonius,[55] upon the ninth of the calends of October [the 23rd of September], a little before sunrise, in the quarter of the Palatine Hill, and the street called The Ox-Heads, where now stands a chapel dedicated to him, and built a little after his death."[56]

Once considered "the nucleus of the Roman Empire," all that remains on the Palatine Hill are the crumbled foundations of formerly marble-skinned villas, temples, and palaces. Today one can wander through the skeletal remains of colonnades, arenas, and basilicas, and marvel at what used to be the structural framework of the mind, heart, and spirit of the once living and breathing Roman Empire. The Palatine Hill is also where Romulus killed his brother Remus to claim Rome as his own after the auguries (bird omens) were not clear enough to determine which of the brothers should be king. Romulus founded Rome that day, April 21, 753 BC. By the end of Augustus's life, Romans were calling him the new Romulus, the second founder of Rome.

Suetonius says that other Romans claim that Octavius was born in a nearby town to the east of Rome called Velitrae. His nursery there is described as "being a very small place, and much like a pantry," and the locals claimed that a violent entity haunted it that would not allow anyone to live there, thus maintaining the sanctity of the house.[57] Whichever place Octavius was born, his rise to fame and power required conflict and cunning. On February 16, 27 BC, "the senators and other citizens gave to the imperator Caesar the title of Augustus, Son of God."[58] Octavius was thirty-six years old.

His father, Gaius Octavius Copia, died when his son was only four, and his mother, Attia, remarried a man named Lucius Philippus. It was his mother's uncle Julius Caesar, though, who saw the potential of Octavius and adopted him when he was a teenager.

After Brutus and about sixty senators assassinated Julius Caesar on March 15, 44 BC, Octavius faced several roadblocks on his path toward ultimate power. He first had to ask permission from Marc Antony to allow him to take control of his portion of Caesar's substantial inheritance.[59] Antony refused at first, but then reluctantly agreed after Cicero—the most powerful senator—humiliated him with vicious rhetoric. Cicero also said wonderful things about Octavius, but it was not from any genuine affection; he merely wanted to weaken Antony. Within the year, however, Cicero would regret playing such a duplicitous game. Antony and Octavius developed a temporary alliance based on their mutual desire to take vengeance on the conspirators who had murdered Julius Caesar. To cement this relationship, Antony demanded that Octavius allow the murder of Cicero. He did. Eventually—and inevitably—these two men who wanted to rule the world squared off against each other. Octavius defeated Antony in the Battle of Actium on September 2, 31 BC.

Octavius now had it all: he had money, a loyal army, and the goodwill of the people for having defeated Marc Antony—the man who had destroyed his own reputation with his sexual and political ties with the Queen of Egypt, Cleopatra. Octavius's next steps would prove to be the most important in establishing his power. He could not just declare himself to be the emperor and expect everyone to submit to his reign. The people and the senate of Rome would put him down as violently as they had his adoptive father. If he were going to truly maintain his power and influence, he had to appear as if he didn't want that power.

The Greatest Showman

In order to avoid getting assassinated, Octavius had to play a discreet game of thrones. His most successful and trusted general, Agrippa, warned him that if he came out too strongly and declared himself a king over Rome, "Our object will seem to have been not to free them [Roman citizens] from conspirators but to enslave them to ourselves. Either supposition entails censure."[60] Censure would mean, at the very least, exile and at the worst, death. Agrippa warned Octavius to be careful and advised him to maintain the appearance of acting democratically.

However, a wealthy patron (not a politician) named Maecenas encouraged Octavius to become a monarch, even though he, too, wanted him to accomplish his goal wisely and carefully. Maecenas told him:

> With this in mind [to become Monarch], together with all the rest that I have told you, heed my advice and let not that fortune slip which has chosen you out of all and set you at the head of all. If you would choose the substance of monarch but fear the name of "kingdom" as accursed, then refrain from taking possession of the latter and be satisfied to employ merely the title of "Caesar." If you need any further appellations, they will give you that of Imperator, as they gave it to your father. They will reverence you also by still another

name, so that you may obtain all the advantages of a kingdom with-out the disfavor that attaches to the term itself.[61]

The advice given to him by Agrippa and Maecenas describes the philoso-phy undergirding Octavius's strategy to increase his power. He wisely chose to be bold yet subtle, decisive yet restrained. He deftly enacted policies that gath-ered power to himself, and yet he avoided (barely) the appearance of tyranny. Any victories he achieved had to appear to be for Rome, not for himself, and he purchased the goodwill of his soldiers with excellent pay and the generous distribution of land.

One of the more subtle tactics he employed was the use of language. For example, four years after the Battle of Actium, the senate began to call him *Augustus*, an original title Octavius had created for himself. *Augustus* implied not only that he revered the gods, but also that he should be revered as a god (although he wasn't officially deified until after his death). *Augustus* means son of God, and every emperor after Octavius included "Augustus" in their impe-rial name. By attaching to himself this never-before-used title, Octavius was effectively, but subtly, establishing himself as not only Rome's political and military leader but also its religious leader. Numa Pompilius, the second king of Rome and the successor to Romulus, had called himself *Pontifex Maximus*, the chief priest of Rome.[62] He was the first Roman king to have put politics and religion into the power of one man. Augustus renewed that long-forsaken combination.

The Age of Augustus is today considered to have begun the year the senate conferred on Octavius the brand new title of Augustus in 27 BC,[63] also confer-ring on him the honor of Imperator. The title he most used to refer to himself, though, was *Princeps,* which means "First Citizen." Some have pointed out the irony of the title by translating *Princeps* as "First among equals." It sounds humble at first, for it seems to affirm that all Romans are equals. But upon further reflection, Princeps is laced with a hint of arrogance, moderated by a surprising aftertaste of acceptability.

Octavius's goal in choosing names and titles like these was to deflect the negative effects of an overtly hated title like king. Image was everything, and

Augustus understood the dangerous waters in which he sailed, with Charybdis and Scylla on either side. On the one side he had to fear offending the all-consuming whirlpool of public opinion, but on the other side he had to avoid the many-headed beast of the senate, which could snatch him up and eat him as easily as anyone could.

Power attained, though, is not easily maintained, and he wasn't content with just being in charge: he wanted to be loved. Octavius understood he would need to strategically take over the established systems of government and appoint loyal Romans to positions of power—men who would govern wisely, and yet were committed to doing his will. He would also need to eliminate anyone he felt was dangerous to his plans. He was not afraid to act violently and forcefully if necessary, but in order to keep the senate at bay, he decided to continue the use of ancient titles such as quaestor, aedile, tribune, praetor, and consul. He didn't want "to seem to be changing the constitution altogether."[64] The bottom line is that he spent the rest of his life carefully crafting his image to bear a resemblance to what people expected an emperor should be.

He became the greatest showman.

Augustus recognized that the political and spiritual landscape of Rome was in a mess after years of civil war, financial chaos, and social upheaval (never mind that he had been at the center of it all), and he knew that a good emperor was supposed to guide the moral character of his people. For example, one of the areas he tried to bring under control was marriage. It wasn't because of any prudish or moral concerns about sexuality, but rather "the Romans were constantly concerned, even obsessed, with the necessity of reproduction—of reproduction within the patriarchal family."[65] In Rome, men could sleep with temple prostitutes (any prostitutes for that matter) and slaves, but they weren't supposed to sleep with other men's wives. To circumvent that restriction, Romans were "frequently changing their wives"—in other words, wife-swapping via the legal channels of divorce and remarriage, thereby appearing to follow Augustus's laws, while instead circumventing his desire for strong marriages and large families.[66] Also, to avoid having children, men were marrying girls who were not old enough to have children, which for Augustus violated the purpose of marriage. Augustus wanted all of this to stop, and he wanted to encourage the production of legal heirs within the construct of the family. And yet because pedophilia, sex with slaves, and prostitution were culturally accepted, Rome had to provide "Places within the city [that] became known as sites for the exposure of unwanted children."[67] Unwanted children were discarded, and although some would die, others were "rescued" to be raised as slaves. Rome was out of control sexually, and, like today, children became the victims of human debauchery.

In spite of all the success Augustus had, his rise to power required him to betray friends and murder senators. He also was a notorious adulterer in contradiction to his laws against adultery. Even his own daughter was accused of sleeping with over half the senate, and he banished her in an attempt to maintain his own image of moral superiority.

One wouldn't know it from his statues, but Augustus was only five feet seven inches tall and would wear platform sandals to give him more height. He was physically frail, superstitious, and rarely went into battle himself in his later years. His carefully crafted image of physical, intellectual, and spiritual superiority was a façade which hid a run-of-the-mill, brutal tyrant. His real talent lay in creating the perception that he was not a tyrant, and the greatest showman knew deep down that it was all an act. Suetonius records:

> On the day that he died, Augustus frequently enquired whether rumors of his illness were causing any popular disturbance. He called for a mirror, and had his hair combed and his lower jaw, which had fallen from weakness, propped up. Presently he summoned a group of friends and asked, 'Have I played my part in the farce of life creditably enough?', adding the theatrical tag:
> If I have pleased you, kindly signify
> Appreciation with a warm goodbye.[68]

He saw himself as an actor leaving the stage, and he wanted the audience to applaud.

The Prince of Bureaucrats

In many ways, Augustus's strategy worked. By the time his reign was over, peace and stability reigned throughout the empire, and his reforms initiated a two-hundred-year era known as the *Pax Romana*, Roman Peace. He had not only carefully managed his public image to maintain his power, but he had also figured out how to tap into the fuel of power—money. He needed loyal governors at home and in the outlying provinces, and he could only maintain their political and military cooperation with money. Lots of it. But how would he accumulate all that money? Augustus became the prince of bureaucrats.

To maintain power over the sprawling Roman Empire and to fully benefit from all of its resources, he reinstituted the ancient practice of taking a census. This wasn't like a modern census where we just count people. It was a way for Rome to assess the financial worth and loyalty (or at least the obedience) of every citizen and subject of the empire. The census form looked more like a modern tax form. These registrations were called *lustrum*, and they took place throughout the empire in five-year cycles which were concluded with a purification ceremony called a *lustrum*.[69] Augustus mentions in the *Res Gestae*[70] (his own account of his life accomplishments) that he personally oversaw three *lustrum*, which were held in 28 BC, 8 BC, and AD 14.[71] These are all twenty years apart, and he doesn't mention any others, although it is known that there were others. These particular ones, though, must have been significant to him. Some historians try to imply that these *lustrums* were not empire-wide, but the fact is that since Augustus was personally involved in ordering and overseeing them, it would be strange if they were not empire-wide. Roman officials called censors were in charge of the censuses, and Rome loved taxing people as much as any bureaucracy ever has. They also loved gauging the loyalty of their provinces with those registrations. It is pointless to criticize Luke's account as if Rome didn't conduct a census in Israel. Of course Rome did! As they did in all of their provinces.

The one Augustus organized in 28 BC—the year before the senate officially recognized him as Imperator—was the first *lustrum* Rome had done in forty-one years. With all the civil unrest that had been going on during those years, it was no wonder that Rome had not had the time to conduct a census.

But with Augustus now in charge, he wanted to convey the image of order and stability. The side benefit, of course, was that the census would bring in much needed revenue, and with money would come power.

The next major *lustrum* began in 8 BC, and the last one began near the end of Augustus's life in AD 14. Suetonius records that just as Augustus was finishing up one census period with the religious ceremonies of purification, he would begin the next. For example, when Augustus was nearing the end of his life, Rome celebrated a lustrum (the completion of a census), and Augustus immediately sent his successor, Tiberius, to the province of Illyricum to begin work on the next census cycle.[72] Augustus was going to join him, but he contracted an illness and became too weak to travel, so he ordered Tiberius to return to Rome.

Mandates

And it came to pass in those days that a decree went out from Caesar Augustus that all the world should be registered. This was the first of a series of registrations that occurred before Quirinius governed Syria.[73] *So all went to be registered, everyone to his own city. (Luke 2:1–3)*

The traditional translation for the italicized portion above is "This census first took place while Quirinius was governing Syria." You will find a close approximation of that in every translation, and it gives the impression that Christ was born during a census that was taken while Quirinius was governor of Syria (a Roman province which included Israel). However, there is a well-known flaw in that translation: There is no record of Quirinius having ever governed Syria while Herod was alive. It is widely accepted that Quirinius did govern Syria, and that he even ran a census, but this was *after* Herod had died. This has caused a major credibility problem for Luke's account. Was Luke confused and therefore got the census wrong, or is there some other explanation?

One explanation suggests that Luke must have been referring to two censuses that were both run by Quirinius, and that Jesus was born during the first one that Quirinius managed while Herod was alive.[74] That's an intriguing idea, and there are some ancient inscriptions that have been found that have led some scholars to place Quirinius in the region when Herod was alive. However, these inscriptions do not mention Quirinius by name, and there is no reason to think that even if he were in the region of Syria in 7 BC that he had anything to do with the management of a census in Judea. There were already two very competent Romans in charge of Syria at that time—Saturninus and Voluminus. Did yet a third high-ranking Roman need to be there, especially to oversee a census? Also, as we will see in chapter 10, Herod was dead by 4 BC, so even if Quirinius could be proven to have governed Syria at a later time from 4 to 1 BC, as this theory suggests, Jesus could not have been born within that range of years. So this understanding of Luke's statement still produces an unyielding puzzle that conflicts with the historical record as we know it.

So let's look at another theory that might more easily explain what is going on in Luke's account and is derived from what we already know. The historical record absolutely confirms that Quirinius governed Syria about ten years after Herod died and that he performed a census. Josephus, an historian who lived and wrote during the first century AD, says:

> *Now Cyrenius [Quirinius], a Roman senator, and one who had gone through other magistracies, and had passed through them till he had been consul, and one who, on other accounts, was of great dignity, came at this time into Syria, with a few others, being sent by Caesar [Augustus] to be a judge of that nation, and to take an account [a registration] of their substance.*[75]

When I first read this, I thought this must be referring to the census Luke mentions. It sounds perfect! However, as I looked more closely, I discovered that this census took place ten years *after* the death of Herod, and since both Matthew and Luke record that Jesus was born while Herod was alive, this cannot be the census at the birth of Christ. Josephus's account, however, does confirm that Quirinius was a high-ranking Roman official who was sent by Augustus to govern Syria and carry out a census there. But the time period given conflicts with the theory that Quirinius did all of this while Herod was alive and ruling over Israel.

The Rise of the Zealots

The census run by Quirinius is nevertheless very important, and there must be a reason why Luke mentions him. According to Josephus, it was ten years into Archelaus's reign[76] when Quirinius and Coponius were assigned to govern Judea and given the task of organizing a registration.[77] Lingering anger and resentment toward Rome was broiling beneath the surface like a volcano ready to blow, and Caesar's decision to tax them caused the upward pressure for justice to exceed the downward pressure of Rome's ability to suppress that anger. When it finally blew, it caused an explosion of events that led to the destruction of the temple in Jerusalem almost 70 years later. The volcano Vesuvius didn't even have such devastating effects on Pompeii.

Why were so many Jews virulently opposed to the Roman census? Religiously, it was because of what it represented and required. An oath of loyalty to Rome and to Caesar was implicit in the act of a census. A census was a survey of the property of the people, and Julius Caesar had excused the Jews from being subjected to taxation, recognizing their demeanor that worshiping God above the state was of upmost importance to them. Participating in a census was to many Jews similar to an act of sacrilege, an expression of disloyalty to the King of the universe, to the very One who had saved them so many times in history and turned them into a nation. Rome was demanding to be put first, above the Lord of lords. Rome was also demanding more and more of the fruit of the Jews' livelihood, which struck the Jews as government-approved slavery. All of this was unacceptable.

Josephus says that the Jewish leaders were able to contain the outrage of the people at first when the Romans required the Jews to participate in the census:

> But the Jews, although at the beginning they took the report of a taxation heinously, yet did they leave off any further opposition to it, by the persuasion of Joazar, who was the son of Beethus, and high priest; so they, being over-persuaded by Joazar's words, gave an account of their estates, without any dispute about it.

The Jewish leaders had suppressed an uprising, or so they thought. Some other Jews remained recalcitrant, though, and they could not be talked out of fighting against the injustice of Roman taxation. Josephus continues:

> *Yet was there one* Judas, a Gaulonite, of a city whose name was Gamala, *who, taking with him Sadduc, a Pharisee, became zealous to draw them to a revolt, who both said that this taxation was no better than an introduction to slavery, and exhorted the nation to assert their liberty; . . . All sorts of misfortunes also sprang from these men, and the nation was infected with this doctrine to an incredible degree; one violent war came upon us after another, and we lost our friends which used to alleviate our pains; . . . But of the fourth sect of Jewish philosophy [the Zealots]*, Judas the Galilean was the author" *(emphasis added).*[78]

What happened during this census was a significant moment in Jewish history—the equivalent of Japan's attack on Pearl Harbor in 1941 or the terrorist airplane attacks on US targets on September 11, 2001. A subversive war started that lasted for another 70 years. Josephus wrote extensively about the horrors that came upon the Jews during this time in his account *The Wars of the Jews*, which culminated with the destruction of the temple in Jerusalem. He traced the entire tragedy back to these Zealots and this revolt led by Judas of Galilee.

So notorious was this Zealot-led rebellion that it even found its way into the pages of Scripture. Forty years after the revolt and soon after the ascension of Christ, the Jewish Sanhedrin arrested the apostles Peter and John for continuing to preach Christ at the temple after they had been commanded not to. During their trial, Luke records a speech by a Pharisee named Gamaliel who referred to a couple of rebellions that had taken place many years before:

> *Men of Israel, take heed to yourselves what you intend to do regarding these men [Peter and John]. For some time ago Theudas rose up, claiming to be somebody. A number of men, about four hundred,*

joined him. He was slain, and all who obeyed him were scattered and came to nothing. After this man, Judas of Galilee rose up in the days of the census, and drew away many people after him. He also perished, and all who obeyed him were dispersed." (Acts 5:35–37)

Fascinating. Gamaliel mentions the same story of Judas and the census that Josephus does as if it were common knowledge. But it must have been more than just a casual memory. Judas of Galilee's rebellion was so formative to the character of the relationship between Rome and Jerusalem that it defined an era. It was the beginning of the rise of the Zealots. It wasn't an obscure event of little import. The census that Quirinius managed was a watershed moment in Jewish history and Luke knew all about it. But Luke was not telling us that Jesus had been born during *that* census but during an earlier one. Jesus was born during a census before the infamous one run by Quirinius. But was that one also run by Quirinius, or has there been a grievous mistranslation of Luke 2:2?

Luke 2:2

Here is Luke 2:2 arranged in the exact order of the original Greek words, although written in English. Each segment matches a Greek word[79]:

> *"This was the first of the series of / registrations / which came to pass / before / governed / the / Syria / Quirinius."*

To rearrange the words a little, which all translators do, this is how the text would read:

> *"This was the first of the series of registrations which occurred before Quirinius took command of Syria."*

However, the common translation is this:

> *"This census first took place while Quirinius was governing Syria."*

Notice how different the common translation is from what the original Greek actually conveys. The common one is less specific, and it isn't clear what it means, as I have already noted.

Returning to the much better translation, "This was the first of the series of registrations which occurred before Quirinius took command of Syria," we can see more clearly what Luke is telling us. Far from being a census "which first took place *while* Quirinius was governor of Syria," Luke is talking about a census that occurred *before* the infamous census that had been managed by Quirinius. That notorious census that Quirinius managed changed the relationship between Rome and Israel forever. It would be like saying, "The census that occurred before Pearl Harbor." Jesus was not born during that Roman census run by Quirinius. Nor does the original Greek allow the idea that the census happened during an earlier census that Quirinius managed. There is no hint of such a possibility in the original Greek at all. Because of this confusion, the English translation has perpetuated a quest to discover a mythical earlier census run by Quirinius.

This passage has been debated for centuries, and the biblical scholar Harold Hoehner in his book *Chronological Aspects of the Life of Christ*[80] promotes the translation and interpretation that I have presented here, namely, that Luke was making a distinction between the census run by Quirinius and an earlier one that he did not manage. Hoehner believes that Luke's true meaning flows naturally from the original language and that it preserves Luke as the premiere historian that he has shown himself to be in so many other instances. So here again is what I believe is the best translation:

> *And it came to pass in those days that a decree went out from Caesar Augustus that all the world should be registered.* This was the first of a series of registrations that occurred before Quirinius governed Syria. *So all went to be registered, everyone to his own city. (Luke 2:1–3)*

So now the question arises: When was that first census to which Luke refers?

Where to Now?

After I first moved to Colorado, my daughter Faye, my wife Beth, and our friends Karen and Charlie volunteered to help rebuild a trail system near Hidden Lake. Charlie and I were assigned a segment that needed to be terraced because of erosion. It was tough, grueling work, but when it was all done the trail was safe for hikers again.

On this 500-year journey we are on, we now need to fix a segment of the trail that has washed out. We have learned a little about the life of Augustus and the importance of a census to his power and to the Roman Empire. We have also seen that there was a Quirinius who conducted a census in Israel ten years after the death of Herod, so that could not have been the one Luke references, the one that actually occurred when Jesus was born. Now we need to identify the census Luke refers to—the one that happened before Herod died and that had been peacefully conducted. To discover that, we need to consider the life and rule of King Herod, and fix one of the most dangerous parts of our trail.

7

The Man Who Would Be King

It is true that Nicolaus of Damascus says that Antipater was of the stock
of the principal Jews who came out of Babylon into Judea; but that assertion
of his was to gratify Herod, who was his son, and who, by certain revolutions
of fortune, came afterward to be king of the Jews, whose history
we shall give you in its proper place hereafter.[81]
—*Flavius Josephus*

I t was a heartfelt, impassioned plea in a court of law from a father to an
emperor: "They have conspired against me. I, their father, who has cared
for them from the generosity of my heart, and the kindness of my soul. They
have been ungrateful and sought to kill me in spite of all my hopes that they
would someday be in control. Such ungrateful souls."[82]

Tears flowed from the audience and tears flowed from the two sons as they
listened to Herod's speech. His children were innocent of such designs, but not
clever enough to discern how their father, King Herod, had come to believe
these evil things about them. As a result, their defense came pouring out of
souls hurt that he had ever considered that they were capable of such evil,
and they pleaded for their lives with the power of a clear conscience. Caesar
Augustus heard both sides and then made his ruling:

Lay your suspicions aside. They are innocent and yet never should they have allowed such suspicions to ever arise. They should take care to be reconciled and show the affection due their exalted father. Forgive each other and show good-will to one another that you might bear a greater degree of affection toward each other than ever before.[83]

Herod and his two sons tearfully embraced and everyone present (almost everyone) was deeply moved by what they had seen. They returned to Jerusalem from Aquilae where the trial had taken place sometime after Agrippa had come to Syria in 12-11 BC, fully reconciled and glad that the ordeal was finally over. Herod was relieved that he didn't have to execute his sons, and he hoped for better days ahead. But he still did not fully comprehend all that had happened.

Herod's eldest son, Antipater, who had been at the trial, was merely pretending to be happy with the outcome. Secretly, he was frustrated that his schemes had failed. He had been spreading lies and rumors about his brothers for months, planting seeds of suspicion in the mind of Herod, hoping to turn him against them. He had almost succeeded. He was patient, though, and would continue his seditious strategy until it worked. He had been *so close*, and maybe with a little more nudging, he might yet succeed. Alexander and Aristobulus were Herod's chosen successors, and they had the added advantage of being the last of the Hasmoneans, which had been the ruling family of Israel for almost 150 years.[84]

That is, until Herod came along.

Herod's Path to Power

Herod's father was a very rich Idumean named Antipater. He was ambitious and subversive, but he also knew that loyalty brought rewards. Alexander, the Hasmonean king of the Jews, appreciated his service and awarded him the governance of Idumea, the southern region below Judea populated by descendants of Esau, Jacob's twin brother (Genesis 25:24–26).

After Alexander died, his wife Alexandra reigned over Israel for another nine years. Once she died, her sons Hyrcanus and Aristobulus fought for the throne but then agreed to rule together. Aristobulus would reign as king while Hyrcanus, the elder son, would be the high priest.[85] It was a satisfactory arrangement for both brothers because Aristobulus was energetic and ambitious, and Hyrcanus was easy going and agreeable. However, the arrangement was not satisfactory to Antipater. He wanted Hyrcanus to be king because through him he saw his own path to power. Antipater saw weakness.

Hasmonean Brothers

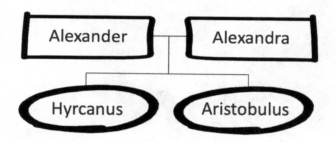

Genealogy Chart 1: The Hasmonean Brothers

To cause dissension between the brothers, Antipater convinced Hyrcanus that Aristobulus was plotting to kill him, even though he wasn't. This induced Hyrcanus to flee to Petra, the capital city of Nabatea, for protection and military aid. The king of Nabatea, Aretas I, was willing to help him because Antipater had carefully nurtured their relationship for years. Also, according to the Greek historian Strabo, the Idumeans and the Arab Nabateans had a shared common ancestry: "The Idumeans are Nabateans, but because of sedition they [the Idumeans] were expelled and joined with the Judeans, adopting their customs."[86] Because Antipater himself was Idumean, he used their shared ancestry to his advantage.[87]

Hyrcanus and Aretas joined forces to attack Jerusalem, but it didn't go well. Aristobulus had generously paid a Roman general named Scaurus to help him threaten Aretas with Rome's disfavor, telling him to go home. Aretas turned back, but once Scaurus was gone, Aristobulus wickedly chased down the retreating army and killed six thousand of the Nabateans.

Even after such foul behavior, Rome could not decide which of the brothers should be king. Both of them sent ambassadors to Damascus to make their case in front of the Roman general Pompey. Hyrcanus sent Antipater, and Aristobulus sent a man named Nicodemus. They both argued well for their candidate, but after returning to Jerusalem, Aristobulus decided he should raise a rebellion against Rome. As a consequence, Pompey besieged the temple in 63 BC.[88] He slaughtered twelve thousand Jews, took Aristobulus and his family back to Rome with him as prisoners, and awarded Hyrcanus the high priesthood.[89] He then appointed Scaurus as the governor of the region to try to keep order.

Earthly Map 1: Judea, Idumea, and Nabatea

With Hyrcanus once again installed as high priest, Antipater was able to continue nurturing the alliances between the Nabateans, Idumeans, and Judeans. Rome also relied on him several times to help deal with Jewish and Nabatean uprisings against Rome. To add to Antipater's regional clout, his wife, Cypros, was the daughter of an eminent Nabatean family, and they had four sons and a daughter together: Phasaelus, Herod, Salome, Joseph, and Pheroras.[90]

Herodians

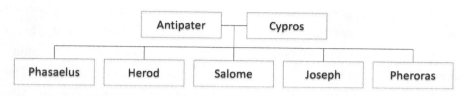

Genealogy Chart 2: Herod's Ancestry

In the years ahead, Antipater's fortunes grew exponentially, especially after he fought alongside Julius Caesar in his war against Pompey. After the war was over, Julius Caesar granted him Roman citizenship and freedom from taxation, and made him the procurator (financial manager) of Judea.[91] This was in the year 61 BC, and his son Herod was fifteen years old.

Even at fifteen, Herod proved himself to be a tenacious leader like his father. Antipater trusted him enough to put him in charge of the region around Galilee, and his older brother Phasaelus managed Jerusalem. Herod immediately won the praise of the Galileans and the favor of Rome by rooting out a band of notorious robbers and killing them all. Meanwhile, Hyrcanus was more than content to let the family of Antipater manage the political affairs of Israel while he served the more peaceful life of a chief priest. It was the Jewish council, however, which saw how Antipater was using Hyrcanus's kindness to gain more power for himself and his family. They also saw the potential threat that his son Herod posed.

Sameas, a righteous man of the Sanhedrin, confronted the young Herod who was on trial for the murder of a rebel Galilean (whom the Galileans were glad Herod had killed, by the way). Josephus records that Sameas told the Sanhedrin, "Take you notice that God is great and that this very man whom you are going to absolve and dismiss for the sake of Hyrcanus, will one day punish both you and your king himself also." Then Josephus adds, "Nor did Sameas mistake in any part of this prediction; for when Herod had received the kingdom, he slew all the members of this Sanhedrin, and Hyrcanus himself also, excepting Sameas."[92]

During the trial, Herod had to flee for his life because Hyrcanus warned him that the Sanhedrin was going to find him guilty and execute him. He pleaded with Rome for help and Rome gave him an army. Herod wanted to go back and kill the Sanhedrin, but his father and brother talked him out of such madness.

The rest of the story of Herod's rise to power follows a similarly winding path through the fortunes of Rome, Judea, and the surrounding nations. In 44 BC, Brutus and Cassius assassinated Julius Caesar. (It was also about this time that Herod's father was poisoned to death by a rival Jew named Malichus.) Caesar's assassination led to wars and turmoil throughout the known world for the next thirteen years, concluding in 31 BC when Octavius defeated Antony in the Battle of Actium.

In the midst of all this international unrest, a new rival to Herod's quest for power arose from the Hasmonean family. This rival was Antigonus. Antigonus was the son of Aristobulus (the brother of Hyrcanus), and after his father died, he believed he was the rightful heir to the throne of Israel, such as it was.

Herod defeated Antigonus's initial attempts to take back Jerusalem, and he saved the life of Hyrcanus. Out of gratitude, Hyrcanus honored Herod so lavishly that the rest of the Jews came to admire him (at least for a little while). With his fortunes on the rise, Herod decided it would be wise to marry into the Hasmonean dynasty hoping to keep the people's affections for him alive. It didn't hurt that Mariamne, the granddaughter of Hyrcanus, was beautiful. They eventually got married and had two sons together, the Alexander and Aristobulus whom we met at the beginning of this chapter.

Herod Marries a Hasmonean

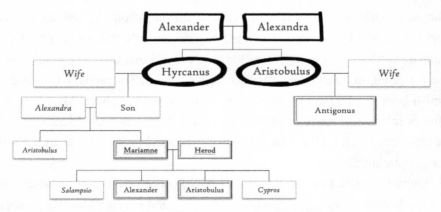

Genealogy Chart 3: The Hasmoneans - Herod Marries Mariamne

Herod's engagement to Mariamne immediately brought him benefits. The famous Marc Antony had come to Syria and a hundred Jewish leaders begged Antony to get rid of Herod. Hyrcanus, though, came to Herod's defense, and since Antony already admired Herod's father, he decided to make him and his brother Phasaelus tetrarchs of the region, essentially allowing them to do the same thing they had already been doing. The seeds Antipater had sown during his life were bearing fruit.

Now that Herod had the support of Rome, he also had the authority to quell rebellions. At this time Antigonus once again attempted to take away power from his uncle Hyrcanus, but now he had the assistance of Rome's archenemy, the Parthians. The Parthians chose to help Antigonus because if they could get rid of Hyrcanus and install Antigonus, that would give them an ally in Judea against the Romans. Herod fought nobly against them: "Herod, with a body of his men, sallied out upon the enemy, who lay in the suburbs [of Jerusalem], and fought courageously, and put many ten thousands to flight, some flying into the city, and some into the temple, and some into the outer fortifications, for some such fortifications there were in that place."[93]

Herod was only able to force a temporary standoff, though, and so in fear for his life, he chose to flee Jerusalem, taking with him his mother, fiancé, and others from his household. The stress apparently was getting to him because on the way to Idumea, he attempted to commit suicide and his entourage had to restrain him. He pulled himself together and went on to shelter his family at the fortress of Masada, and then he himself went on to Petra to ask for help against the Parthians and Antigonus.

Meanwhile back in Jerusalem, his brother Phasaelus and the High Priest Hyrcanus had been taken prisoners by the Parthians. Herod had been wise to flee. Antigonus maimed Hyrcanus by cutting off his ear so that he could never again serve as high priest,[94] and Herod's brother Phasaelus committed suicide by crushing his own head against a stone to prevent the shame of being executed. Jerusalem was firmly in the hands of Antigonus and the Parthians—for now.

The Nabateans refused to help Herod retake Jerusalem, so in desperation he fled to Alexandria, Egypt, to ask for help from Cleopatra. Since he was still in the good graces of Antony, and since Cleopatra and Antony had already struck up their famous love affair, he felt he could count on her for support. She allowed Herod to build a ship with the assistance of loyal friends, and he sailed to Rome to petition Antony for aid.

Antony threw all of his support behind Herod, especially considering the fact that Herod's enemy, Antigonus, had made an alliance with the enemies of Rome. He decreed that Rome would assist Herod in his bid to be the king of the Jews. At this point—40 BC—it was just a promise, but it was a promise that would soon come true. Indeed, so notable was this promise that when the senate dismissed, Herod went out of the senate house walking *between* Marc Antony and Octavius (the future Caesar Augustus). Herod's bid for king had just been approved by the most powerful men in the world, and to make it official, they threw a huge feast for him and made sacrifices to the gods. This moment became the first day of Herod's reign according to the reckoning of the Romans. He was now thirty-six years old.[95]

During the next three years, a series of battles and skirmishes ensued between Antigonus and Herod. They fought battles throughout the holy land and thousands of Jews died on both sides. Herod's younger brother Joseph was killed near Jericho, but in the end, Herod prevailed with the help of the Roman legions. He besieged Jerusalem and the temple mount in the same way that Pompey had done twenty-seven years earlier, and then through sheer persistence, Jerusalem fell to Herod and the Romans in the summer of 37 BC. They captured Antigonus, took him to Rome, and executed him. Herod was now officially the king of the Jews.

Herod's Reign

Herod had now successfully taken the throne from the Hasmonean dynasty[96] and had won the favor of Rome due in part to his ability, ironically, to keep the peace. He was able to keep the Romans from killing the Jews, and he was able to prevent the Jews from giving the Romans a reason to kill them. The Romans appreciated his willingness to do what was necessary to suppress uprisings, and the Jews tolerated him, not merely out of fear, but also because he was incredibly generous. Money talks.

The Sanhedrin faced an odd tension: on the one hand they hated Herod, but on the other hand he was spending a lot of money on building projects. In a school-ground-bully-kind-of-way, Herod would pummel you if you didn't love him, but in a spoiled-brat-rich-guy-kind-of-way, he was willing to buy your love too. As a result, the Sanhedrin worked hard to keep a lid on the angry radicals who wanted to get rid of him, and he continued to lavish the country with new cities and buildings. However, in his attempts to keep Rome happy, he built temples to the Roman gods too. He even named one of his cities Caesarea in honor of Caesar Augustus. The Jews, of course, were appalled that their king would do such a thing for a man who thought he was a god.

In essence, Herod was an egotistical pragmatist, and he would do whatever was necessary to keep himself in power.

When he became king in 37 BC, Hyrcanus was alive and well, but now he was living in Babylon as a free man. After maiming him, the Parthians had chosen to treat him kindly because of his noble lineage.[97] While in Babylon, he reconnected with the Jewish exiles who had remained behind after the decree of Cyrus, and it turned out they loved him. Thousands of Jews still lived there, and they considered him their priest and king, not Herod.

Hyrcanus was laid back enough, though, that once Rome had officially made Herod king of the Jews, he was excited and thought that Herod would welcome him back with open arms and maybe even appoint him as high priest again. He had no idea who he was dealing with, even after all these years. Hyrcanus had two grandchildren: Mariamne—whom Herod had recently married—and Aristobulus, a tall, handsome, intelligent, sixteen-year-old boy. His existence meant that the Hasmonean line still had a viable heir to the throne. So Herod pretended to freely welcome the exiled family back to Jerusalem but only because he wanted to kill them all. Even Mariamne. And he succeeded.

His servants "accidentally" drowned the eighteen-year-old Aristobulus (younger brother of Mariamne) after he had been made high priest and proved himself to be honorable and impressive.[98]

- Herod finally executed Hyrcanus for treason by making it *appear* that Hyrcanus had committed treason, even though he had not.[99]

- He allowed Mariamne to be put on trial and executed her because he had been persuaded that she was plotting against him. Her only crime, though, had been an inability to disguise her contempt for the man who had murdered her grandfather and brother.
- Alexandra (Hyrcanus's daughter-in-law) tried to persuade Rome to kill Herod by tattling on him to Cleopatra, hoping she would turn Antony against him. That failed. Later, Alexandra made one more attempt to set herself up for a possible return to power when Herod became seriously sick. But when Herod found out about her hopefulness at his demise, he had her executed.[100]

He had succeeded at killing all of the Hasmoneans except for his own two sons—and that was soon to change.

In the thirteenth year of his reign (25 BC), Mariamne was executed and then a series of famines and calamities hit the region. However, instead of gathering all of the food to himself like a typical monarch or tyrant would have done, Herod saw an opportunity to win the affections of the people, which he deeply desired. He therefore rationed his own supplies and had bread baked for the elderly, making sure they were all well taken care of. As a result of his kindness, the rich and poor equally became dependent on him and they loved him for it. He even cut to pieces much of his golden furniture and used the money to buy food from Egypt. These actions won him serious praise from the people, so much so that they even overlooked his former offenses. This was the best he ever had it.

After these calamities ended and he had won the affections of the people, he decided it was time to marry again. (Herod had six wives altogether.) He chose a gorgeous Egyptian.[101] He also began an aggressive building program of fortresses, palaces, pagan temples, and entirely new cities like Caesarea.

The pinnacle of his building projects was to renovate the temple for the Jews. Their current temple had been completed in 517 BC, but it had been attacked, looted, and burnt multiple times throughout the centuries (even Herod had besieged it in 37 BC). It was sorely in need of some renovations, so much so that he forewarned the Jews that he would need to tear it down to its foundations. He promised that the new one would surpass even Solomon's in size and value, but they were worried that he would tear it down and leave it unfinished. Knowing this, he reassured them by not starting the demolition until all the supplies had arrived on site. He started building during the eighteenth year of his reign (20 BC) and spared no expense.[102] The resulting structure was magnificent! And he finished the temple in record time, in just a year and a half.[103]

Family Feuds

As we saw at the beginning of this chapter, Antipater had failed to get Alexander and Antigonus executed in Rome in 12-11 BC, but that didn't thwart him from continuing to try. It took Herod's oldest son Antipater two more years, but he eventually convinced Herod that Alexander and Aristobulus were plotting his demise. Josephus says, "Antipater used stratagems perpetually against his brethren, and that very cunningly."[104]

During the next two years, Antipater went to another level of evil by causing Herod to fear even his closest servants. Herod's household became a disaster zone in which no matter what he did he could never find "a single quiet day or hour, but occasions of one fresh quarrel or another arose among his relations."[105] Herod became suspicious of everyone (except for Antipater, oddly enough), and he would torture and kill trusted friends and servants to try to figure out who was really after him. To confuse matters more, Antipater spread false stories among the servants—who thought that he was telling them the truth—so that when Herod would torture them, they would confess a planted lie. Death ran through the halls of the palace like an undisciplined child; Antipater's designs seemed flawless. Herod lived in a constant state of terror, haunted by images of his sons sneaking up on him with swords drawn.

During this time (10 to 8 BC), Herod also fell into disfavor with Augustus because of some lies told about him by an Arab named Sylleus. Herod sent ambassadors to Rome to defend himself against Sylleus's slanderous accusations, but this is also when matters in his own household were getting worse. Fortunately, Herod's ambassadors were able to succeed in convincing Augustus of the truth, and Augustus then turned his anger on Sylleus who would have to pay back his debts to Herod and eventually submit to execution by Aretas.[106]

The outcome of it all was that Herod was once again in Augustus's good graces, and Josephus tells us that Herod, "in his prosperity, took advantage of this change for the better, and the freedom he now had, to exercise his hatred against them [his sons] after an unheard-of manner."[107] Herod considered his opinion of Alexander and Aristobulus's behavior as sufficient evidence of their guilt, and this time he didn't even allow them the opportunity to defend themselves. Antigonus had finally succeeded against his brothers, and Herod's paranoia had gotten the best of him. He had his sons strangled in Caesarea Sebaste, on the coast of Israel in 8 BC.

The Census

Antipater was now the sole heir to the throne, and Herod trusted him completely, but Antipater found himself in an unexpectedly ironic position: the people had loved Alexander and Aristobulus, but they didn't trust Antipater, and he now lived in constant dread that Herod might figure out that he had been the source of all the recent turmoil and dissension. Now he had to somehow get rid of Herod.

To accomplish this, Antipater allied himself with a group of powerful women in the palace.[108] Herod's brother Pheroras was under their control (one of the women was his wife), and Antipater ingratiated himself with them. They were also closely aligned with a very powerful group of religious Jews called the Pharisees. Josephus says of them:

> they [the Pharisees] were in a capacity of greatly opposing kings. A cunning sect they were, and soon elevated to a pitch of open fighting and doing mischief. Accordingly, when all the people of the Jews gave assurance of their good-will to Caesar, and to the king's government, these very men did not swear, being above six thousand; and when the king imposed a fine upon them, Pheroras's wife paid their fine for them.[109]

The phrase "the Jews gave assurance of their good-will to Caesar" refers to Rome's policy of requiring an oath when conducting a census:

Male citizens were required to state under oath their full name, age, tribe or district of residence, the name of their father or patron, and a monetary valuation of their property. They also provided information about their wives and those children who were still subject to their authority (in patria potestate), *but widows and orphans were listed on their own because they were not subject to a husband's or father's authority.*[110]

Dionysius tells us that the oath was "required by law that they had submitted a true valuation in good faith."[111] In good faith—or as Josephus says, "in good will"—means that all the Jews agreed to have their families recorded along with an honest valuation of their worth. However, six thousand Pharisees wanted nothing to do with it. The Pharisees were putting their own lives on the line by doing this, and King Herod fined them. That was his responsibility as someone who the Romans expected to keep the Jews in line. But Pheroras's wife decided to pay their fine for them, and the census went off peacefully because the rest of Israel was perfectly okay with what Rome was expecting of them.

So here we have in 7 BC Rome conducting a census in Israel while Herod was alive. At this time there were also two Romans managing the affairs of Syria, Saturninus and Voluminus, which was not unusual. In the previous chapter we saw that Augustus began a new lustrum in 8 BC (AUC 746), and now we know that Herod, Saturninus, and Voluminus participated in this census/registration by managing its application in Israel a year later. Jews were allowed to go to their ancestral homes to register, which was a very efficient managerial tactic. Rome is known to have used a similar method in Egypt.[112] Remember, Rome perpetually conducted censuses in five-year periods because the empire was so vast, but this was even flexible because there were so many factors like war, natural disasters, and uprisings which could influence the ability to manage a census. When the Pharisees refused to comply with the requirements of the census, they knew they were putting their lives at risk and that Rome would have to do something about it—violently, of course. Pheroras's wife may have saved their lives by paying their fine.

To comply with taxation meant allowing Rome to maintain a certain level of control over your nation, and the Pharisees knew this. It was an issue they wrestled with, and not just during the life of Herod during this first census. The Pharisees also asked Jesus about it years later during his ministry. They came to him and said:

> *"Teacher, we know that You say and teach rightly, and You do not show personal favoritism, but teach the way of God in truth: Is it lawful for us to pay taxes to Caesar or not?"*
>
> *But He perceived their craftiness, and said to them, "Why do you test Me? Show Me a denarius. Whose image and inscription does it have?"*
>
> *They answered and said, "Caesar's."*
>
> *And He said to them, "Render therefore to Caesar the things that are Caesar's, and to God the things that are God's." (Luke 20:21–25)*

Wise words. The Pharisees were trying to trap Jesus in the same way they had trapped themselves all those years ago: they had refused to pay taxes because it meant swearing loyalty to Rome. Maybe if Jesus were to reveal himself as a zealot subversive, Rome might kill him for them. A sneaky plan.

But here's the important question for us: Was Christ born during this census? To add to the probability that this is the correct census, we have the testimony of a later historian and church father Tertullian. He lived around AD 200, and he was a determined defender of the faith. In one of his defenses, he makes the claim that "there is historical proof that at this very time a census had been taken in Judea by *Sentius Saturninus*, which might have satisfied their inquiry respecting the family and descent of Christ."[113] Amazing, right? He refers to records in his day that could be checked, and that Saturninus was the Roman governor at the time of the census. Why doesn't he refer to Quirinius as being the one in charge of the census? Isn't that what Luke is supposed to have said? Doesn't Tertullian know about that verse? Of course he did!

English, obviously, was not a language in AD 200, and the Bible wasn't even translated into Latin until the late 300s, so Tertullian would only have read the Gospel of Luke in the original Greek. Without batting an eye, he confidently asserts that the records show that Saturninus was the governor at the time of Christ's birth. Tertullian shows no awareness of any contradiction with Luke's account. Why? Because there was none. As we saw earlier, a straightforward translation of the Greek language says, "*This was the first of a series of registrations that occurred* before *Quirinius governed Syria.*" Tertullian must have understood the passage in the way explained in the last chapter. Rome is also known to have conducted provincial censuses in fourteen-year cycles. They did this in Egypt, as historian and Bible scholar William Ramsay points out.

> *Recently, three different scholars announced about the same time, and independently of one another, the discovery that periodical enrollments were made in Egypt under the Roman empire, and that the period was not of fifteen years, as in the later system of indictions, but of fourteen years. The same Greek term is used in the Egyptian documents and in Luke to indicate the census: they were called "Enrollments," Apographai.*[114]

This would mean that in 7 BC, Rome conducted a peaceful census, and then fourteen years later in AD 6–7, there was another census conducted by Quirinius. Luke is distinguishing the first mentioned peaceful census from the later violent one run by Quirinius.

The Puzzle Pieces Are Connecting

So, all the prophetic and historical clues point to 7 BC as the year Christ was born: 442 years earlier Nehemiah dedicated the wall around Jerusalem, and now we know that a peaceful census occurred during Herod's reign in 7 BC. Even if one were to argue that Jesus could have been born later in 3 or 2 BC, by that time Herod was dead (as we will confirm in chapter 10). Also, since Luke's language says this was the first census in a series, it must have been the beginning of Rome's more extensive intrusion into the national life of the Jews, a new policy begun by Augustus, which is why six thousand Pharisees initially protested.

As intriguing as all this evidence is, there is more that I need to present in order to conclusively prove that 7 BC is the year Jesus was born, but for now let's pause in our quest for the year and turn our attention to the month and day he was born. Why did the early church choose December 25? And if that is the wrong date, what is the correct one?

STAGE III

The Plan Comes Together

8

Tradition!

Joseph also went up from Galilee, out of the city of Nazareth, into Judea, to the city
of David, which is called Bethlehem, because he was of the house and lineage
of David, to be registered with Mary, his betrothed wife, who was with child. So it
was, that while they were there, the days were completed for her to be delivered.
And she brought forth her firstborn Son, and wrapped Him in swaddling cloths,
and laid Him in a manger, because there was no room for them in the inn.
—Luke 2:4–7

W hat an elegantly simple account of the birth of Christ. Its artistry is
clean, with clear imagery and efficiency of language. Think about how
many words, plays, movies, and books have been derived from these
few words, plainly spoken. Think about how much the world changed after
that moment occurred.

What do you see in your mind's eye when you read that Joseph and
Mary "went up from Galilee, out of the city of Nazareth, into Judea, the
city of David, which is called Bethlehem"? You may see Mary riding a
donkey, with Joseph walking alongside holding the lead line, or some vari-
ation on that. This is perfectly reasonable. But did you notice that Scripture does not mention a donkey? I don't believe this means that Mary

and Joseph did not travel with a donkey, but it does speak to the power of tradition—and of suggestion.

Another powerful image of the Christmas story we have is based on the whole "no room for them in the inn" thing. You probably envision a bedraggled and concerned couple hurrying into Bethlehem the day before she is to give birth, and no one seems to care. Joseph and Mary desperately try to find a room at an "inn," which we may envision to be like a Super 8 motel or a tavern, but everyone seems unconcerned about the needs of a nine-month pregnant woman. So the couple wander into the surrounding hills, desperate, and all they can find is a cave or a stable to bed down in for the night during the winter, maybe hoping to find someplace else the next day. However, Mary gives birth, and later that evening shepherds and kings show up bearing gifts. Does this describe what you see in your imagination when you read the Bible verses, maybe with some story details a bit different?

I would like to suggest an alternative scenario. The young couple arrives in Bethlehem several weeks before Mary is due, but the town is crowded with travelers on their way to Jerusalem for the upcoming fall festival season[115] and the added burden of the census. Many homeowners have chosen to rent out rooms for extra money at this time of year, but it was so busy that a normal room was unavailable and the cost may have been out of reach for Mary and Joseph.

It took some searching, but they were able to find an owner who may have been a family member and who would allow them to stay in their basement (for some it would have been their first floor), which also functioned as a stable. The space was affordable, comfortable, and safe. The animals would have been out in the pastures since it wasn't winter, and Joseph and Mary lived there while they did their civic duty to register and pay their taxes. It would not have been wise to travel back to Nazareth just before Mary was to give birth, so they remained in Bethlehem, comfortably ensconced in their humble lodgings intending to give birth there. They even made do by using the built-in stone manger as a crib once their baby was born. Remember that Joseph and Mary were practical, hard-working, simple people.

I know this sounds strange, but it was a common feature in Bethlehem for people to have basement/stables in their own homes because of the natural cave structures available in the region. Historian James C. Martin says: "Such mangers are found in animal shelters, and in first-century Bethlehem of Judah, animal shelters were typically associated with caves. *In this region, many families built their homes over caves.* The cave was used as a basement in which the family's animals were kept."[116]

Luke uses the Greek word *kataluma*[117] which means "guest room," not "inn." In Luke 22:11, the disciples used such a guest room in a private residence for the Last Supper. If Luke had wanted to convey the idea that the holy family was coldly turned away from a motel and had to wander into the hills to find a cave, he could have used the Greek word for a public lodging place, *pandocheion,*[118] as he does in 10:34 with the story of the Good Samaritan. But no such coldheartedness is found in the nativity story. In reality, Luke describes a common practice in ancient Israel (and in ours), which was for homeowners to take advantage of hordes of people coming to town by renting out an extra room in their home, like a modern Airbnb. And since the town was so crowded, with no upper rooms available, Mary and Joseph settled for a more affordable basement/stable/cave.

Also, we need to notice an easily overlooked phrase in Luke 2:6, "So it was, that *while they were there*, the days were completed for her to be delivered." There is definitely room for interpretation as to how long Joseph and Mary were in Bethlehem before she gave birth, but they must have been in their accommodations for at least a few weeks. The census would have been managed by officials who would have been in a small town like Bethlehem for several weeks, and there certainly is no requirement to think that Mary and Joseph were desperately looking for a place at the last minute. Why do we assume that they would have waited until Mary was almost due before they made a two-week trek from Nazareth to Bethlehem? Maybe the timing of the census demanded they be there at a certain time, but they would have had plenty of notice. They knew the census was happening, and they traveled to Bethlehem maybe a couple of months after Mary returned from staying with Elizabeth—perhaps in her seventh month of pregnancy. They were wise, careful, and responsible human beings who were capable of thinking ahead, and that changes the scenario completely. Instead of conveying reckless desperation, the verse conveys practical foresight.

The reality is that many of the images we have of Christ's nativity were created during the Middle Ages, which was an era not typically all that concerned with portraying the authentic lifestyle of first-century Israelites. We must also remember that Mary is the one who is telling Luke what happened, and in a few words she gives no sense of bitterness, resentment, nor even a feeling of desperation or abandonment: "Why didn't someone help us! We were so desperate!" Instead, without complaint, she shows us that she and Joseph were law-abiding citizens doing their civic duty, and they made do with what was available to them in spite of their circumstances. They were giving to Caesar what was due to Caesar at the cost of great hardship to themselves, and they adapted the best they could to the situation they were in, willingly and with foresight.

We must also keep in mind that being born in an animal shelter wasn't some random misfortune because there weren't any social services available or kind people around. It was God's plan for his Son to be born in a stable, not a palace. God came to us in humility and modesty, not pride and superiority. He came to subdue thrones and to show us that a true leader is a servant. God worked all circumstances toward his Son being born in a manger. As the archbishop of Constantinople, John Chrysostom, eloquently said around AD 386:

> But what am I to say, or what am I to speak? For the miracle strikes me senseless. That Ancient of days has become a child, He who sits on a high and lofty throne is placed in a manger, the intangible and simple and uncompounded and incorporeal One is turned about by human hands, He who tore the bonds of sin asunder is entwined in swaddling-clothes, since He will this. For He wants to make dishonor honor, ill-repute to put on glory, the boundary of hubris to show the way of virtue. And so He enters my body so that I might contain His Word.[119]

Chrysostom's beautiful sentiment highlights what the birth of Christ means: God humbly became one of us, swaddled in cloths, lying in a manger.

He came to rule by coming to serve. A flamboyant entry would have invalidated that goal. A modern author, Justin Earley Whitmel, expresses the same awe: "There's no one who surrendered more freedom than Jesus, who went from the all-powerful second person of the Trinity to the vulnerable form of a helpless infant. He went from speaking the universe into existence by his Word to not being able to speak a word."[120]

But when did all of this happen?

December 25th?

In regard to the year Christ was born, I believe that the historical record best supports 7 BC, which I will provide more evidence for in chapter 10. Now, though, I would like to focus on identifying which month and day Jesus was born.

Chrysostom and Tradition

The church tradition, obviously, is December 25th, but why was that chosen? I discovered that during the first three hundred years of the church, its leadership were undecided on the date of Jesus's birth. It wasn't firmly established as a church tradition until John Chrysostom pronounced it as the official position of the Western church in 386. But why did he choose December 25th? Was he basing his decision on careful scholarship and a preponderance of evidence? He tells us why in his homily (a style of sermon that resembles a modern TED Talk) entitled "Homily on the Birthday of Christ (a)":

> *Long ago I set my heart on seeing this day [December 25th], and not just seeing it, but seeing it with such a great gathering of people. I continually prayed that our place of meeting would be filled just as we now see it filled. So this has come to pass and had its consummation. Although it is not yet the tenth year since this day became clear and familiar to us, through your zeal, it has now flourished as though it was given from the beginning many years ago.[121]*

Here he states to a packed house that December 25th had only recently been chosen as the official date of Christ's birth, even though it had been a day long recognized. This giant of the faith also acknowledged that choosing the date had been a hotly debated topic:

> *Your heartfelt zeal for this day is a great sign of your love for the one who is born. . . . You want, of course, to hear about this day. I well know that many are still debating with each other about it, some arguing against, some for. Everywhere there is a lot of conversation about this day, some saying accusingly that the day is a new innovation which has only recently been introduced, while others contend that it is ancient and venerable, that the prophets spoke in advance about his birth and that from the beginning it was plain and clear to those living from Thrace to Cadiz.[122]*

Chrysostom proclaimed that December 25th had finally won the debate over when Jesus was born. Prophets revealed it, and Christians accepted it from one side of the empire to the other. He acknowledged that there were other theories out there, but not in order to continue the debate but to end it.

However, we need to look a little more closely at the reasons he gives for the choice of December 25th. Chrysostom states, "I have three convincing arguments to share with you through which we will know for sure that this is the time at which our Lord Jesus Christ, God the Word, was born." In summary, these are his reasons for accepting December 25th as Jesus's birthday: (1) "The news about the feast was swiftly circulated everywhere"; (2) The census records were stored in Rome and could be confirmed; and (3) Jesus was born in Bethlehem.[123] Let's consider each of Chrysostom's points.

1. The news about the feast was swiftly circulated everywhere.
This is an argument from popularity and success. Celebrating December 25th had been well received by Christians for ten years before Chrysostom preached about it, and since the date was growing in popularity—it had gone viral, shall we say—he remarks that this is a sure sign that God was blessing their choice. He equates the success of the Christ mass with Gamaliel's speech to the Sanhedrin, who urges the Jewish leaders to take a neutral stance toward Peter and John and allow their message to be confirmed by whether it succeeds or not. If it suc-

ceeds and the gospel spreads, then their message is from God, but if Rome shuts down the new religious movement, then it is not from God.[124] Chrysostom says regarding the success of Christmas services over the last decade, "the power of the message won over everything . . . and demonstrated a strength of its own." In other words, the December date for celebrating Jesus's birth was becoming popular, so it must be God's confirmation that it was an accurate choice.

Chrysostom has a point. Celebrating Jesus's birthday on December 25th was becoming popular in his day, and it has continued to grow in popular appeal since then. Moreover, church attendance is highest at Christmas (and Easter), and many people who are not Christian are more willing to attend church at Christmas if invited by a friend.[125] I think Chrysostom would be pleased at the day's continued popularity (but maybe disappointed at the decreased attendance the following week), and he would most certainly consider this a sign that he and other church leaders in his day had made the right choice.

Nevertheless, this popularity and longevity does nothing to tell us why December 25th is better than other candidates. It was chosen, and it has been successful, but I wonder if similar success would have attached itself to a different date if church leaders had promoted it. In fact, the early church leaders had proposed other dates, including January 2, April 18, April 19, and May 20.[126] And while December 25 eventually became the accepted date, it did not happen quickly. It's mentioned on a calendar in 354 as having first been celebrated in Rome in 336. "It would not appear to have been celebrated in Antioch until approximately 375. By 380 it was being observed in Constantinople, and by 430 in Alexandria. It was still unknown in Jerusalem early in the fifth century—it was not until the sixth century that the Nativity was finally . . . celebrated on 25 December."[127]

So far, except for the official adoption of December 25th as Jesus's birthday, we have no confirmed historical reason for its adoption. How do we know that Jesus was really born on that day?

2. *The census records were stored in Rome and could be confirmed.*
Chrysostom's second argument points to the presence of hard evidence in Rome that anyone could check if they wanted to:

For anyone who wishes to do so it is possible to consult the ancient codices which are stored publicly in Rome, to learn the time of the census and so to know this for certain. . . . But listen and do not doubt that we have received the day from those who have accurate information about these things and live in that city. Those who pass their lives there have observed this day from early times on the basis of ancient tradition and it is they who have shared the knowledge about this day with us.[128]

If we could find these records, that would be a momentous bit of evidence! Tertullian (ca. 160–220) also referred to such documentation, but only as a way to strengthen the argument that Christ had come in the flesh. He says nothing about a specific date. Chrysostom, however, implies that they had Roman census records which would confirm the date as December 25th, and yet if such documentation was easily available, why was there even a debate? If records could be checked, why didn't church scholars do that? The reality is that other early church scholars believed in different dates for Christ's birth (we will look more closely at them shortly), so why wasn't the argument settled long before Chrysostom's speech? He says that if anyone wanted to make the journey from Constantinople to Rome (not an easy trek in those days), they could see the census record and get the needed confirmation. In the meantime, his proposal amounts to this: "Trust me and the authorities who have confirmed it."

Chrysostom is right that Rome did keep very detailed census records as demonstrated by Egyptian papyri which have survived. According to Roger Bagnall and Bruce Frier:

There is ample evidence to support the instinctive modern notion that people must have submitted their census declarations in their legal domiciles, an idea reinforced of course by the Lucan narrative of Jesus' birth, in which "everyone went to register, each to his own city" (Luke 2:3). The fragmentary Edict of Vibius Maximus from 104, ordering Egyptians to leave Alexandria to register, preserves in part the relevant passage: "The house-to-house census having started, it is essential that all persons who for any reason whatsoever are absent from

their nomes [districts] be summoned to return to their own hearths,
in order that they may perform the customary business of registration
and apply themselves to the cultivation which concerns them."[129]

Detailed records, which included names, ages, occupations, and a valuation of property (some records even identify scars), have not only been discovered in Egypt, but there is also evidence of census records having been stored in the temple of the Nymphs in Rome.[130] Nevertheless, nothing discovered so far would confirm Chrysostom's claim that Joseph and Mary are on a list dated in December.

3. Jesus was born in Bethlehem.

This point is completely biblical and true. Jesus was born in Bethlehem according to prophecy (Micah 5:2) and in actual fulfillment (Luke 2:4). There is no obscurity or doubt. However, such a fact says nothing about the date Jesus was born. It says where he was born, not when.

So we are still left to wonder why the Western church chose December 25th.

A Pagan Source?

One theory that became popular in the 1600s and has become widely accepted as a fact among the Reformed and evangelical traditions is to attribute the December 25 choice to pagan influences within the church. That theory regards "the institution of Christmas as a particularly significant example for how certain elements of Christianity originally developed out of an ancient pagan context."[131] Perhaps you have heard this theory taught as an absolute certainty, but there are good reasons to reconsider whether the church chose December 25th *because* it was a pagan holiday.

Pagan winter festivals were celebrated near the winter solstice, which was about December 22 or 23 at the time of Jesus,[132] but proximity doesn't mean the church chose the 25th for that reason. God's law commands that Passover be celebrated fourteen days after the first appearance of the new moon. Pagans similarly guide their festivals by new moons, full moons, equinoxes, and solstices. Does that mean we should blame pagan influences for why the Jews celebrated biblical festivals? K. R. Harriman is critical of the effort to accuse the church of having pagan reasons for choosing December 25th. He points out, "we have no clear evidence that a festival dedicated to Sol Invictus (Mithras) was celebrated on December 25 prior to the Christian celebration of Christmas on that date."[133] Pagan literature doesn't put the birth of *Sol Invictus*, a minor Roman deity, on December 25th as many people have proclaimed.

The earliest document that clearly identifies December 25 as the date of Christ's birth is a Christian document called *The Chronography of 354*, an illustrated codex calendar that a calligrapher named Furius Dionysius Filocalus had illuminated.[134] In "Part 12: Commemorations of the Martyrs," the first reference is to *"natus Christus in Behleem Iudeae"* (the nativity of Christ born in Bethlehem of Judea) on the *"VIII Kal. Ian"*—that is, eight days before the Kalends of January. Kalends is the first day of a month, so in our vernacular it means eight days before January 1. The ancients counted inclusively, so the date arrived at is December 25.

Also, in the same document in "Part 6: The Calendar of Philocalus," it lists the birthday of "Invicti" on December 25. Who is *Invicti*? The name means "unconquerable," and it is assumed that this is a reference to *Sol Invictus*, a minor Roman solar deity, also known as Mithras. At first glance this appears to confirm that the Western church decided on December 25 because it was the birthday of *Sol Invictus,* but Steven Hijmans points out, "December 25 was neither a longstanding nor an especially important official feast day of Sol. It is only mentioned in the *Calendar of 354* and as far as I can tell the suggestion that it was established by [the emperor] Aurelian cannot be proven."[135]

Harriman also points out that the ancient pagans never even used that date:

Saturnalia was not celebrated on December 25. According to Macrobius, Saturnalia was originally celebrated on the fourteenth day before the Kalends of January (December 19 on the Julian calendar), but it was lengthened to a three-day celebration (starting on December 17) and the festivities ultimately extended for seven days (December 17–23; Saturnalia 1.10.) Notice that, even in its most extended form, it never overlaps with December 25. It is certainly in the neighborhood, and it certainly was a popular Roman festival, but it does not explain why December 25 should be chosen.[136]

There certainly is no doubt that the pagans had winter festivals and that they worshiped the sun, moon, and stars, but guilt by proximity does not mean that the church chose it for that reason.

Harriman, Hijmans, and others do admit that pagan influences have attached themselves to Christmas over the centuries, but their case is that it is a byproduct, not a cause for the religious observance. He also points out that during the first few centuries of the church, leaders paid scant attention to the celebration of Christ's birth because celebrating a birthday itself was considered a pagan practice. This explains why there is such a mystery surrounding the date of his birth. It was debated for hundreds of years, but it was a subsidiary topic. Anyway, my goal is not to trace how pagan elements have crept into Christmas over the centuries.[137]

From what I have been able to figure out, the church attempted to resolve the question of the date of Christ's birth sincerely and without nefarious, pagan intent. During the church's first few centuries, it had a healthy and rigorous debate about Jesus's birth, just as Chrysostom pointed out. Along with December 25, other dates were considered.

Typologies

Historical typology means "the events of the Old Testament are seen to be typified in the New Testament, and there is a correlation between the Old Testament events of liberation and the New Testament events of salvation."[138] For example, the Exodus typifies Christ freeing us from the slavery of sin; Jonah was swallowed by a fish typifies Jesus being in the grave until the third day (Christ himself uses this typology in Matthew 12:39–40). Jesus also made a clear typological connection between himself on the cross and the bronze serpent raised up in the wilderness: "And as Moses lifted up the serpent in the wilderness, even so must the Son of Man be lifted up, that whoever believes in Him should not perish but have eternal life" (John 3:14–15).

Historical typology is more than merely seeing analogies and poetic allusions to teach spiritual lessons. Instead, it focuses on taking historical events and seeing their prophetic fulfillment in later historical events. The premiere example would be the Passover lamb. There were real Passover lambs that were sacrificed by the Jews on the evening of Abib 14 when they were slaves in Egypt. They took its blood and brushed it onto their doorposts and lintel. As a consequence, the angel of death passed over the Jews but took the life of the firstborns of all the Egyptians. On the same day thousands of years later, Christ died on the cross for our sins on Abib 14 before sunset. In this scenario, God's judgment was poured out on his own Son, and the angel of death will pass over all those who believe in his holy name.

The early church saw these connections, promoted them, and developed them on multiple levels which would then strengthen the prophetic and typological meanings, but it appears that the early church abandoned historical typology in regard to the birth of Christ. Instead of trying to identify when Christ was born by correlating it with Old Testament events, they began to use weaker symbolic connections that sounded spiritual but were not necessarily correct. For example, Harriman points out that early Christians "worked with a triad of dates, such that Jesus's Incarnation/conception happened on the same day as his death and then his birth was a distinct date nine months afterwards."[139] This kind of parallelism—a person dying on the same date that he or she had been conceived or born—might have been derived from Deuteronomy 31:2 when Moses says, "I am one hundred and twenty years old *today*. I can no longer go out and come in. Also the LORD has said to me, 'You shall not cross over this Jordan.' " This is the day Moses wanders off alone into the hills to die—or some say to be taken up like Elijah—on his birthday. Parallelisms like this can happen, and they might even have significance, but we should not confidently say that since God did this for Moses, he would also do it for the Messiah. There are definitely comparisons to be made between Moses and Jesus: Moses was a shepherd; Jesus is the Good Shepherd. Pharaoh tried to kill baby Moses; Herod tried to kill baby Jesus. These are meaningful, but the birthday and death-day correlation is not as strong as the connection between the Passover lamb and Jesus. One is highly speculative, while Jesus as the Passover lamb is clear and well established.

Harriman goes on to point out that the earliest references to the date of the birth of Christ put his birth near the spring equinox and Passover.[140] Harriman directs us to Clement of Alexandria (AD 150–215), who lays out several suggested dates about when Christ was born, baptized,[141] and crucified. The challenge we face in translating these dates to our calendar is that Clement used Egyptian months because he lived in Alexandria, Egypt. Here's what Clement says:

There are those who have determined not only the year of our Lord's birth, but also the day; and they say that it took place in the twenty-eighth year of Augustus, and in the twenty-fifth day of Pachon. . . . Further, others say that He was born on the twenty-fourth or twenty-fifth of Pharmuthi.[142]

Regarding the date of the crucifixion, in this same passage Clement says:

And treating of His passion, with very great accuracy, some say that it took place in the sixteenth year of Tiberius, on the twenty-fifth of Phamenoth and others the twenty-fifth of Pharmuthi and others say that on the nineteenth of Pharmuthi the Saviour suffered.[143]

Ignoring the fact that Clement believed Jesus ministered for only one year (Luke says Jesus was baptized in the fifteenth year of Tiberius, and Clement says he was crucified in the sixteenth year),[144] notice that most of these dates fall on *the twenty-fifth*. Interesting, right? One of the possible combinations from these older sources designates that Christ was born on *Pharmuthi* 25, and he died on *Pharmuthi* 25—the same date. Also noteworthy is that all of the potential candidates are in the spring. *Phamenoth* is approximately March, *Pharmuthi* is approximately April, and *Pachon* is approximately May. Therefore, with these few dates, Clement reveals to us that within the first one hundred and fifty years of Christianity, Clement and his sources associated Jesus's death and birth with the spring equinox, since *Phamenoth* 25 equates to March 21.

Another complexity in all this, though, is that later church leaders decided that Clement used a word for "birth" that could also mean "conception." If that is what Clement meant—conception instead of birth—then nine months later Jesus would have been born in the Egyptian month of Choiack 25, which is at the winter solstice—December 21. Kurt Simmons puts all the pieces together:

In the Roman calendar, the civil dates of the vernal and autumnal equinoxes were March 25 and September 24, and the summer and winter solstices June 24 and December 25, respectively. We say 'civil dates'

*as distinguished from natural dates, meaning the dates marked in the
calendar for religious holidays when government offices were closed
versus the actual astronomical events they nominally marked.[145]*

I believe this may be why the church eventually chose December 25. The
church currently celebrates the Annunciation (when Gabriel told Mary that
she would conceive Jesus) on March 25, which is the *civil* spring equinox.
Nine months later the baby would be born, and therefore Christmas is on
December 25, the *civil* winter solstice. Therefore, the December choice has
nothing at all to do with converting the celebration of Mithras into a celebration of Christ. The church during Chrysostom's day decided that Clement
meant Christ was conceived on Phamenoth 25, not born, and the tradition was
set that exists to this day.

However, even if we accept that explanation, it still doesn't explain why
Clement's sources chose the spring equinox. Was their choice based on historical records, or was it purely symbolic because new life begins in the spring?
And what were the sources that Clement cited? Can we find those? And did
they mean to tell us that Christ was conceived in the spring as the church later
decided, or that he was born in the spring?

Clement names one of his sources as a man named Basilides, who happened to be the leader of a gnostic sect of Christianity. Gnosticism was a major
religious philosophy with which some of the early church fathers fiercely contended. Gnostics taught that Christ was the great Illuminator and brought revelation to mankind, but he was distinctly different from the historical Jesus we
see in the Gospels. The early church father Irenaeus (ca. 130–202) specifically
refutes Basilides in chapter XXIV, "Doctrines of Saturninus and Basilides,"
in his work *Against Heresies*. Irenaeus summarizes the teachings of Basilides,
which sound identical to what is in the surviving gnostic books *The Gospel of
Judas* and *The Secret Book of John*. When Irenaeus wrote, one of the primary
doctrinal battlegrounds was not about when Christ was born, but rather that he
was God in the flesh and how that should be understood. It was a doctrinally
charged time in church history. Church leaders saw themselves as combatants
in a spiritual war, seeking to defend the faith against corruption.

What's curious is that Clement quoted a gnostic teacher. I'm not implying that Clement supported the gnostics, any more than the apostle Paul supported all the views of some of the pagan poets he quoted (Acts 17:28). All truth is God's truth, and sometimes individuals who disbelieve in him still say true things. As it turns out, Clement and Basilides both lived in Alexandria, Egypt, and their lives overlapped. Alexandria was the ancient equivalent of the modern internet. It had the largest library in the ancient world. So Clement would have had access to all kinds of documents, including the census records, some of which are still in existence to this day.[146] So, I wonder, do any of the gnostic writings or other documents that have survived refer to the date of Christ's advent? Can we find where Basilides said this? Could the gnostics have recorded the date of Jesus's birth? Well, unfortunately, the writings of Basilides have not survived, but from other gnostic writings that have, I still haven't found any specific dates for Jesus's birth mentioned, nor have I heard of anyone else identifying such a date. Another dead end.

But beyond Basilides, who else was Clement quoting? We don't know because he doesn't say. However, we do know that he not only had access to the library of Alexandria, but he also lived at the same time as Ptolemy (100–170), "an Egyptian astronomer, mathematician, and geographer of Greek descent."[147] Ptolemy lived in Egypt which was the world's best at keeping calendars. Maybe Clement found some other scroll or book that had recorded the date of Christ's birth that is now lost to us. Matthew records that the holy family fled to Egypt to avoid Herod's persecution, and it is likely that they would have fled to Alexandria because there was a large Jewish population there. Perhaps some records were left behind by Jesus's family. As exciting as all these possibilities are, the library of Alexandria was destroyed in the 400s and only the privately owned scrolls and documents have been preserved. What we have left reveals nothing about our question.

Short of finding a long-lost document, we must explore the date of Jesus's birth in a different way. Going back to the accusation that the church chose the date of Christ's birth based on pagan symbolism, could the dates Clement mentions about the conception/birth near the spring equinox have been chosen by his sources because of their pagan symbolism? The spring definitely contains birth, king, and shepherd connotations for the ancient Babylonians:

The new moon closest to the spring equinox marks the start of the calen-
drical New Year. And befitting this sacred juncture, it is the season most
closely associated with the king, who is now inaugurated and empowered
by the gods to rule for another term. . . . As a seasonal symbol [for spring]
the lamb [Aries] reflects the fact that a majority of newborn lambs, kids
and calves appear in the cattle-fold in the springtime. . . . Its radiant fleece
. . . represents the newborn sun springing into manifestation.[148]

That sounds much more like the birth of Christ than any winter solstice symbolism I've read. I am not trying to say Clement chose his dates based on this
kind of mythic symbolism but maybe his sources had. If so, this could make a
strong case that Clement might have believed that Christ was born in the spring,
not conceived in the spring. Spring symbolism fits the birth of Christ much better
than winter solstice symbolism, which is more closely associated with the pagan
underworld: "The sacred cycle of the stars comes to a close with the appearance
of the wintertime constellations. . . . This is the time when the disembodied souls
of mankind are spirited away from the environs of the earth and are driven up
into the circumpolar regions of heaven to join their ancestors."[149] The ancient
pagans made associations based on nature metaphors, but here we run into the
same difficulty I have been trying to avoid—weak associations. Just because the
pagans attached symbolic meaning to the seasons that sound like they *could* be
metaphors for Christ doesn't mean that the church chose the date of Christ's birth
because of that. Maybe there were biblical reasons for their choice after all.

Zacharias Revisited

We need to return to Zacharias, who I last talked about in chapter 2. One of the
things I didn't mention then was that Luke gives us a template with which to
determine when Christ was born. If you remember, Zacharias was chosen by
lot to serve during his priestly division's (Abijah's) week of service. Gabriel
appeared to him and told him his wife would conceive. He returned home, Elizabeth got pregnant, she went into worshipful seclusion for five months (Luke
1:24), and then in the sixth month, after Gabriel appeared to Mary (vv. 26, 36),
Mary moved in with her for about three months until John was born (vv. 56–57).

Then Mary went back to her home in Nazareth, Joseph committed to stay with her, and they traveled to Bethlehem where she gave birth a month or so later. In total, it was fifteen months from when Elizabeth conceived until Jesus was born. It's a neat and tidy framework, and if we could figure out when Zacharias served, then we could figure out the month in which Christ was born. Voila!

Tradition says that Zacharias served as high priest and that he had his vision on the Day of Atonement, which occurs sometime during September/October. If that is true, then six months later Mary would have conceived in March, and then nine months later given birth to Jesus in December, just as the church has taught! However, is this tradition correct? Was Zacharias a high priest and did he serve on the Day of Atonement? Luke had a perfect opportunity to tell us if Zacharias was the high priest, but he doesn't. Instead he says, "So it was, that while he [Zacharias] was serving as *priest* before God in the order of his division" (v. 5). Being high priest was a high-profile political position appointed by the king, and Luke would not have left that out. Also, one of the responsibilities of the high priest was to burn incense, but he would never have been chosen by lot to do so. Therefore, it seems more likely that Zacharias was an ordinary priest who was faithfully performing common priestly duties that had to take place every day in every year, and it was simply his turn to officiate. Also, there is nothing from Luke's text that tells us Zacharias served on the Day of Atonement or at any other special convocation for that matter. In effect, based on the information given to us by Luke, there is simply no way to know when Zacharias served.

However, there might be another way to figure out when the division of Abijah was chosen to serve in the course of a regular year. Theoretically, the math is fairly straightforward. There were twenty-four divisions of priests as originally laid out in 1 Chronicles 24:1–19. In verse 10, the eighth division was allotted to Abijah, and each division was to serve for one week. So, starting on the first day of the first month (Abib), the first division served, and so on. However, the catch is that since there are fifty-two weeks in a solar year,[150] each priestly division had to serve twice a year, about six months apart. Which half of the year did Zacharias serve in Luke's account? The first half or the second? Luke doesn't say.

To complicate matters more, 24 (priestly divisions) x 2 (serving twice in a year) = 48 (weeks), not 52.[151] What happens during those extra four weeks? Every division would serve during the weeklong pilgrimage convocations of the Feast of Unleavened Bread, Pentecost, and the Feast of Tabernacles, but those only account for about another twenty-one days. How did the ancients adjust for all of the mismatches and imperfections of the calendar? Can we go back and reconstruct the cycle of divisions?

Miraculously, there are two calendrical documents—labeled 4Q320 and 4Q321—preserved in the Dead Sea Scrolls, which lay out exactly which Jewish months each division was to serve.[152] The Dead Sea Scrolls are ancient documents that were found in several caves near the Dead Sea in Israel. Many of the documents discovered were portions of Old Testament books, and the community thought responsible for copying and preserving these scrolls is known as the Qumran community, which many scholars think were Essenes— an ascetic community of Jewish men.[153] The Torahtimes Messianic Ministry confirms that "It is fair to assume that the Qumran calendar used the same rotation of priestly divisions current in Jerusalem."[154] Much study has been done on the Qumran calendrical documents, and some scholars have tried to use them to determine when Zacharias might have served in Luke's account,[155] but here's the problem: not only did each priestly division serve twice a year, but the month of their service shifted *every* year. The Qumran documents utilize a six-year cycle, and what they reveal is that every family division, including the division of Abijah, would serve over the course of six years in every month. For example, if they served in the fifth month, then twenty-four weeks later they would serve in the tenth month, then the next cycle would be in the fourth month, then the ninth month, etc. In other words, they did not serve at a regular date every year.

The Qumran documents give us an insight into the meticulous efforts involved in keeping track of the divisions of priestly service, but they are not useful for our purposes unless we already know the year that Christ was born or have been told when Zacharias served. If we could determine either one of those independently of the Qumran documents, then we could use them to find the other. Therefore, we are stuck with the same dilemma: we must figure out when Christ was born based upon other historical and scriptural criteria, and then some of these other puzzle pieces will fall into place.

Sitting by the Trail and Enjoying the View

Let's take another breather, sit down, remove our packs, take a drink, and get our bearings. What have we discovered so far? We have learned that the early church had multiple traditions for when Christ was born. Some church leaders believed he was born in the spring, and others interpreted that to mean he was *conceived* in the spring and then *born* in the winter nine months later. That appears to be why the church chose March 25 as the Annunciation and December 25 as the Advent, but were they correct? I don't believe they were. Indeed, I have come to believe that the Bible has told us all along the exact month and day Christ was to be born, and it was *not* December 25. The only reason we haven't seen this before is because of a particular—almost universally believed—foundational assumption that needs to be exposed as an unproven assumption, not a certainty. Once we eliminate that assumption, then the date reveals itself quite naturally and convincingly.

9

The Temple of God

Concerning this temple which you are building, if you walk in My statutes,
execute My judgments, keep all My commandments, and walk in them
then I will perform My word with you, which I spoke to your father David. And I
will dwell among the children of Israel, and will not forsake My people Israel.
—*1 Kings 6:12–13*

A s we learned in the last chapter, historical typology makes connections between historical events and subsequent fulfillments. The church made clear connections between the Passover lamb and Christ, and these connections are strong and do not rely on personal opinion or subjective nuances that might only be products of someone's imagination. And yet, in regard to the *birth* of Christ, there have not been any similarly strong typologies put forward. December 25 remains unconnected to any biblical symbols. Nevertheless, I believe there is a strong typology that reveals to us the month and the day on which the Messiah would be born, but its significance has been missed because of deeply embedded assumptions that have steered us away from it.

With an initial survey of Scripture, we can easily find prophecies that point to the birth of the Messiah but not to any particular date. Here's one of these:

"Therefore the Lord Himself will give you a sign: Behold, the virgin shall conceive and bear a Son, and shall call His name Immanuel" (Isaiah 7:14). Matthew marks the fulfillment of this prophecy in his Gospel (Matthew 1:20–23).

Author Fred John Meldau lists other birth prophecies in his book *The Prophets Still Speak*:

> Consider the following references: "Thou art he who took me out of the womb" (Isa. 49:5); "And now, saith the LORD who formed me from the womb to be his servant" (Isa. 49:5); "The LORD hath created a new thing in the earth, A woman shall compass a man" (Jer. 31:22); ". . . until the time that she who travaileth hath brought forth" (Mic. 5:3).[156]

There are also less obvious references, such as when Matthew quotes Jeremiah 31:15 after Herod slaughters the innocent children of Bethlehem:

> **"A voice was heard in Ramah,**
> **Lamentation, weeping, and great mourning,**
> **Rachel weeping for her children,**
> **Refusing to be comforted,**
> **Because they are no more." (Matthew 2:18)**

In addition to these, some of the more notable references to Jesus's birth are found in the names and titles he is given:

- *Immanuel*: God with us (Isaiah 7:14)
- The offspring of David (2 Samuel 7:12–13; Revelation 22:16)
- The Word became flesh (John 1:1–14)

The apostle John makes no mistake about it: "In the beginning was the Word, and the Word was with God, and the Word was God. . . . And the Word became flesh and dwelt among us" (John 1:1, 14). This is from John's prologue in his Gospel. In short, John tells us that the Word of God—that is, God's Son—became a man. Short, sweet, and to the point. God the Son took on human form to show us the true character of the Father, full of grace and truth. As Jesus said of himself, "He who has seen Me has seen the Father" (14:9). He has come to dwell with us. God has not forsaken us.

The birth of Christ resulted in the presence of God on earth in the Incarnation. Jesus wasn't a man who became God; he was God who became man. He didn't teach us how to follow a path toward our own personal ascension; he *is* the Path. He *is* the Truth. He *is* the Life. He is the origin, the goal, and everything in between. And he didn't fall from the heavens like a star; he was born of a woman. These are profound theological truths, and Jesus reinforces them by making a typological connection to himself.

After he tosses out the moneychangers in the temple court in Jerusalem, some Jews ask him, "What sign do You show to us, since You do these things?" (2:18). Jesus answers:

> *"Destroy this temple, and in three days I will raise it up."* Then the Jews said, *"It has taken forty-six years to build this temple,[157] and will You raise it up in three days?"* But He was speaking of the temple of His body. *(vv. 19–21)*

There it is: Christ refers to himself as the temple, therefore the temple points us to the Incarnation. The temple and all of its features symbolize the meaning of Christ, and at the heart of the temple, the holy of holies, is the presence of God on earth. God dwelt in the temple; likewise God dwelt within the body of Christ. Jesus was 100 percent man; he was also 100 percent God. Two distinct natures co-existing in the same Person.

The prophet Zechariah speaks of the return of the Jews from the Babylonian exile and the rebuilding of the temple:

> *"Sing and rejoice, O daughter of Zion! For behold, I am coming and I will dwell in your midst,"* says the LORD. *"Many nations shall be joined to the Lord in that day, and they shall become My people. And I will dwell in your midst. Then you will know that the LORD of hosts has sent Me to you." (Zechariah 2:10–11)*

Zechariah declares that the presence of God would dwell in the midst of the Israelites when the temple was completed, but his words are also a prophetic utterance that describes the future Incarnation: God would dwell with us—all humanity—at the birth of Christ.

But Jesus isn't only typified by the temple but also by the high priest. The book of Hebrews teaches that Jesus is greater than the angels, and he is the Creator who "laid the foundation of the earth" (Hebrews 1:10). The Creator became the created so "that He, by the grace of God, might taste death for everyone" (2:9). This qualifies Jesus to be the ideal high priest who serves at the temple, for he was faithful in all things and kept the law of God without one mistake. Morally he was perfect, and ceremonially he was perfect. Also, when John baptized Jesus, he was officially transferring the priesthood to Jesus:

> *As Pope Benedict XVI points out in his book* Jesus of Nazareth: The Infancy Narratives, *St. John the Baptist was the bridge connecting the priesthood of the Old Covenant to the New Covenant priesthood of Jesus Christ. The Nativity of John the Baptist is the perfect time to reflect on his priestly role, because it was a priesthood he inherited from his parents.*[158]

The author of Hebrews makes it a point to tell us that Jesus is the eternal high priest according to the order of Melchizedek whose name means "the king of righteousness" (6:19–7:3). Melchizedek was not from the line of Aaron, and yet he was a priest of the Most High God. As David said in Psalm 110:4 of the Messiah's reign, "You are a priest forever according to the order of Melchizedek." (Some believe Melchizedek was the preincarnate Christ himself, but that is a debate we will not deal with here.)

The bottom line is that Jesus was qualified to faithfully fulfill the intermediary role of a priest, thereby representing the perfect, unchangeable priesthood (7:26–28).

The author of Hebrews makes other typological connections:

- Jesus is the physical fulfillment of the temple ordinances, furnishings, ceremonial items, and divine services (9:1–5).

- Jesus not only fulfills the Sabbath but *is* the Sabbath: "For he who has entered His rest has himself also ceased from his works as God did from His" (4:1–10). In chapter 4, the Sabbath is referred to with personal pronouns. The author doesn't say "it's rest" but "His rest," just like he uses personal pronouns to talk about the Word of God in verses 12 and 13.
- Animal sacrifices are no longer necessary because Christ *is* the sacrifice. "Not with the blood of goats and calves, but with His own blood He entered the Most Holy Place once for all, having obtained the eternal redemption" (9:12). Christ offered himself as the perfect sacrifice so that we could draw near to God "with a true heart in full assurance of faith" (10:22).

And yet as amazing as all these typologies are, and I'm sure there are more, how do they help us to know *when* Christ was born? For that help, we need to return to the Old Testament.

Leviticus 23

In the law of God, God's people were to faithfully keep eight holy convocations which are summarized in Leviticus 23. God instituted each one of them to commemorate important events in the history of Israel and to remind the Hebrews of his blessings, his judgments, and his purposes. They were to be celebrated yearly at the time God commanded, with specific practices that taught the people spiritual lessons associated with each convocation.[159]

The chart that follows is based on Leviticus 23 and will be a useful reference. The first column (Biblical Name) lists the names of the Jewish months as mentioned in the Bible before the Babylonian exile. The next column (Post-Exilic) lists the names which began to be used in the Bible after the Babylonian exile (ca. 500s BC), and then next (Post-Biblical) are the names which are currently being used but were not used in the Bible. I will use the biblical, pre-exilic names as much as possible. I have also listed our months (Roman Months), but keep in mind that Jewish months started at the first appearance of a new moon. A new moon is the sliver of a moon that appears above the western horizon as the sun sets. The Essenes called it "the fingernail of God." We don't use the new moon to calculate our calendar, but God commanded that it be used to figure out when to determine his sacred convocations.[160] What needs to be noted is that each convocation must be celebrated on a specific month and day, and they each start at sunset. Here's the chart.

	Biblical Name (Pre-exilic)	Post-Exilic	Post-Biblical	Roman Months	Convocations
1	Abib (Ex. 12:2; 13:4)	Nisan (Esther 3:7)		March/April	Passover (14th); Feast of Unleavened Bread (15-21); Feast of Firstfruits (16 or 17. Cannot be on a sabbath.)
2	Zif (I Kings 6:1)		Iyyar	April/May	
3	Third Month (Ex. 19:1)	Sivan (Esther 8:9)		May/June	Pentecost (Sivan 6 or 7). Fifty days after Feast of Firstfruits.
4	Fourth Month (II Kings 25:1-4)		Tammuz	June/July	
5	Fifth Month (Num. 33:38)		Av (Ab)	July/August	
6	Sixth Month (Ez. 8:1)	Elul (Neh. 6:15)		August/September	
7	Ethanim (I Kings 8:2)		Tishrei	September/October	Feast of Trumpets (1st); Day of Atonement (10th); Feast of Booths (15-22).
8	Bul (I Kings 6:38)		Cheshvan	October/November	
9	Ninth Month	Chislev/Kislev (Neh. 1:1)		November/December	
10	Tenth Month (II Kings 25:1-4)	Tebeth (Esther 2:16)		December/January	
11	Eleventh Month (I Chr. 27:13-15)	Sebat (Zech. 1:7)		January/February	
12	Twelfth Month	Adar (Esther 8:12)		February/March	
13	*Intercalary month*	*Adar II*			*An extra month is added 7 times in a 19-year period, every 2-3 years.*

Table 4: Jewish Months – Leviticus 23

The convocations are briefly summarized in the chart above, but they do need some further explanation, which is presented in the next few sections.

Spring Convocations

- Abib 14 at twilight: The Passover lamb was to be sacrificed fourteen days after the new moon. By extension, God is telling us exactly when Jesus was going to be crucified. It doesn't tell us the year, but it does tell us the month and day.

- Abib 15–21: The Feast of Unleavened Bread. This is a seven-day feast with the first and seventh days as special Sabbaths.
- Abib 16: The Feast of Firstfruits, which is the day after the first day of the Feast of Unleavened Bread, but it cannot be celebrated on a Sabbath. Therefore, if the 16th is a regular Sabbath day, it would have to be celebrated on the next day, a Sunday.
- The Third Month, 6 or 7: The Feast of Weeks (Pentecost) is the fiftieth day counted from the Feast of Firstfruits.

Fall Convocations

- Ethanim 1: The Feast of Trumpets begins on the night of the new moon at twilight. It's the Jewish New Year celebration today known as Rosh Hashanah.
- Ethanim 10: The Day of Atonement. A sacred fast. The most holy day of the year.
- Ethanim 15–22: The Feast of Tabernacles. The first and eighth days are special Sabbaths.

It is clear from the New Testament that the spring feasts were typologically connected to Christ's death:

- Jesus was the Passover lamb sacrificed for our sins.
- The people of God then ate unleavened bread. Jesus made us pure (unleavened) by his sacrifice (1 Corinthians 5:7–8).
- Then there is the Feast of Firstfruits that Christ fulfilled at his resurrection on a Sunday. Paul says, "But now Christ is risen from the dead, and has become the *firstfruits* of those who have fallen asleep. . . . But each one in his own order: Christ the firstfruits, afterward those who are Christ's at His coming" (1 Corinthians 15:20, 23).
- From the Feast of Firstfruits a forty-nine-day countdown began. On the fiftieth day, the Hebrews celebrated Pentecost, which commemorates the giving of the law on Mt. Sinai (Exodus 19:16–20). This usually falls about the 6th or 7th day of the Third Month and was typo-

logically fulfilled when the Holy Spirit entered the hearts of believers (Acts 2). Just as God gave us the law on Mt. Sinai written on stone, God sent the Holy Spirit, which is God's law written on our hearts (Hebrews 10:16; Ezekiel 36:25–27).

But what about the three *fall* convocations? Let's spend a little more time looking at them.

The Fall Convocations

In this section I will defend my key premise: God told us exactly the month and day on which Christ would be born. In Leviticus 23, just as God told us the month and day Jesus would be crucified—Passover on Abib 14—God has also told us the month and day when Jesus would be born: the Feast of Trumpets on Ethanim 1.

I know my conclusion directly contradicts what so many people believe about the meaning of the Feast of Trumpets, and I do not make this argument lightly. I fully recognize that many brethren believe that Christ will fulfill the fall convocations at his second coming. Michael Norten summarizes well this widely accepted view: "The spring feasts picture the events surrounding Jesus Christ's first coming, and the fall feasts picture the events surrounding His second coming."[161] This viewpoint has been the common interpretation I've heard my entire life—and I have believed it too, until recently. I found that it suffers from a fatal flaw, which we will get to shortly.

One of the reasons given for believing that Christ will return at the Feast of Trumpets is what Paul says in 1 Corinthians 15:51–52: "Behold, I tell you a mystery: We shall not all sleep, but we shall all be changed—in a moment, in the twinkling of an eye, *at the last trumpet*. For the trumpet will sound, and the dead will be raised incorruptible, and we shall be changed."

Paul also says: "For this we say to you by the word of the Lord, that we who are alive and remain until the coming of the Lord will by no means precede those who are asleep. For the Lord Himself will descend from heaven with a shout, with the voice of an archangel, and *with the trumpet of God*. And the dead in Christ will rise first" (1 Thessalonians 4:15–16). We can add to this the Seven Trumpets of Revelation (Revelation 8:1–9:21; 11:15–19).

So with all these trumpets announcing Christ's return, our transformation, and the resurrection, it's little wonder that people think Paul's "last trumpet" is a reference to the Feast of Trumpets. It's in the very name! But should we really retranslate 1 Thessalonians 4:16 to say, "For the Lord Himself will descend from heaven with a shout, with the voice of an archangel, *at the Feast of Trumpets*"? Is that what the "trumpet of God" actually means?

Feast of Trumpets

Trumpets—called shofars in the Old Testament—were used for a lot of things in ancient Israel: the beginning of a new month, a Sabbath day, a battle cry, and a day of celebration. There were different *kinds* of blasts, different *numbers* of blasts, and different *shapes* of horns: curved horns from a ram and straight horns from an antelope. And each blast communicated a different meaning.[162] Playing trumpets was quite an elaborate skill. It required special training, and they were blown at many times other than during the Feast of Trumpets.

Because of the multitude of ways trumpets were used during many Jewish occasions throughout the year, Paul may not have been referring to the Feast of Trumpets at all. The apostle never specifically says Christ will return at the Feast of Trumpets; he just tells us that Christ's arrival will be announced with a shout and the blast of the trumpet of God. The connection to the feast is an assumption. So let's look more closely at what the Bible says about this feast and see how it was celebrated in the Old Testament.

Leviticus 23:23–25 says:

> The LORD said to Moses, "Say to the Israelites: 'On the first day of the seventh month you are to have a day of sabbath rest, a sacred assembly commemorated with trumpet blasts. Do no regular work, but present a food offering to the LORD.' " (NIV)

From this passage it appears that the sole purpose of the prescribed day is to be a special Sabbath day that is set aside at the new moon of the seventh month every year. Numbers 29:1 says, "On the first day of the seventh month hold a sacred assembly and do no regular work. It is a day for you to sound the trumpets" (NIV).

Psalm 81:1–4 gives us a little more information:

Sing for joy to God our strength;
  shout aloud to the God of Jacob!
Begin the music, strike the timbrel,
  play the melodious harp and lyre.
Sound the ram's horn **at the New Moon,**
  and when the moon is full, on the day of our festival;
this is a decree for Israel,
  an ordinance of the God of Jacob. (NIV)

The Feast of Trumpets is when sacrifices were to be made and devotion to the Lord was to be announced with joyful music. Where's the battle cry for the final battle at the end of all things? In 1 Thessalonians, Paul's words seem more like a jolt in the routine, a battle cry that rings out from Christ himself and that brings the dead back to life and the living to union with him. It doesn't sound like the Feast of Trumpets at all.

That is hardly a conclusive point, but here is the bigger problem with believing Paul is connecting the final trumpet with the Feast of Trumpets. Jesus told us specifically about his return, "of that day and hour no one knows, not even the angels in heaven, nor the Son, but only the Father" (Mark 13:32). Jesus is clearly teaching his disciples that not even he knows when the end of all things will happen. Matthew 24:36 and Luke 12:40 record the same lesson: no one will be able to predict the "day and hour" when that final trumpet will blow and Christ returns, not even Jesus (at least at that time in his human life).

So here's the fatal flaw: Since we know exactly when the Feast of Trumpets is celebrated—the new moon of the seventh month—then why would Paul use it to tell us when Jesus would return? Did Paul know what Jesus didn't? Not a chance! Paul would not contradict Jesus, and it was Jesus who made it clear that the time of his return was knowledge reserved for God the Father. No one else, not even Jesus or Paul, had access to that mystery.

We can see this truth even more clearly when digging more deeply into what Jesus meant when he said "No one can know the day or the hour." Greek words sometimes carry nuances that are difficult for translators to capture, and in this case the English word "hour" is an extremely poor translation of the Greek. The Greek word means "*any period,* fixed by natural laws and revolutions, whether of the year, month, or day."[163] In other words, when Jesus uttered the words "But of that day and *hour* no one knows," he was emphatically stating that "No one will be able to figure out *the year, season, month, day, or moment* of my return. Not a bit of it. Nothing. It will be a surprise that not even I, the incarnate Son of God, knows." In the clearest possible terms, he was unequivocally telling us lowly mortals that "You won't be able to figure out when I will return. It's *impossible!*"

Edgar Whisenant, who wrote the infamous book *Eighty-Eight Reasons the Rapture Will Be in 1988,* is an example of someone (and there are others) who claimed he had a work-around of this biblical limitation to our knowledge. Whisenant uses some dazzling cup-shifting street magic to try to prove that Jesus really meant that we wouldn't be able to *intellectually* figure out the day or the hour, but that we would be able to *spiritually* know when he would return (which Whisenant connects with the rapture). Ironically (to be kind), he goes on to reveal the exact day, hour, and year of Christ's return, apparently so that all the rest of us unenlightened folk would intellectually know.

So when does Whisenant say Christ's return will be? On the Feast of Trumpets in the year 1988. Most of his book is about why he believed Jesus would return in 1988, but I don't think we need to take any time to bother with debunking that. Indeed, instead of repenting, Whisenant continued this charade for almost a decade, pushing the year forward, year after failed year, while always maintaining that Jesus would return on the Feast of Trumpets. And even to this day many preserve Whisenant's same basic premise, even those who distance themselves from Whisenant's "spiritually" perceived year.

The other problem with believing that Christ will return on the Feast of Trumpets is this: If he doesn't return at the Feast, then we can breathe easy and say, "Maybe next year Jesus will return," which is the exact opposite of the attitude Jesus wanted us to have. He wants us to expect his return at any moment, which is what he taught in every parable on the subject. Therefore, the premise that Christ will return during one of the fall convocations is flawed at its very foundation.

When I was finally able to set aside this assumption and recognize it as an impossibility, I was then freed up to ask the forbidden question: What if the fall convocations are fulfilled by Christ's *birth* instead of by his second coming? It is an undisputed certainty that the holy convocations of Leviticus 23 all point to Christ and some aspect of his ministry. Since the spring feasts point to his death and resurrection, I explored the possibility that the fall convocations point to his first coming. That was almost an unthinkable prospect when it first occurred to me, but the seed was planted, and it gradually grew until it became the key to solving the riddle of the month and day when Christ was born.

Day of Atonement

Before we see how the Bible uses the fall convocations as a typology of Christ's birth, let's take a quick glance at the remaining two fall convocations. As we have seen, trumpets were to be blown on the Feast of Trumpets, but they were also to be blown nine days later on the Day of Atonement.[164] However, the Day of Atonement is different than any of the other convocations because it is a fast, not a feast. It is the most sacred day of all the holy convocations, and God says, "you shall afflict your souls, and offer an offering made by fire to the LORD" (Leviticus 23:27). The Jewish historian Josephus refers to it simply as "The fast,"[165] and God takes this day seriously: "For any person who is not afflicted in soul on that same day shall be cut off from his people. And any person who does any work on that same day, that person I will destroy from among his people" (vv. 29–30). He takes our redemption seriously, and he expects us to take it seriously too.

The Feast of Tabernacles

Five days after the Day of Atonement, the Feast of Tabernacles commences for a seven-day feast, punctuated with another Sabbath on the eighth day (vv. 33–36). The Jewish word for this pilgrimage feast is Sukkoth, and it commemorates the forty years of wandering in the wilderness. It is considered the most joyous of all the seven convocations. It is a week of rejoicing in God's provision for delivering Israel from bondage (Deuteronomy 16:13–15), but it is also a time of learning the hard lessons of life (1 Corinthians 10:1–11).

Now let's look a little more closely at how these fall convocations were celebrated in the Old Testament and how they reveal to us when Christ would be born, not when he would return.

Dedicating Solomon's Temple

Solomon started building the temple in the fourth year of his reign, and it took seven years to complete (1 Kings 6:37). After it was finished, the priests needed to place the ark of the covenant in the holy of holies. This was a big deal. The ark had not had a permanent residence for over four hundred years since the time of Moses. During the wandering in the wilderness, it had been carried on poles and kept in the tabernacle. During the time of the conquest, Jewish tradition says it was kept in Gilgal (Joshua 4:18–19).[166] After the conquest and during the time of the Judges, the ark was in Shiloh with the tabernacle (Joshua 18:1; 1 Samuel 4:3–4) until the Philistines captured it for seven months. They finally sent it back to Israel where it remained in Kirjath Jearim for twenty more years (1 Samuel 5:1–7:2). Finally, David built a new tabernacle for the ark in the City of David where it was brought with much fanfare (1 Chronicles 15–16). It remained there until Solomon built the temple.

Placing the ark in the holy of holies was a momentous event in Jewish history, and Solomon rose to the occasion. Significantly, Solomon chose to dedicate the temple in the month of Ethanim[167]:

> *Now Solomon assembled the elders of Israel and all the heads of the tribes, the chief fathers of the children of Israel, to King Solomon in Jerusalem, that they might bring up the ark of the covenant of the LORD from the City of David, which is Zion. Therefore all the men of Israel assembled with King Solomon at the feast in the month of Ethanim, which is the seventh month. (1 Kings 8:1–2)*

As we have seen, the feasts of the seventh month started on the first day of the month at the new moon. It is significant that Solomon chose to dedicate the temple on Ethanim 1, and to bring in the ark of the covenant, the throne of God's presence, to dwell within the heart of the temple:

> *Then the priests brought in the ark of the covenant of the LORD to its place, into the inner sanctuary of the temple, to the Most Holy Place, under the wings of the cherubim. For the cherubim spread their two wings over the place of the ark, and the cherubim over-shadowed the ark and its poles. . . . Nothing was in the ark except the two tablets of stone which Moses put there at Horeb, when the LORD made a covenant with the children of Israel, when they came out of the land of Egypt.*
>
> *And it came to pass, when the priests came out of the holy place, that the cloud filled the house of the LORD, so that the priests could not continue ministering because of the cloud; for the glory of the LORD filled the house of the LORD.*
>
> *Then Solomon spoke: "The LORD said He would dwell in the dark cloud. I have surely built You an exalted house, and a place for You to dwell in forever." (vv. 6–7, 9–13)*

Quite the event! God's glorious presence announced with trumpets, coming down in a cloud to indwell the earthly temple in the holy of holies, surrounded by cherubim. It must have been quite the spectacle. The arrival of God on earth! God with us, and it was on the Feast of Trumpets when this happened.

Solomon also gave a lengthy prayer of dedication that every person should read in its entirety. Here's an excerpt: "But will God indeed dwell on the earth? Behold, heaven and the heaven of heavens cannot contain You. How much less this temple which I have built!" (v. 27). The temple and all its furnishings are magnificent, and yet Solomon recognized that a mere structure can never contain the fullness of God's presence. The earthly temple is a shadow of God's heavenly throne room, but nevertheless Solomon says that the God who dwells in the heavens will dwell in this earthly temple *forever.*

That's interesting. Forever? Nebuchadnezzar destroyed Solomon's Temple in 587 BC only about four hundred years later, and who knows what happened to the ark of the covenant. So it appears that Solomon's statement, "I have built You . . . a place to live *forever*," isn't merely an optimistic statement or hyperbole and instead prophetically points to Christ.

As we saw earlier in this chapter, Christ referred to his body as the temple, and it is he alone who will endure forever. His first, temporary human tabernacle died, but then after his resurrection he bodily ascended to the heavenly places. To him we now continually direct our prayers. Instead of praying toward the temple in Jerusalem where God's presence once dwelt, now we pray to Jesus in the heavens: "And whatever you ask in My name, that I will do, that the Father may be glorified in the Son. If you ask anything in My name, I will do it" (John 14:13–14).

The strength of this historical typology now presents itself: just as God's presence came to dwell in Solomon's Temple when it was dedicated on Ethanim 1, God's presence came to dwell on earth in the temple of a baby wrapped in swaddling cloths lying in a manger, also on Ethanim 1. Just as Leviticus 23 shows us that Christ would be crucified on Abib 14, it also shows us that Christ would be born on Ethanim 1. The parallels are striking, but there's more.

Dedicating Nehemiah's Wall

Although I believe that the above typology makes a strong case for when Christ was born, it is still not a sufficient argument. It can't be the only connection made, so we need to make more. In chapter 4, we talked about the significance of Nehemiah completing the walls of Jerusalem in relationship to Daniel's prophecy, and we surmised that the 442-year countdown—the 62 prophetic weeks—began the year after the wall was dedicated. The celebration lasted an entire Sabbath Year and was celebrated as if it were the Year of Jubilee. I know this is confusing, but since a year count begins on Ethanim 1 and goes to Ethanim 1, that would mean that Ethanim 1, 449 to 448 BC, is the first year, and Ethanim 1, 8 to 7 BC, is the final year of Daniel's predicted 442 years.

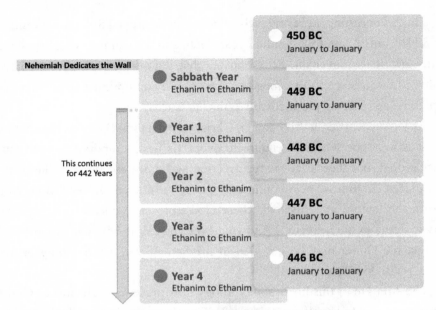

Timeline 5: Nehemiah's Dedication to Jesus's Birth (part 1)

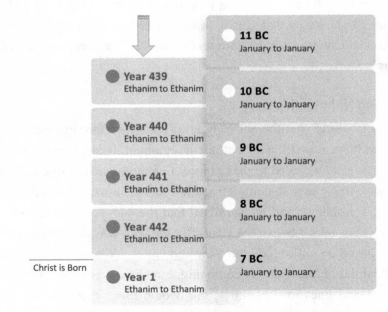

Timeline 6: Nehemiah's Dedication to Jesus's Birth (part 2)

So now let's look more closely at the dedication of the wall. Nehemiah 8:1–2 says:

Now all the people gathered together as one man in the open square that was in front of the Water Gate; and they told Ezra the scribe to bring the Book of the Law of Moses, *which the* LORD *had commanded Israel. So Ezra the priest brought the Law before the assembly of men and women and all who could hear with understanding* on the first day of the seventh month.

Just as Solomon had chosen Ethanim 1 to dedicate the temple, Ezra and Nehemiah chose the seventh month to dedicate the wall and to read the Word of God, which is another typology for Christ: "The Word became flesh" (John 1:14).

Ezra started reading from the Word on the first day (Nehemiah 8:2), and by midday the people were weeping. Think of this moment: they had been exiles in Babylon for 70 years, then Cyrus allowed them to return to Jerusalem where it took them twenty-two years to complete the temple. It was 62 years after that when Nehemiah finally asked the Persian king Artaxerxes to allow him to return to Jerusalem. And then after the wall was completed, they gathered in a restored Jerusalem to dedicate the wall, and they wept.

On day one—the Feast of Trumpets—they listened to the Law of God, and they decided to put their newfound commitment into immediate action. God had commanded in Leviticus 23 that on the fifteenth day of the seventh month they were to dwell in booths for a week—the Feast of Tabernacles. "They kept the feast seven days; and on the eighth day there was a sacred assembly, according to the prescribed manner" (8:18). Toward the end of the month, they once again read God's Law and rededicated themselves to obeying all that it commanded. Nehemiah 9 then gives an overview of Jewish history as a reminder of what God had done for them and how amazing it is that they were back in Jerusalem with the temple and the wall completed. In chapter 10, they renewed their commitment to keeping God's Law, and they signed a covenant agreement. Nehemiah 10:30–31 highlights some of the commitments they were intending to keep:

We would not give our daughters as wives to the peoples of the land,
nor take their daughters for our sons; if the peoples of the land
brought wares or any grain to sell on the Sabbath day, we would not
buy it from them on the Sabbath, or on a holy day; and we would
forego the seventh year's produce and the exacting of every debt."

This passage reveals why I believe Ezra and Nehemiah initiated the Year of Jubilee after they dedicated the wall. They were resetting all debt and returning land to the rightful families, which is something only done during a Year of Jubilee.[168] After that year was over, the new countdown began for the prophetic 62 weeks.

They also read the Word of God, which is more than just words on a page: it is the Lord unveiling his presence, not just his will. Hebrews 4:12–13 says:

For the word of God is living and powerful, and sharper than any
two-edged sword, piercing even to the division of soul and spirit, and
of joints and marrow, and is a discerner of the thoughts and intents of
the heart. And there is no creature hidden from His sight, but all things
are naked and open to the eyes of Him to whom we must give account.

Notice the personal pronouns used to describe the Word of God. It isn't the Bible which sees all but the living Word: Christ himself. In other words, the Lord's presence came into the midst of the Israelites on that day through the power of his Word. Likewise, on Ethanim 1, 442 years later (62 prophetic weeks), the glory of God's Word descended from heaven, and the Word became flesh and dwelt among us, "and we saw His glory, glory as of the only begotten from the Father, full of grace and truth." God's Word in the flesh. God with us.

Isaac

But there still has to be more connections than that. As you may already know, the patriarch Isaac, the promised son of Abraham, is typologically connected to Christ's crucifixion. God commanded Abraham to sacrifice Isaac, his promised son, to test Abraham's faith. But at the last-minute God restrained him and proclaimed that he would provide the sacrificial ram. Christ became that ram nearly two thousand years later when God sacrificed his own Son to provide for our redemption from sin.

But there is yet another event in Isaac's life that I have come to believe connects Jesus to him: Isaac's circumcision. According to God's law, every male child is to be circumcised eight days after he is born. Genesis 17:10–12 says,

> *This is My covenant which you shall keep, between Me and you and your descendants after you: Every male child among you shall be circumcised; and you shall be circumcised in the flesh of your foreskins, and it shall be a sign of the covenant between Me and you. He who is eight days old among you shall be circumcised, every male child in your generations.*

The Lord also told Abraham and Sarah during this encounter that a child of their own flesh would be born by that time the following year (v. 21).

Intriguingly, Jewish tradition teaches that "Abraham was said to have circumcised himself on the tenth of Tishri [Ethanim], the day later celebrated as the Day of Atonement, when the sins of the people are forgiven."[169] If that tradition is correct, then it would be a year later that Isaac was born on Ethanim 1, and he would have been circumcised eight days later. The Jewish Virtual Library article about circumcision says, "Abraham circumcised his son Ishmael, all the males of his household, and his slaves. In the following year when Isaac was born, *he was circumcised on the eighth day.*[170]

Now let's put this into the context of Luke 2:21: "And when eight days were completed for the circumcision of the Child, His name was called Jesus, the name given by the angel before He was conceived in the womb." Jesus Christ was circumcised eight days after he was born according to the law, and if he was born on Ethanim 1, this would line up with when Isaac had been born and circumcised. Therefore, Isaac doesn't merely foreshadow Christ's sacrifice; he may very well foreshadow Christ's birth and circumcision.

Forty Years

But wait, there's more! On the fifteenth day of Ethanim, the Feast of Tabernacles began with a holy convocation. The Feast of Tabernacles is a celebration of the forty years of wandering in the wilderness. It is considered the most joyful convocation of all the Jewish feasts, but let me remind you of Daniel's prophecy. There were 7 sevens (50 years), *a gap*, and then 62 sevens (442 years). I didn't see this next connection, nor anticipate it, until after I objectively laid out the dates. I did all of the groundwork without assuming any answers, so when I saw this my jaw dropped. Here it is. Cyrus conquered Babylon in 539 BC,[171] and 50 years later Daniel's first prophetic 7 weeks ended in 489 BC. If I'm right and the 442-year countdown restarted in 449 BC after Nehemiah's dedication of the wall of Jerusalem, that would mean from 489 to 449 BC is 40 years. The Jews wandered in the wilderness for 40 years, and the wonder of it all is that this could foreshadow how long the Messiah would live among us too. If Jesus was born in 7 BC and crucified in 33 AD, that would mean he was crucified six months before the beginning of his fortieth year. If one were to calculate his age the way we do now, we would say he was forty.[172]

I have been taught my entire life that Jesus was thirty when he was baptized and thirty-three years old when he was crucified (AD 30–33). It all sounds so nice and tidy. But did you know that one of the earliest church fathers, Irenaeus, argued that Jesus may have been in his forties when he was crucified?

Irenaeus was born between 115 and 125 AD, in Smyrna (modern Izmir, in Turkey). Irenaeus often heard the aged Polycarp preach. Polycarp was a close associate of the apostle John, and Irenaeus treasured this close connection with an eyewitness of Christ's time on earth.[173]

Irenaeus testifies that he got his information about the age of Jesus from elders who had known the apostle John himself:

[I learned this from] those who were conversant in Asia with John, the disciple of the Lord, [affirming] that John conveyed to them that information. . . . Some of them, moreover, saw not only John, but the other apostles also, and heard the very same account from them, and bear testimony as to the [validity of] the statement.[174]

Irenaeus explains what he learned from those elders: "He [Jesus] did not then want much of being fifty years old; and, in accordance with that fact, they said to Him, "Thou art not yet fifty years old, and hast thou seen Abraham?"[175] Irenaeus is quoting the Pharisees in John 8:57, who were dumbfounded by Jesus's audacious claim that he had seen Abraham. They sarcastically ridiculed him by saying, "You are not even fifty years old! LOL." If Jesus had been a mere thirty years old, they would have mocked him for that, but as it was, they mocked him for being in his forties, having not reached his fifties yet.

Irenaeus makes his argument, though, not to tell us when Christ was born, but to point out that Jesus had ministered for more than one year. Declercq says, "In the second and third centuries, the synoptic chronology [Jesus ministered for one year] was without question the dominant tradition."[176] This is called the short chronology, and Irenaeus was one of the few who called the short chronology into question—he even considered it heretical. He pointed out that John's Gospel records three Passovers during the life of Jesus, so how could Jesus have only ministered for one year? Irenaeus was a revolutionary on this point, and he was eventually vindicated by Eusebius in the fourth century, and it has since become the dominant view.

However, I believe it is important to take into consideration all that Irenaeus said on this issue. He didn't just teach that Jesus ministered for three years. He also implied that it was more than three years, and he believed this on the testimony of men who claimed they heard it from the apostles, including John. That's quite the claim, and we should not discard his point lightly.

Therefore, since I have suggested that Jesus was born on Ethanim 1 in 7 BC, now an entirely new vista appears on the horizon, and we need to explore the ramifications. Luke tells us that Jesus was about thirty years old when he was baptized in the fifteenth year of the reign of Tiberius (Luke 3:1), which is now identified as occurring in AD 28. If you do the math, from 7 BC to AD 28 is thirty-five years. So was Jesus exactly thirty as Clement calculated, or was he thirty-five? Was Luke wrong for saying Jesus was *about* thirty, or have the calculations of later church leaders superficially created the problem? Let's unravel this final dilemma and put a punctuation point on the month, day, and year Christ was born.

Point Lookout

It is a beautiful view from here, so let's sit for a minute and take a look at all the places we have traveled so far:

- Jesus fulfilled the Feast of Trumpets when God's presence came down to indwell the temple of the Son's human body. Jesus is the Word become flesh.
- Jesus fulfilled the Day of Atonement at his circumcision. He was purified and sanctified, fulfilling the promise of the covenant given to Abraham.
- Jesus fulfilled the Feast of Tabernacles when he dwelt among us, taking on all of our fleshly weaknesses and yet never did he sin. God wandered in the wilderness of our flesh, teaching, healing, and showing us the way to find joy.

This has been quite the journey. However, even though the end of the trail is not much further, we have one more challenge to overcome. So shrug on your pack, and let's finish this trek.

10

The Gordian Knot

But Herod deprived this Matthias of the high priesthood, and burnt the
other Matthias, who had raised the sedition, with his companions, alive.
And that very night there was an eclipse of the moon.

—*Josephus*

W hen I first sought to sort out the historical record and figure out when
Christ was born, the death of King Herod was one of the major strands
I wanted to untangle. When I pulled on that strand, however, it tight-
ened up everything else. It was like when I used to untangle one-hundred-foot
extension cords for my job in Marina del Rey, California. I'd spend half an
hour just twisting and pulling and flailing cords around.

Calculating Herod's death became my Gordian knot. What is the Gordian
knot? The History Channel website gives a nice summary:

*As the story goes, in 333 B.C. the Macedonian conqueror [Alex-
ander the Great] marched his army into the Phrygian capital
of Gordium in modern day Turkey. Upon arriving in the city, he
encountered an ancient wagon, its yoke tied with what one Roman
historian later described as "several knots all so tightly entangled*

145

that it was impossible to see how they were fastened."

Phrygian tradition held that the wagon had once belonged to Gordius, the father of the celebrated King Midas. An oracle had declared that any man who could unravel its elaborate knots was destined to become ruler of all of Asia.

According to the ancient chronicler Arrian, the impetuous Alexander was instantly "seized with an ardent desire" to untie the Gordian knot. After wrestling with it for a time and finding no success, he stepped back from the mass of gnarled ropes and proclaimed, "It makes no difference how they are loosed." He then drew his sword and sliced the knot in half with a single stroke.[177]

Oh, how I have wanted to do that! But that's not really solving the problem, is it? I couldn't have gone to my boss with an electrical cord all stretched out in little pieces and said, "It's untangled!" But that is what many have chosen to do when they encounter the problem of Herod's death.

According to modern scholarship, Herod died in the spring of 4 BC, but so many people have decided, "No he didn't," and then they have given reasons why one shouldn't trust the historian Josephus and his account of Herod's life. That's a possibility because Josephus was fallible, but as we will see, his account of Herod's life is accurate and his timeframes are consistent. Therefore, since Herod died in what we call 4 BC, then Jesus could not have been born in 1, 2, or 3 BC, and that excludes a lot of theories about when Christ was born, including the one that we have keyed our entire calendar to: AD 1.

Dionysius Exiguus (ca. 465–530) was a Scythian monk who is credited with being the first one to key the beginning of our calendar to the birth of Christ. For the first 500 years, the church was primarily concerned with identifying the correct year of the crucifixion and resurrection, but they used the Roman, Greek, and Babylonian calendar systems to identify how many years had passed since the passion of the Christ. In other words, no one ever used BC or AD for the first 500 years after Christ was born.

Dionysius is the first one to count years from Christ's birth, and he decided that his table should start 532 years after Christ was born. There was a mathematical reason he chose 532 years, as we look at in chapter 11, but there remains a controversy about how trustworthy his choice was. Was it based purely on mathematical calculations? Or was it based on some historical documents he had access to?

Georges Declercq, faculty member at the University of Brussels, argues that "Dionysius was guided first and foremost by practical considerations related to the reckoning of Easter rather than by a desire for historical accuracy."[178] That is a fascinating point. Declercq documents that Dionysius mathematically calculated the date of the crucifixion and then counted back to the date of his birth. To put it plainly, our entire calendar is keyed to a mathematical model, not some well-known historical data that the early church had access to. There wasn't some document they had which told them when Jesus had been born. Therefore, if history proves he was wrong, that means we are not obliged to sustain his conclusions.

New Testament scholar Harold Hoehner articulates the modern understanding of our calendar: "The commencement of the Christian era was January 1, 754 A.U.C. (anno urbis conditae = from the foundation of the city [of Rome]) and Christ's birth was thought to have been on December 25th immediately preceding [Dec. 25, 753 AUC]. So 754 A.U.C. became A.D. 1 in the calendar of Dionysius."[179] Hoehner is right in the sense that this is how we view the origins of our calendar *now*, but the actual origin is not as clear-cut as he makes it sound. Dionysius never used the designation "754 AUC." That is a later development—a pattern that was laid over the complex calculations of Dionysius and other mathematicians, made for scholarly consumption. This is confusing stuff!

To reveal the depth of the problem: If our modern calendar is based on the *historical* date of Christ's birth, why then do we put Herod's death in 4 BC? It is curious that if the early church calculated that Jesus had been born on December 25, AD 1 as Dionysius calculated, how come Herod's death is about four or five years earlier? This seems odd considering that Scripture clearly teaches that Herod was alive when Jesus was born (Matthew 2:1). See how tangled the Gordian knot can be?

Did Herod die in 4 BC, or is that an historian's mistake? Or is something else going on altogether?

Were the calculations of Dionysius and other early church fathers wrong, or are they as close to correct as we can possibly get?

This is a gnarly knot with lots of technical and emotional strands to untangle. You pull on one and the others tighten up and somebody will inevitably get mad.

Rick Larson in his 2007 DVD *The Star of Bethlehem* was the first person who really caught my attention on this issue. He persuaded me that Christ had been born in June of 2 BC. I believed him for years because he offered evidence that was so convincingly presented that it seemed undeniable. However, for his theory to work, he had to dismiss the traditional date of Herod's death, and he claimed that new scholarship showed that Herod died in 1 BC. I believed him. See how easy it is to use a sword to solve the Gordian knot? He believed his star theory was true, therefore he claimed that Herod did not die in 4 BC, so that allowed his theory about the star to be true. Problem solved!

I'm thankful for Larson's video and his comments because it compelled me to look a little more deeply into why certain scholars thought 4 BC was wrong. I started my work to strengthen his theory, not to refute it. So I read numerous sources and bought the Starry Night software[180] that Rick Larson used. My intention was to recreate his theory about the star of Bethlehem and prove that Herod died in 1 BC as he claimed. Instead, what I discovered is that Herod's death fits perfectly into 4 BC and that it cannot be moved like a peg on a board. It isn't just historically accurate; it is *astronomically* accurate. Therefore, one cannot say, "I do not like Herod's death there, so I will move it here." Herod's life happened in the context of Roman history, and Josephus integrates the events surrounding Herod's death into a timeline of other events that can be confirmed by other sources. Therefore, to move the death of Herod to 1 BC tightens the knot more than ever before and creates time differentials with unsolvable conundrums, causing more problems than it solves. To see why, we need to look more closely at the last days of King Herod.

The Last Days of Herod

It took a long time, but Herod at last came to realize that his oldest son, Antipater, had been the cause of all the chaos and bloodshed in his family. Herod had implicitly trusted him for years, but that trust had led Herod to execute his two beloved sons in 8 BC, thereby ending the last of the Hasmonean line. The truth that Antipater had been behind all the chaos came to light in a most unusual way.

After the Pharisees refused to participate in the census run by Saturninus while Herod was king in 7 BC, Herod came to realize that Pheroras's wife had been the chief cause of their petulance. She revealed where her true loyalties lay when she paid the fine for the Pharisees' rebellion against the census. Now Herod distrusted her and wanted his brother to divorce her. When he refused, Herod backed off his demand and instead banished them both. He was polite about it but firm, and he and his brother were not supposed to see each other again this side of death. Herod, however, broke his own rule and went to visit him when he heard that Pheroras had become sick. This act of kindness saved Herod's life.

During this time, Antipater set in motion two plots to kill his father. First, he convinced Herod's brother to poison Herod, and second, as a backup plan, Antipater conspired with Sylleus (whom Caesar Augustus had recently put under the responsibility of King Aretas of the Nabateans, if you remember) to bribe Herod's guards to assassinate Herod. To deflect suspicion from himself, Antipater had a friend write a letter to Herod, implying that Augustus wanted Herod to send Antipater to Rome. Being in Rome would not only make Antipater appear innocent when his father died, but it would also allow him to be in Rome to get the all-important backing of Augustus right away. Both plots went awry and instead exposed Antipater to be the liar that he was.

When Herod showed kindness to his brother and visited him while he was sick, Pheroras couldn't go through with murdering his brother. So Pheroras demanded that his wife destroy the poison he had acquired. However, she kept some back, poisoned Pheroras, and intended to poison Herod if the opportunity arose (and herself if it came to that). Pheroras soon died from a "mysterious illness," and Herod allowed his wife to return to the palace. Her servant girls knew the truth, though, and they informed him that she had poisoned Pheroras. As a result, Herod went on another torturing spree: "at length one of [the people he tortured], under the utmost agonies, said no more but this, that *she prayed that God would send the like agonies upon Antipater's mother*, who had been the occasion of these miseries to all of them."[181] This one inadvertent revelation caused Herod to realize that Antipater had been behind all the plots, including manipulating him to execute Alexander and Antigonus. Antipater's backup plan of having a guard kill Herod also backfired.

In the meantime, Antipater was still in Rome and completely unaware that he had been rooted out. He was a practiced liar, but as with any deceiver, once the person you are lying to knows you are lying, your lies become more obvious than ever. Herod (a good politician himself) played along with Antipater's deceptions in order to catch him in his own machinations. Josephus tells us that while Antipater was coming back from Rome, "Quintilius Varus was at this time at Jerusalem, being sent to succeed Saturninus as president of Syria, and was come as a counselor to Herod, who had desired his advice in his present affairs."[182] Quintilius Varus governed Syria from 6 to 4 BC,[183] so Antipater's trial occurred during the transition of power in the spring or summer of 6 BC when travel by ship was safer.

Antipater showed up in his father's palace fully expecting to be warmly welcomed back, but instead Herod formally accused him and told him that his trial would begin the next day with Varus as the judge. At the trial, Herod spoke first and lamented how much trauma his own child had brought into his life in spite of all the favors he had bestowed on him. Antipater—even though it was clear that his plots had been uncovered—still tried to convince Herod that he had only meant to protect his father from harm. Such is the heart of a deceiver—denial until the bitter end.

Nicolaus, Herod's lawyer, decimated Antipater's defense:

Yet were you, O Antipater (as you yourself have confessed), the informer as to what wicked actions they had done. . . . Nor do we say this as accusing you for being so zealous in your anger against them, but are astonished at your endeavors to imitate their immoral behavior; and we discover thereby that you did not act thus for the safety of your father, but for the destruction of your brothers.[184]

A flood of testimony now poured forth from everyone who knew anything about anyone in an attempt to save their own lives. With Antipater's guilt fully exposed, Varus had had enough, stood up, and left for Antioch, the Roman capital of the Syrian province. The life of Antipater was now in the hands of Herod, who did not immediately execute his son but rather sent letters to Caesar Augustus to explain what had happened and to await further instructions. While he waited, he imprisoned Antipater in Jericho.

In 6 BC, Herod was in the seventieth year of his life. That would mean Herod was born in 75 BC (counting inclusively). Josephus is consistent because he also tells us that Herod was fifteen years old when his father Antipater made him governor of Galilee.[185] We know that this was in 61 BC because this was also the ninth year of the High Priest Hyrcanus.[186] Hyrcanus had begun his priesthood "on the third year of the hundred and seventy-seventh Olympiad, [when] Hortensius and Quintus Metellus, who was called Metellus of Crete, were consuls at Rome.[187] According to the Roman historian Cassius Dio, Hortensius and Metellus were consuls in 69 BC, which falls in the third year of the 177th Olympiad. The multiple sources and cross-checks confirm the synchronization of Josephus and modern scholarship. The timeline on the following page will be helpful as we walk through these events.

A Rebellion, a Dream, a Fast, and an Eclipse

Now that Herod was seventy years old and had been betrayed by almost everyone he had ever trusted, except his sister Salome, Josephus says "he grew fierce, and indulged the bitterest anger upon all occasions." He was also hated by nearly everyone in Jerusalem. His poll numbers were in the tank, at maybe .0001 percent. The remaining few who supported him were in close proximity to him and could be killed if they said otherwise.

I believe part of the reason for his plummeting poll numbers and "bitterest anger" was because, if my theory is correct, sometime after the trial of Antipater in the middle of 6 BC, a group of magi from Babylon showed up who informed him that the true king of the Jews had been born. After the magi betrayed him, he ordered the execution of young boys "in Bethlehem and in all its districts" (Matthew 2:16). Few things are more insidious than the indiscriminate slaughter of young children. (More about those events in the final two chapters.)

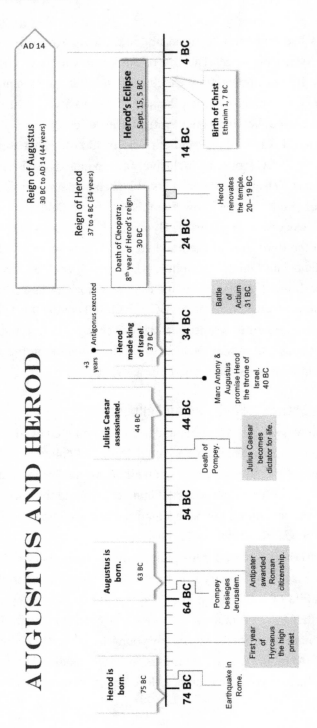

Timeline 7: Overview of the Lives of Augustus and Herod

It was in 5 BC that everything started falling completely apart for Herod. A small group of Pharisees led by two men, Judas and Matthias, were emboldened to "pull down all those works which the king had erected contrary to the law of their fathers."[188] The primary object of their offense was that Herod "had erected over the great gate of the temple a large golden eagle, of great value, and had dedicated it to the temple."[189] Some Jews believed this to be a blasphemous insult, and they decided to tear down the golden eagle and cut it into pieces with axes. Judas and Matthias were caught, along with forty others, for carrying out this deed. At their trial, they said they were more than willing to be executed because they believed that what they had done was righteous. Herod, however, didn't have them immediately executed because he knew how explosive the Jews could be. So instead he sent them to his prison in Jericho where his son Antipater was also being held.

Herod then called together all the other Jewish leaders: "and when they were come, he made them assemble in the theater, and because he could not himself stand, he lay upon a couch." Herod was very sick in 5 BC, and he couldn't walk. At this particular meeting, he recounted all the good things he had done for the Jews over the course of his reign and argued that what these rebels had done was an ungrateful insult against God. The leaders agreed with him so they would not also be thrown into prison.

Confusingly at this time, there was also another Jew named Matthias who had been politically appointed by Herod. High priests were supposed to be selected by "the unanimous agreement of the seventy elders, . . . but [Herod] made it his practice to install and remove high priests as the fancy took him."[190] Therefore, Herod fired Matthias after he had recused himself from serving during the most sacred fast of the year, the Day of Atonement.

Matthias chose to recuse himself from serving as high priest because "This Matthias the high priest, on the night before that day when *the fast* was to be celebrated, seemed, in a dream, to have conversation with his wife; and because he could not officiate himself on that account, Joseph, the son of Ellemus, his kinsman, assisted him in that sacred office."[191] Josephus tells us that the High Priest Matthias had had a conversation with his wife in a dream, and we are left to wonder why such a thing would disqualify him from fulfilling his responsibilities. Josephus explains earlier in *Antiquities* that God "also directed them [high priests] not only to observe purity in their sacred ministrations, but in their daily conversation, that it might be unblamable also."[192] Priests were to be holy even down to the spirit of their conversations. Matthias apparently was concerned that he had made himself impure because of a conversation he had had with his wife *in a dream*. Must have been quite the conversation!

So, during which fast did all of this happen? As we have seen, there are eight convocations in Leviticus 23 (if we count the Sabbath), but the Day of Atonement is celebrated as a fast, not a feast, and it is considered to be the most holy day of the Jewish year. There is a debate about whether Josephus was referring to this one, or to one of the other fasts that the Jews hold throughout the year. Zechariah 8:19 mentions several fasts, but there are others too, such as the fast of Esther, also known as Purim. Josephus refers to another fast that was being celebrated when Pompey took Jerusalem "on the third month, on the day of the fast" (bk. 14, chap. 4.3 [66]) which can only be a reference to Shavuot (Pentecost) in the Jewish third month. However, since Josephus only says "the fast" without any other qualifiers when he is talking about when the eclipse happened, it makes sense that his Greek and Roman audience would be drawn to think of the best known Jewish fast of the year—the one that took place on Ethanim 10, the Day of Atonement. Commentator and historian Paul Maier confirms this interpretation: "This fact, that one Joseph was made high priest for a single day, on occasion of the action here specified, that befell Matthias, the real high priest, in his sleep, the night before *the great day of atonement*, is attested to both in the Mishna and Talmud" (emphasis added).[193]

Matthias's decision had made Herod so angry that he not only fired Matthias the priest, but he also decided to finally execute Matthias the rebel, along with all of the other Pharisees imprisoned in Jericho who had torn down the golden eagle. His patience had worn out. Josephus then says, "And that very night there was an eclipse of the moon." This one phrase is the most crucial element in solving the mystery of the year of Christ's birth. This event loosens the Gordian knot.

Fortunately, eclipses are predictable celestial events that can be pinpointed with modern software quite accurately. There are many types of eclipses, but the full lunar eclipse was the most dramatic portent in the ancient world. They are called a Blood Red Moon and "were counted as the most baleful sign manifested by the heavens, as they predicted the violent death of the king."[194]

A *solar* eclipse can only happen near the time of a new moon when the moon floats between the earth and the sun. They only last fifteen minutes to half an hour, and only happen during the day because the moon blots out the sun. They can safely be looked at with eye protection. I had the opportunity to observe one on August 21, 2017. The sight was eerie. All the birds went silent, and the shadows of leaves did this weird multiplicity thing called a "shadow band." I took the following photo of shadows cast by the leaves of my tree on my back fence during the solar eclipse. It shows what shadow bands look like. They are curved and the light through the leaves appears to multiply.

Photograph 1: A Solar Eclipse Causes "Shadow Bands"

A *lunar* eclipse, on the other hand, can only happen near the time of a full moon when the earth comes between the moon and the sun. This type of eclipse can last for hours. I observed one on May 15, 2022, and it was indeed ominous.[195] It can only be seen during the night because the shadow of the earth blots out the moon. This is the kind of eclipse Josephus refers to.

The traditionally accepted date of the lunar eclipse that Josephus mentions is considered to be March 13, 4 BC, near the fast of Esther (Purim).[196] This might work if Josephus was referring to the fast of Esther, but that eclipse was only a partial eclipse (which is not as portentous as a full eclipse), and it happened at about 2:30 in the morning only one month before the next Passover on April 11, 4 BC. This is important to notice because even though Josephus doesn't tell us exactly how long Herod lived after the eclipse, he does tell us what Herod did during that time, and it needed way more time than one month to play out. The following is Josephus's account of what happened to Herod between the eclipse and his death.

Herod's Final Months

At this time, right after the eclipse, Herod's suffering increased exponentially.

> *Herod's sickness greatly increased upon him after a severe manner, and this by God's judgment upon him for his sins; for a fire glowed in him slowly . . . [which] augmented his pains inwardly . . . [and] brought upon him a vehement appetite to eating. . . . His entrails were also exulcerated, and the chief violence of his pain lay on his colon; an aqueous and transparent liquor also had settled itself about his feet, and a like matter afflicted him at the bottom of his belly. Nay, further, his privy-member was putrefied, and produced worms.[197]*

Herod sent for physicians and allowed himself to be taken to the hot springs at Callirrhoe on the east side of the Dead Sea about fifty miles from Jerusalem. Not a quick journey in those days, especially for an invalid. He spent a while there, but nearly died after being dipped in warm oil. He then was taken to Jericho, thirty-seven miles back toward Jerusalem, where his son Antipater was jailed and where Herod spent the rest of his life.

It was in Jericho that he became a full-blown madman, and devised a depraved and barbarous plot:

> *He then returned back and came to Jericho, in such a melancholy state of body as almost threatened him with present death, when he proceeded to attempt a horrid wickedness; for he got together the most illustrious men of the whole Jewish nation, out of every village, into a place called the Hippodrome, and there shut them in.[198]*

With the Jewish leaders imprisoned in the hippodrome,[199] Herod then commanded: "I shall die in a little time, so great are my pains; which death ought to be cheerfully borne, and to be welcomed by all men; but what principally troubles me is this, that I shall die without being lamented, and without such mourning as men usually expect at a king's death."[200]

Herod knew everyone despised him, so to rectify that he wanted all the Jewish leaders who had been locked up in the hippodrome to be killed upon his death. However, he didn't want his death to be announced until after all the leaders were killed so that the country would be in mourning for them. While grieving their deaths, his death would be announced so it would appear as if the people were weeping for him! He made his soldiers swear to enact his diabolical fiction upon his death.

Herod revived a little after he got the news that Caesar Augustus had given him permission to execute his son Antipater, giving him a reason to live at least a few more days. His pain was getting worse, though, and he tried to commit suicide. His first cousin stopped him, and Antipater (who was still in the prison at Jericho) heard rumors that his father had died. So he tried to bribe his jailer to release him from prison. But the jailer didn't like Antipater at all and instead turned him in. Herod became so infuriated that he had Antipater executed immediately. He then changed his will and died five days later. Thus ended the life of King Herod.

Immediately after Herod's death, Herod's sister Salome and his wife Alexas wisely freed the Jews held captive in the hippodrome at Jericho. They knew how insane his request had been. Herod's chosen heir, Archelaus, then organized a grand funeral to honor his father. However, Archelaus needed to be officially recognized by Caesar Augustus as the new king, and he wanted to go to Rome right away to secure that designation. The Jews delayed him, though, and they appealed to him for tax relief and to manage things differently than his father had. He told them that he would honor their requests upon his return from Rome, but they were impatient and unafraid of him. They revolted against him even though it was during the Passover of 4 BC. He suppressed their uprising by killing three thousand Jews. Not a great beginning to his reign, and it's a good thing Jesus and his family were in Egypt at the time (Matthew 2:13–15).

As you can see, given the final months of Herod's life, there is simply not enough time for all of these events to have occurred between the traditionally accepted eclipse on March 13, 4 BC and Herod's death a couple of weeks before Passover on April 11. Quite frankly, it's impossible.

There are a couple of other contenders for Herod's eclipse that should be considered. One possibility is March 23, 5 BC, which was a full eclipse that transpired at about 8:30 in the evening. It happened the day *after* Passover, though, and so it couldn't be the right one because Herod died a couple of weeks *before* Passover. It also has the opposite problem of the March 13th partial eclipse of 4 BC: it doesn't seem like the events of Herod's last days needed an entire year to unfold.

I, therefore, believe that the full lunar eclipse on Friday, September 15, 5 BC at 10:30 in the evening is the most probable candidate for the one Josephus mentions. I am not certain why it hasn't been given more consideration, but it fits the bill perfectly. The new moon was on Ethanim 1, 5 BC (September 3), and the Day of Atonement (the fast) was on Ethanim 10 (September 12). There was an eclipse a few days later at 10:30 p.m. on September 15, exactly as Josephus described. If this is the correct eclipse, then that would mean Herod's last days as described above would have taken place over a six-month period, which is plenty of time for them to have occurred.

But there are those individuals who steadfastly believe that Jesus was born in 3 or 2 BC, and some of them believe that a partial lunar eclipse on December 29, 1 BC fits the criteria for Herod's eclipse. It did occur near the fast of the tenth month of the Jewish calendar, but it was below the horizon at 4:30 in the afternoon, so nobody in Jerusalem would have seen it.

Others, though, believe that the full lunar eclipse on January 10, 1 BC is the best candidate because it, too, occurs a couple of days after the fast of the tenth month.[201] This date would allow enough time for Herod's last days to unfold before he died, and such a date would also allow enough time for the magi to have visited Herod before the eclipse if Jesus were born in either 3 or 2 BC. However, January 10 has two major weaknesses that reduce its credibility: (1) Josephus tells us specifically that Herod reigned thirty-four years after the execution of Antigonus, which happened in 37 BC. Counting inclusively,

Herod's life, and therefore his reign, ended in 4 BC. So Herod would have been dead before Jesus was born. (2) Josephus doesn't tell us specifically what fast he is referring to, but that actually might be our most important clue. He says, "That very day which the Jews observed as a fast." From this we can infer that he meant the Day of Atonement because it is the best known Jewish fast, and he would not have needed to put a qualifier on it as he does for the fast in the third month. There is also no contextual reason to think he was referring to the fast of Esther.

Therefore, the eclipse on September 15, 5 BC is by far the best candidate. It meets all of the necessary criteria:

- Matthias recuses himself from serving as high priest for the Day of Atonement because he is ritually unclean and therefore cannot enter the holy of holies, which is only done once a year on the Day of Atonement.
- Herod fires and replaces Matthias the high priest after he finds out, and then executes Matthias the rebel and all his followers.
- The eclipse on September 15 allows enough time for all the events in Herod's last months to unfold before he dies several months later before the next Passover, but not too much time elapses (the Goldilocks principle).
- The full lunar eclipse needed to be visible in Jerusalem.

The life and death of King Herod, therefore, becomes, ironically, one of the best ways to figure out when Christ was born. We cannot put Christ's birth on the Feast of Trumpets in 5 BC because that is when Herod's eclipse occurs, and there was no census at that time. Herod would have been heading to Jericho to deal with his health problems.

Moving back a year, Christ could have been born in the fall of 6 BC, which would have given enough time (a year) for the magi to arrive before the September 15, 5 BC eclipse, but there wasn't a census in 6 BC. Varus had already taken over as governor, and the historian Tertullian tells us that Saturninus was in charge of the census when Christ was born.

Therefore, 7 BC must be the year Christ was born. It works even if one were to maintain that Christ was born on December 25 of that year. There would be enough time for the magi to have arrived in Jerusalem in 6 or 5 BC, and very few people maintain that the magi were present at the birth of Christ in spite of what the typical manger scene and many movies portray. If the magi had been at the manger scene, by the way, they would have had to have arrived in Jerusalem at least a week before Jesus was born, which is inconsistent with what Matthew tells us. In his Gospel he writes: "Now *after* Jesus was born in Bethlehem of Judea in the days of Herod the king, behold, wise men from the East came to Jerusalem, saying, 'Where is He who has been born King of the Jews?' " (Matthew 2:1).

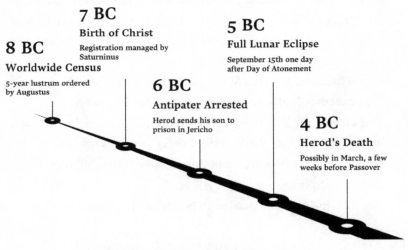

7 BC
Birth of Christ

5 BC
Full Lunar Eclipse

8 BC
Worldwide Census

Registration managed by
Saturninus

September 15th one day
after Day of Atonement

5-year lustrum ordered
by Augustus

6 BC
Antipater Arrested

Herod sends his son to
prison in Jericho

4 BC
Herod's Death

Possibly in March, a few
weeks before Passover

Timeline 8: Basic Timeline of Herod's Last Days

The Baptism of Jesus

Now we need to untangle another strand of the Gordian knot: How old was Jesus at his baptism—the event that initiated his ministry? To do this, it is essential to remember that *none* of the early church fathers thought in terms of BC or AD. Indeed, that notion was not even suggested until the Scythian monk Dionysius Exiguus decided he no longer liked the accepted calendar reference used by the scholars of his day, which was *Anni Diocletiani* (AD), which means Years of Diocletian.[202] In the late first century, Diocletian was a Roman emperor who had been particularly violent and cruel to Christians, so Dionysius figured why should the church honor an anti-Christian emperor whenever they referred to the date of Easter? He decided that it would be better if AD should stand for *Anno Domini*, "In the year of the Lord." Pretty clever, really, and although his new format now rules our calendars today, his idea didn't catch on for another two hundred years until the Venerable Bede (ca. 700) helped to establish its use by frequently using the phrase "in the year of our Lord."[203] As much as I admire the cleverness of BC and AD, however, it has led to much of our confusion about when Christ was born.

Time Will Tell

I am not going to rely on BC or AD in the following section. You may desperately want me to attach BC or AD to the following events because it is what gives us a sense of location in the flow of events. It's our historical compass, and I have used BC/AD dates up until now because it is what we are familiar with. But there is an important reason why I won't use BC and AD in this next section: It isn't how the ancients kept track of time. Once we go back to their methods, the birth of Christ actually falls perfectly into its place, no problem at all. Seriously, if we stay with the terminology they used and stop trying to convert everything to BC/AD, it all makes sense. So please pretend for a little while that BC/AD does not exist, and imagine yourself using the old ways of keeping track of time by using the length of a king's reign, how many years happened between events, the order of Roman consuls, and four-year segments called Greek Olympiads. These were the way it was done before the birth of Christ and for at least the first seven hundred years after Christ. It will be challenging to do, but it is the best way to expose why so much confusion has arisen about the date of Christ's birth.

Luke tells us that Jesus was baptized in the fifteenth year of Tiberius and later adds that Jesus was about thirty years old when he was baptized (the event that launched his ministry):

> *Now in the fifteenth year of the reign of Tiberius Caesar, Pontius*
> *Pilate being governor of Judea, Herod [Antipas] being tetrarch*

of Galilee, his brother Philip tetrarch of Iturea and the region of Trachonitis, and Lysanias tetrarch of Abilene, while Annas and Caiaphas were high priests, the word of God came to John the son of Zacharias in the wilderness. (Luke 3:1–2)

Now Jesus Himself began His ministry at about thirty years of age, being (as was supposed) the son of Joseph, the son of Heli . . . . (v. 23)

Clement of Alexandria (ca. 200) uses this passage to calculate the birth of Christ, and he makes it sound quite straightforward: "And our Lord was born in the twenty-eighth year, when first the census was ordered to be taken in the reign of Augustus. . . . Accordingly, in fifteen years of Tiberius and fifteen years of Augustus; so were completed the thirty years till the time He suffered."[204] How easy is that! Clement had earlier explained that he believed Augustus had reigned for 43 years from the death of Cleopatra,[205] so subtract 15 from 43 and we arrive at the 28th year of the reign of Augustus. Problem solved! Clement used a simple calculation to figure out when Jesus was born. If we look more closely, Clement started the reign of Augustus with the suicide of Cleopatra. This would make sense because Clement lived in Alexandria, Egypt, and her death was one year after Augustus defeated Antony at the Battle of Actium.

All of the other subsequent church fathers accepted his calculations. For example, Tertullian (ca. 200) says, "Let us see, moreover, how in the forty-first year of the empire of Augustus, when he has been reigning for xx and viii (28) years after the death of Cleopatra, the Christ is born."[206] When Tertullian refers to the forty-first year of the empire of Augustus, he must have been dating the beginning of Augustus's reign from the Battle of Mutina (April 21, 43 BC), in the year following the assassination of Julius Caesar. But both Clement and Tertullian agree that Jesus was born 28 years after Cleopatra committed suicide.

Eusebius (ca. 300) speaks the same way but with one alteration of his own: "It was in the forty-second year of the reign of Augustus and the twenty-eighth after the subjugation of Egypt and the death of Antony and Cleopatra."[207] Eusebius says it was the forty-second year of Augustus's reign, but he must have been starting his reign from the assassination of Julius Caesar. Tertullian and Eusebius had different starting points for the reign of Augustus, but each of them said that Christ was born 28 years after the death of Cleopatra.

Dionysius uses the same calculations as Eusebius, and in the "Preface of Felix" in Dionysius's famous Easter tabulations, Felix says, "In the middle of the 194th Olympiad, i.e. in the forty-second regnal year[208] of Octavianus Augustus [28th from death of Cleopatra] our Lord Jesus Christ was born."[209]

Moving forward 200 years, the Venerable Bede (ca. 700) also stays with the "42nd regnal year; 28th year from the death of Cleopatra" model, for he says that Claudius concluded the conquest of Britain "in the fourth year of his reign, which is the forty-sixth from the Incarnation of our Lord."[210] From his fourth year back to Augustus's 28th year, there are 46 years. So the early church for at least the first 700 years is consistent within itself. Jesus was born in the 28th year of Augustus because that was 30 years before Christ was baptized. Voila! The controversy about the year of Christ's birth did not even exist for the first 700 years!

It wasn't a controversy but that does not mean it was the right date. It looks like the early church fathers made no effort to confirm Clement's date by studying history. Apparently they never checked to see if Herod was alive in the 28th year of Augustus's reign (which he wasn't), or whether Augustus had ordered a census in the 28th year (which he hadn't). They just went with Clement's calculations, and they seemed to be indifferent to the historical dilemma they were creating. Indeed, as we will see, they had all the information necessary to figure out that the 28th year of Augustus was wrong.

Josephus tells us (and the early church fathers, including Eusebius, relied heavily on him) that Herod was in the seventh year of his reign when the Battle of Actium was fought: "At this time it was that the fight happened at Actium, between Octavius Caesar and Antony, in the seventh year of the reign of Herod."[211] That would mean that the death of Cleopatra was in the eighth year of the reign of Herod. Herod's reign officially began in the year that Antony executed Antigonus. Antigonus was the Hasmonean successor, and once he was dead, Herod was the undisputed king. Josephus also tells us that Herod reigned for thirty-four years after the death of Antigonus: "When he [Herod] had done these things, he died, the fifth day after he had caused Antipater to be slain; having reigned, since he had procured Antigonus to be slain, thirty-four years."[212]

The timeline on the next page lays out the sequence of events. Also, remember that Josephus counts inclusively, meaning he doesn't start with zero. The first year is counted as 1.

Herod therefore died in the 27th year of Augustus *according to the information available to the early church fathers*, and yet they appear to have ignored that fact. If Jesus had been born in the 28th year of Augustus, then Jesus would have been born one year after Herod died, a clear violation of Luke and Matthew's accounts. How did the church fathers miss this? My theory is that they were so committed to their belief that Jesus was exactly thirty years old at his baptism in the fifteenth year of Tiberius that this superseded any other considerations. They were committed to their calculations, not to history.

So a lot is riding on answering the following question: does Luke 3:23, where we are told that Jesus began his ministry when he was "about thirty years of age," mean that Jesus was *exactly* thirty years old when he was baptized? The Greek word *hōsei* means "about," and the other Greek term *triakonta* means "thirty." Matthew uses *hōsei* to say that Jesus fed "*about* five thousand men, beside women and children" (Matthew 14:21). When this Greek adverb modifies a number, it means approximately, not precisely. Could the crowd have been 4,500 people or 5,500? We don't know because the language is intentionally imprecise.

Luke uses the same Greek word in 1:56 when he says, "Mary abode with her [Elizabeth] *about* three months," leaving the impression that she stayed with Elizabeth for another week or two after John was born. Luke 23:44 says, "And it was *about* the sixth hour [when Jesus died]," leaving the impression that Jesus died near that hour, give or take some minutes before it or after it.

So, what did Luke mean by "about thirty"? Samuel Andrews in his book *The Life of Our Lord Upon the Earth* says, "that the statement the Lord was about thirty years of age is to be taken in a large sense, and that He may have been of any age from thirty to thirty-five, when He began His labors."[213]

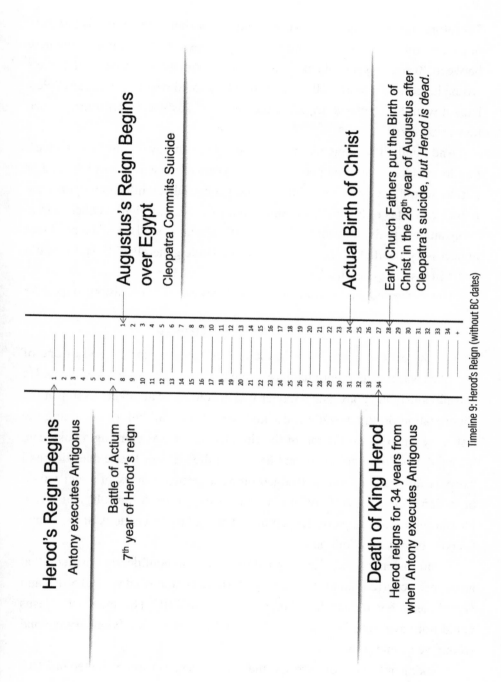

Timeline 9: Herod's Reign (without BC dates)

Therefore, far from rigidly locking us into Jesus being thirty at his baptism, or even within a few months of being thirty, Jesus could have been anywhere between 30 and 35 years old and that would not violate Scripture at all. Luke's word choice was intentionally vague, so why should we make it precise? Perhaps it would be better to translate the verse, "Jesus was in his thirties when he was baptized."

And finally, I imagine that if we were able to sit down with Luke and ask him to clarify if Jesus had been thirty-five years old when he was baptized or not, he would have said thoughtfully, and yet casually, while sipping on wine in between bites of bread, "Yea. Sure. That sounds about right." Others agree: "Any attempt to dogmatically assert Christ's age at 30 at his baptism produces unnecessary conflict in the Gospels and the Bible generally."[214] And I would add, "In history generally."

This further loosens the Gordian knot, and now we can allow history to speak.[215]

Taking a Water Break

One of the oddest things I saw in the Grand Canyon near the end of one of my hikes was a man intentionally refusing to stop and get a drink of water. He was obviously in agony, and a ranger was encouraging all hikers to stop at the water station on this heavily trafficked part of the trail before beginning the last, very steep leg to the top of the rim. The hiker was carrying a coke can, his head was drooping down, and he had all the signs of heat exhaustion and extreme fatigue. And yet he trudged on as if getting a drink of water would be a sign of weakness. Foolish man not to stop, refresh himself, and take a look around. So let's pause for a moment and take one last look at the Grand Canyon before we climb out.

From historical and astronomical data, we can confidently conclude that an eclipse occurred right after the Day of Atonement in what we call 5 BC, and Herod died a few months later before Passover in 4 BC. This means that Jesus could not have been born in 5, 4, 3, 2, or 1 BC. That is a boundary beyond which we cannot pass.

Looking at 6 and 7 BC, we saw that since a census was conducted in 7 BC, that must be the year Christ was born.

We have also seen that the dedication of Solomon's Temple and the dedication of Nehemiah's wall both typologically point to Christ being born on Ethanim 1.

Putting it all together according to our modern calendar system, the date for Christ's birth would be September 25, 7 BC.[216] At first this may appear to break some sacred biblical truth, but our current calendar is based on traditions and calculations made hundreds of years after Christ was born. The early church fathers in the east and west tried to calculate the date of Christ's birth, but it appears that they were more concerned with rigidly adhering to Jesus being exactly thirty years old at his baptism than with using history to confirm the date. As Declercq says:

> *Chronology was only of incidental interest to Dionysius. His main concern was to advocate the Alexandrian method of Easter reckoning in the West. . . . The year of the incarnation was from that perspective only a computistically irrelevant detail, which was useful as a numerical system to denote the individual years in the table. . . . For him the year of the incarnation was but a number in a liturgical document.*[217]

Luke, therefore, is once again proven to be right: Jesus was in his thirties (not exactly thirty), and there was a census during the reign of Herod that occurred years before the infamous census that had been run by Quirinius. Five miles from Jerusalem, the Savior of the world had been born, and yet political intrigue and power plays had blinded the eyes of the Jewish leadership in a quagmire of deceit so deep that they never even realized that their own Messiah had arrived. They had completely lost their focus.

So now that we have established the historical context and the date of Christ's birth—and seen how well it fits into its slot in history—we need to turn our attention to the only group of people who realized that the Messiah had come. Almost everyone else missed it, but they did not. Indeed, they were so attentive that they had been anticipating his arrival for over 500 years.

Last Days of King Herod

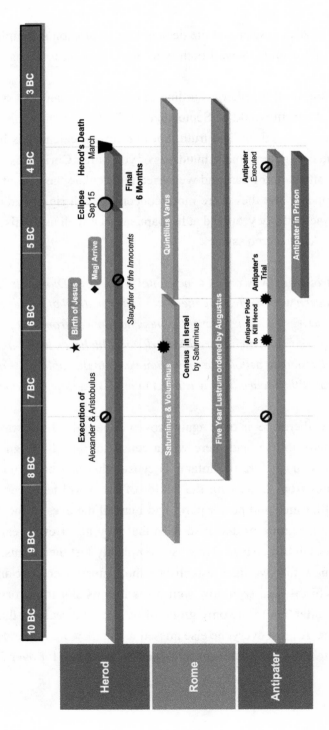

Timeline 10: King Herod's Last Days

STAGE IV

Underneath the Starry Skies

11

Masters of Time

Now after Jesus was born in Bethlehem of Judea in the days of Herod the king, magi from the east arrived in Jerusalem, saying, "Where is He who has been born King of the Jews? For we saw His star in the east and have come to worship Him."
—*Matthew 2:1–2 NASB*

The caravan arrived in Jerusalem as all caravans do, in a broiling cloud of dust and fragrant smells, snorting, crowded animals, the crack of leather, and shouts of merchants. It was business as usual. The camels and horses moved goods across the desert trade routes that formed a vast web of communication connecting the known world, facilitating the flow of gossip and money, the very life blood of civilization. The human circulatory system has not changed in two thousand years.

There was also safety in numbers. Large caravans hired soldiers to help ward off bandits. Dangerous times had armies marching everywhere: Romans, Jews, Arabs, and Parthians. Everywhere. Always marching. War. Turmoil. Progress. Control. Rebellion. Freedom. Conflict. Love. Hate. Competition. Cooperation. And who knew when a Roman legion or a throng of rebels might decide to resupply their forces with your goods? Bribery, force, and sheer good luck made trade a risky but bountiful way to make a living.

A group of turbaned men found each other amid all the other activity. They made sure they were all there, and that their provisions were properly unloaded and then moved off of their animal transport. They needed to find accommodations so they could prepare to present themselves to the king they sought. It might take days or weeks, but they were eager to start as soon as possible.

They had heard rumors about King Herod, of course, but they also knew (or thought they knew) that no ruler was ever as bad as his enemies made him out to be nor as good as his allies wanted him to be. They had heard that Herod had executed two of his sons and their mother, but Rome had allowed it, so he must have had good reasons for it—reasons that outsiders might not discern. They also had heard that he had recently imprisoned his eldest son for subversion. But they weren't there to visit Herod because they thought he was moral or righteous. Who would ever expect that of an earthly king?

In spite of all they had heard of him, they wanted to extend a hand of goodwill. They had seen a sign in the heavens that had proven to them that all of their calculations and generations of waiting had finally come true. Also, because Herod had recently built the city of Bathyra to guard the primary northern trade route between Babylon and Jerusalem, they were now able to make the journey safely. The dangerous Trachonites, who had been harassing pilgrims for decades, could no longer attack caravans without violent retaliation by a well-trained contingency of Jewish horsemen led by a Babylonian Jew named Zamaris. Herod had given him tax-free status if he would build a city and keep the Trachonites in check. It worked for the next century.[218]

Because of Herod, therefore, times were good, and the Babylonian Jews appreciated him for it. They had not always been fond of him and had, in fact, supported his rival Hyrcanus at one time, but that was in the past.

These travelers themselves, however, were not Jewish. They were members of an ancient guild of magi *(magos)* who some say traced their origins back to Persia. They may have originated there, but magi lived in cities all over the world now, and this group of magi was likely to have been nationally and ethnically diverse. They weren't kings, but they served in royal courts and had many of the same privileges as princes. At one point during their long history, they had even been powerful enough to legitimize the reign of kings, conferring on them the authority and credibility granted only by the gods.

In the broadest sense, magi were priests. Priests concerned themselves with temple rituals, but they also studied the movements of the stars in the hopes of discerning their influence on the fate of kings and nations. Some of them were trained in the craft of interpreting dreams, and others were trained in necromancy—the analysis of natural omens which could influence the course of a kingdom. In a very loose comparison, they served the same role as our modern political analysts, psychologists, and presidential advisors who study trends and the external influences on people's behavior. Of course today we use more technologically advanced tools, but the underlying desire is the same: to study patterns in order to help leaders make informed decisions. The ancients also took into consideration the movements of the stars and planets, but has that changed? Look at all the roadside palm readers and daily horoscopes. Maybe we aren't so different after all.

Be that as it may, the group of magi who showed up on the doorstep of Herod were specialists in astronomy/astrology,[219] but they were of a different kind. In spite of their pagan heritage, they appear to have been well-versed in the Hebrew Scriptures, and they traveled all the way to Jerusalem to worship the Jewish Messiah.

Babylonian omen charts do not make predictions about the Jews, so how did these magi know that the Messiah had been born? And why would guild members of a group that the Bible strongly condemns make a seven-hundred-mile journey filled with danger and hardship just to honor the birth of the heir to the throne of a conquered nation? This is a mystery we need to explore.

From Where Were the Magi?

To be right up front about it, I believe the magi were from Babylon, but that isn't without controversy. Some traditions claim they were from Persia and others even further east than that. The following quote is from a translation of *The Revelation of the Magi*, "[which] is a lengthy narrative that claims to be the personal testimony of the Magi themselves on the events of Christ's coming."[220] Translator Martin Landau believes it "was probably written in the late second or early third century."[221]

> *The names of the wise men and kings were called as follows: Zaharwandad son of Artaban; Hôrmizd son of Sanatruq; Auštazp son of Gudaphar; Aršak son of Mihruq; Zarwand son of Wadwad; Arîhô son of Kosrau; Artahšišat son of Hawîlat; Aštanbôzan son of Šîîšrawan; Mihruq son of Humam; Ahširaš son of Sahban; Nasardîh son of Baladan; Merôdak son of Bîl. These are kings, sons of Eastern kings, in the land of Shir, which is the outer part of the entire East of the world inhabited by human beings, at the Ocean, the great sea beyond the world, east of the land of Nod, that place in which dwelt Adam, head and chief of all the families of the world. And these sons of kings received commandments, laws, and even books from their fathers.[222]*

This mystical group of men apparently dwelt in Eden beyond the edge of the world, although if one reads Genesis 4:16 carefully, Nod is east of Eden. Oh well, close enough. But if one removes the hyperbole, an interesting core of possible truth remains. There were more than three wise men, and they had "received commandments, laws, and even books from their fathers." We will come back to that idea later.

The point is that this kind of fanciful storytelling was a trend for centuries after the birth of Christ, and it effectively established the image in our minds that the magi were kings from some far-off exotic land. Sadly, these kinds of legends have overly dramatized an otherwise very no-frills account given by Matthew: "Now after Jesus was born in Bethlehem of Judea in the days of Herod the king, *magi from the east* arrived in Jerusalem" (Matthew 2:1). That's it. "Magi from the east." That's the phrase that grew into "kings from the great sea beyond the world, east of the land of Nod." It is an interesting study to walk through how these fanciful stories developed. Dwight Longenecker in his book *Mystery of the Magi* gives a helpful history of the development of the myth of the magi during the first few centuries of the church, pulling back the veil of legend so we can see who the real magi might have been. He believes they were astrologers from the nearby Arab country of Nabatea, which was just east of the Dead Sea.

Although I have come to a different conclusion than him about which city the magi were from, his theory makes a lot of sense. According to Longenecker's argument, the magi who showed up in Jerusalem were from the city of Petra of the Arabian Nabateans, and they were extending a hand of friendship to Herod. As we have seen in earlier chapters, the Nabateans did have close political and economic ties to Israel, although they weren't always friendly with the Jews. The Nabateans had even at one time conquered Jerusalem, and if it hadn't have been for the heroic efforts of a then young Herod, Jerusalem would have remained in their hands.

All of these components, along with the relative peace between the two countries at the time of Christ's birth, make a compelling case for Longenecker's belief that the magi had been from Petra. In 8 BC, Herod had even been in Rome working alongside the king of the Nabateans, Aretas IV.

But familiarity is also the weakness in Longenecker's theory. No magi from Nabatea would have been so easily fooled when Herod pretended to be excited about their announcement that a king had been born. How could anyone who truly knew Herod ever think he would be excited that the true king of Israel had come into the world? Herod had spent his life killing all contenders to the throne, and the Nabateans knew that. Nabatean magi, therefore, would not have been so naïve, nor would they have needed an angelic revelation to tell them that Herod couldn't be trusted. Magi from farther away, however, might more easily be fooled.

This isn't a conclusive argument, though, and what I appreciate about Longenecker's book is that he does present enough evidence to discard the image that the magi were exotic mystics and kings from far-off lands beyond the edge of the world. As Longenecker points out, "Like the story of Saint Nicholas, who became the modern Santa Claus, the story of the wise men grew into legend and expanded into myth. From Syria and North Africa to Europe and then around the world, Matthew's simple story not only grew but also influenced world culture."[223]

So, this still leaves us the need to explore further the question, where were the magi in Matthew's account from? The magi were an interesting group of people.

The Greek historian and geographer Strabo (ca. 64 BC–AD 21) believes that they originated in Persia, and he describes them as "having felt tiaras [turbans] wrapped around them that come down their cheeks on either side far enough to cover their lips."[224] Yet an older source, Herodotus (484–425 BC), tells us that the magi were a people group which originated in Media, north of Persia.[225]

Wherever they originated, they functioned as priests by making sacrifices and offerings to the gods, and they could be called upon to interpret dreams and omens, give advice to kings (and be impaled for giving bad advice[226]), and decipher signs in the heavens, such as a solar eclipse as they did with Xerxes on his way to fight Greece.[227] These responsibilities were not unique to the magi. The Egyptians and Chaldeans (Babylonians) also had such priests: "Moreover, the priests of the Egyptians, the Chaldaians, and the Magoi, being different from the rest in some sort of wisdom, came to be leaders, honored by those before our time."[228]

Why were the magi honored and considered so authoritatively wise? Because they were supposedly able to discern the will of the gods by observing natural phenomenon, deciphering dreams, and interpreting the positions of the stars, planets, sun, and moon. They had special insight into what the gods wanted kings to do, and major nations such as Egypt, Babylon, and Persia needed their insights.

The East

The best way for me to explain why I believe the magi were from Babylon instead of Persia or Nabatea is to build for you a general mental image of the world at the time. I've noticed this in myself, but sometimes I get the impression that long ago people were somehow different than us. I have almost a cartoonish image that is more of a caricature than anything based in reality. For example, I had the impression that the ancient world of the Middle East and beyond was a collection of disconnected nations that hardly knew anything about each other. The world back then was primitive, divided, local, and mysterious. I even had a feeling of greyness, and I think it was because of the dust and the stones of all the ruins.

But through my historical work I have come to realize that the reality of the ancient world was far different. That world was colorful, noisy, and vibrant with extensive trade routes and collaboration between nations with healthy and robust cultural and political interactions. Yes, there were wars and rumors of wars, just as there are today, but they also had a sophisticated and integrated world market economy where many nations freely traded with each other, shared knowledge, and had to necessarily be concerned about giving away trade secrets, being raided by thieves, and haunted by the ever-present concern of the influence of kings and emperors on international relations and world markets. There were multiple religious groups, some more violent and zealous than others, and some more academic and thought-provoking. Some were based on traditions, and some loved the new best thing to come along.

There were also the pragmatic people who understood how things worked and who could care less about what the gods might think of what they did or how they did it. There were the vagabonds, the criminals, the charlatans, and the mercenaries. There were the artists, the athletes, the actors, the soldiers, the musicians, the sculptors, the historians, and the scholars. And then there were the poor, the outcasts, the abused, the abusers, the pedophiles, the prostitutes, gangsters, politicians, and slave traders. Unwanted infants and older children were discarded on the streets, and abortions occurred. People bustled around, kept busy, insulted each other, judged each other, were entertained by violence and bloodshed, and looked out for themselves more than they looked out for others. All of the characteristics of modern civilization were characteristics of ancient civilization because people are people. We may have new gadgets and fancier devices which make our forms of travel and communication quicker and more efficient, but their overall purpose meets the same human needs and desires. It amazes me how modern the ancient world really was.

The ancients also mapped out their world, and although our mapping ability is far more sophisticated and precise, they laid out regional boundaries pretty much the same way we do now. What we call the Middle East, however, they used to call Arabia. We think of Arabia as only covering the Arabian Peninsula, but two thousand years ago it included the Middle East. Two geographers from the second and first centuries BC—Eratosthenes and Strabo—both set Arabia's northern boundary as extending from Damascus to Babylon (near modern-day Baghdad), and its eastern boundary followed the Tigris and Euphrates rivers down to the Persian Gulf. The western boundary was Syria along the Mediterranean coast. Strabo says, "The entirety of Arabia lies above Judaea and

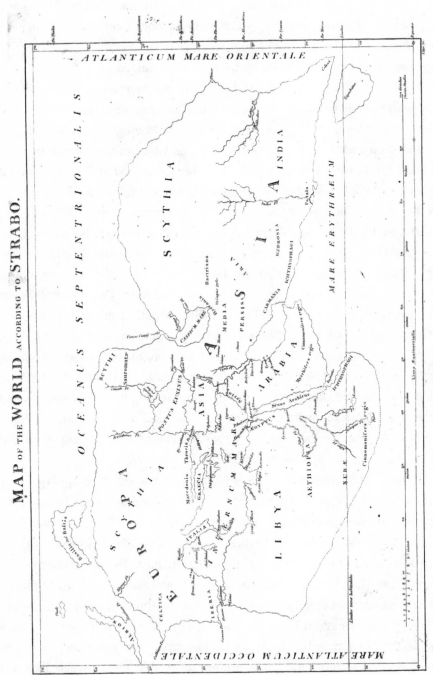

Earthly Map 2: The Ancient Middle East Boundaries According to Strabo and Erastothenes

Hollow Syria, as far as Babylonia and the riverine valley of the Euphrates, and toward the south except for the Tent Dwellers in Mesopotamia."[229]

The preceding map is Dr. Playfair's (1738–1819) re-creation of the geographer Strabo's ancient world.[230] Notice the boundaries of Europa, Libya, Arabia, and Asia. Also notice Media and Persis near the middle of the map.

Here is a closer look at the regions with which we are most concerned:

Earthly Map 3: Babylon Is in Arabia

You can see that Arabia is the name of the large region we now call the Middle East. Media and Persis are in a completely different geographical region beyond Mesopotamia. In other words, Babylon was geographically in Arabia, not Persia, even though the Parthians ruled Babylon at this time (as we saw in chapter 7). Why does this matter?

I would like to bring your attention to a second-century Christian apologist named Justin Martyr (ca. 100–165).[231] He was only one generation removed from the apostles, and he was a philosopher who converted to Christianity. His most important work is *The Apology*, which is a defense of Christianity during a time when it was an illegal religion. He also wrote the *Dialogue with Trypho*, which starts with Justin's conversion and then explores Christian doctrines in the form of a philosophical conversation.

In his *Dialogue*, Justin Martyr refers to the magi as having come from *Arabia*: "Now this king Herod, at the time when the magi came to him from Arabia . . . . Accordingly the magi from Arabia came to Bethlehem and worshipped the Child."[232] (There are many more such references in his writings.)

Since Justin Martyr lived within a generation of the apostles, he may best reflect what people nearest to the time of the first church understood when Matthew says "the East." They would have known he was referring to the region between Israel and Mesopotamia, aka Arabia, which included many different regions and cities.

To show that this was a concept shared by the Jews for centuries, Judges 6:33, 7:12, and 8:10 refer to some of the enemies of Israel as "children of the east." There is also mention of Midianites (who were from the region we now call Saudi Arabia) and Amalekites (who were just below Israel), but the book of Judges also mentions the "children of the east." Who were they? *Ellicott's Commentary for English Readers* explains: "Ben Kedem [children of the east] (Gen. 25:6; Job 1:3) is a general name for Arabs, as Josephus rightly calls them."[233] The *Pulpit Commentary* confirms this: "we gather that the country lying to the east of Palestine as far as the river Euphrates was called the east country, and that the various tribes of Arabs and others who peopled that desert were called 'the children of the east.' "[234]

Justin Martyr mentions Damascus as part of Arabia just to the north of Jerusalem. He does so while commenting on a prophecy by Isaiah and linking it to the magi mentioned in Matthew:

> But now the prophecy [Isaiah 8:4] has stated it with this addition: "Before the child knows how to call father or mother, he shall take the power of Damascus and spoils of Samaria." And you cannot prove that such a thing ever happened to any one among the Jews. But we are able to prove that it happened in the case of our Christ. For at the time of His birth, magi who came from Arabia worshipped Him, coming first to Herod, who then was sovereign in your land, and whom

the Scripture calls king of Assyria on account of his ungodly and sinful character.[235]

Justin Martyr is arguing that the "spoils" the magi brought were their gifts of gold, frankincense, and myrrh. The magi were showing submission to the Jewish Messiah with their gifts—it was their tribute.

The psalmist says:

He shall have dominion also from sea to sea,
And from the River to the ends of the earth.
Those who dwell in the wilderness will bow before Him,
And His enemies will lick the dust.
The kings of Tarshish and of the isles
Will bring presents;
The kings of Sheba and Seba
Will offer gifts.
Yes, all kings shall fall down before Him;
All nations shall serve Him. (Psalm 72:8–11)

The ESV study Bible commentary says, "Psalm 72 gives examples of places in the world as the ancient Israelites knew it, as parts of the world standing for the whole world."[236] The list of kings, therefore, is representative of all nations. Justin Martyr also calls Herod the "king of Assyria," meaning that he is the king of paganism because of his wicked deeds. He stands as a representative of all that is opposed to God. In contrast, Matthew uses the magi from the east to represent all gentiles who will choose to believe in the Lord. Herod represents unbelievers; the magi represent believers. Gentiles will turn to the true God and forsake their own wisdom and moral values. God calls people from all nations, tribes, languages, and people to worship him.

Gold, Frankincense, and Myrrh

The first-century geographers Eratosthenes and Strabo also tell us where the gifts of the magi originated: "Kattabania produces frankincense, and Chatramotitis myrrh, and these and other aromatics are traded with merchants."[237] Frankincense and myrrh were valuable commodities from Kattabania in the far south of the Arabian Peninsula (the Myrrhifera region noted on Earthly Map 2), and these aromatics were transported all over the world, including to Rome. Every religion used frankincense and myrrh in their ceremonies, and the Arabians had a corner on that market. Rarity combined with high demand made some people very rich, particularly in trade centers like Nabatea and Damascus. But these aromatics should not be associated with any particular nation but with *religion* in the broadest sense. The gifts of the magi were religious gifts with religious overtones, and they represented the wealth of the world laid at the feet of the true King of kings.

So, in summary, the magi were from Arabia, which, as we have seen, included Damascus, Nabatea, and Babylon. They could have come from any of these cities or from any of the others in the region, but I believe they came from Babylon. Herod had recently made the route between Babylon and Jerusalem safe so that Jews could travel more securely to celebrate the sacred convocations, and this would have made the seven-hundred-mile journey much safer for the magi too.

But most importantly of all, I believe the magi were from Babylon because that is where the prophet Daniel once lived.

The Daniel Connection

Many Jews were taken away to Babylon before and after Nebuchadnezzar destroyed Solomon's Temple in 587 BC, and it is where Daniel lived the majority of his life. Near the end of his life, he had several visions. The first one was during the first year of Belshazzar, who was the grandson of Nebuchadnezzar (Daniel 7:1), and then Daniel had another vision in the third year of Belshazzar, just before Cyrus the Great conquered Babylon on October 9, 539 BC (8:1). Then during the first year of Cyrus the Great and Darius the Mede,[238] Daniel realized that God was fulfilling his word to Jeremiah the

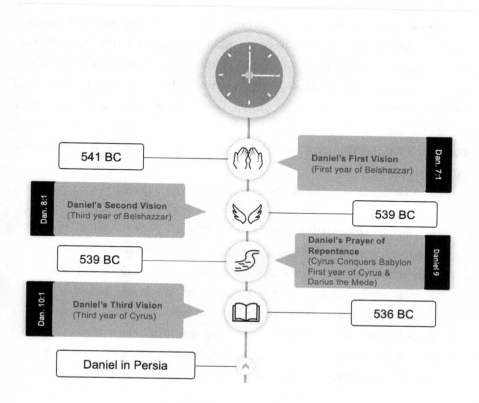

Timeline 11: Daniel's Visions[274]

prophet (9:1–2), so he repents for Israel, and then the angel Gabriel arrives and tells him the prophecy of the 70 weeks (vv. 24–27). It is then during the third year of Cyrus that Daniel has another vision, "on the twenty-fourth day of the first month [Abib], as I was by the side of the great river, that is, the Tigris" (10:4, cf. v. 1).

Susa is a Persian city on the Tigris River, and tradition tells us that Daniel spent the last years of his life in Susa (modern-day Shush in Iran), where his tomb is to this day.[239]

Daniel, by God's will, becomes the prophet to whom God revealed his exact plan concerning when the Messiah would come. Other prophets gave the Messiah's characteristics and mission, but Daniel gave the Messiah's timing.

Daniel lived in Babylon and had been trained by the greatest minds of his day, the Chaldeans (1:4). They were the intelligentsia, the PhDs, the mathematicians, the priests, and the counselors to kings. But not only had they trained him; he had become chief among them. Why? Because God had revealed knowledge to him that no amount of study or human reason could have ever accounted for. His insights were beyond human capabilities, and after Cyrus conquered the Babylonians, Daniel was transferred to Persia and his influence continued there.

Chris Brennan, in his book *Hellenistic Astrology*, says about the Chaldeans:

> *During the Hellenistic period the term 'Chaldean' (Chaldaios) came to be widely used to refer to astrologers or to the astrological profession in general. The word was originally used as a designation for a geographical area in Mesopotamia or an ethnic group that originated there. Later it came to be used to refer to a class of priests from Mesopotamia who were thought to specialize in divination and astrology; eventually, from the first century CE onward,* it largely became a generic term used to refer to all astrologers."[240]

He further explains: "To a lesser extent there were probably similar connotations underlying the use of the term *magi* in the Gospel of Matthew (first century CE), which was used in the Christian nativity story to refer to a group of astrologers from the east."[241] Isn't that interesting? Chaldeans and magi, according to Brennan, appear to have been used as generic terms for astrologers near the time of Christ. The likely reason for this is that after Cyrus the Persian conquered the Babylonians, the two groups would have merged into one entity, or at least come to be seen that way to the common person. If you remember, Cyrus the Great, king of Persia, conquered the Babylonian empire in 539 BC. Daniel within a few years was living in Persia.

So, here's my theory: the magi were astrologers and priests from Babylon who had learned from Daniel exactly when the Jewish Messiah would be born. The idea that they looked up at the stars and saw some rare alignment, causing them to realize that the Jewish Messiah had been born, is false. Instead, they knew

God's Word and were keeping track of the passage of time. They expected the Messiah to come when he did, or, at the very least, they had a good approximation of when he would arrive. And the sign they saw confirmed their expectations.

At the beginning of this chapter, I quoted a book called *Revelation of the Magi,* which says, "And these sons of kings received commandments, laws, and even books from their fathers." As exaggerated as some things in that book may be, at the core of it there seems to be a truth: the magi who arrived in Jerusalem were at the end of a long line of magi who had been keeping track of time since the prophecies of Daniel.

But why were they believers? Why were they paying attention to Daniel's prophecies at all? What had converted them? Scripture tells us that Daniel had saved the lives of all the Chaldeans. It's a famous story but worth revisiting. Nebuchadnezzar had had a dream that he wanted the Chaldeans to interpret, but he wasn't going to tell them what it was. They had to tell him not only what the dream was but also its interpretation. If they failed, he was going to kill them all. Somebody reported this to Daniel, and he prayed, and God revealed the dream and the interpretation to him, thus saving the lives of the entire priestly class of astrologers. Nebuchadnezzar was impressed and proclaimed, "Truly your God is the God of gods, the Lord of kings, and a revealer of secrets, since you could reveal this secret" (2:47).

Similarly, when Daniel was an old man after Cyrus had conquered Babylon, he was thrown into the lions' den because some government officials had politically manipulated Darius the Mede. But when God delivered Daniel, Darius proclaimed of Daniel's God:

> *For He is the living God,*
> *And steadfast forever;*
> *His kingdom is the one which shall not be destroyed,*
> *And His dominion shall endure to the end. (6:26)*

Certainly after saving their lives and the conversion of both of these kings, at least some of the priests he had saved would have turned to the Lord God Almighty and worshiped him above all other gods. I believe the fact that a group of magi came to Jerusalem so they could worship the Messiah provides evidence enough that at least some of them believed in Daniel's God. They were the intellectual and spiritual descendants of a specialized guild of magi who continued to use their knowledge of the stars to keep track of the passage of time and to transfer that knowledge to future adherents of the faith. Chris Brennan points out: "A related issue is the apparent existence of mystery traditions within the astrological community, and the possibility that many of the ancient doctrines were kept secret, with some of the astrological schools being kept private or underground."[242] Astrologers were known to form independent guilds which specialized in certain interpretive endeavors. They worked with kings, which was a tricky business, but their insights would gain them access to power, money, and influence. There were schools—guilds—of astrologers with specialized sets of knowledge that they wanted to keep proprietary, much like tech businesses or media groups do today. The first-century Greek geographer Strabo says, "There are also a number of groups of Chaldean astronomers, some of whom are called Orchenians, Borsippenians, and a number of others, as if considered different sects, each with their own dogma about the same things."[243] This may be how the magi knew when Christ was born: The magi who showed up on Herod's doorstep were members of a specialized guild that had been keeping careful track of the passage of time since the time of Daniel.

All astrology must first start with the accurate mathematical calculations of the positions of the stars and planets in relationship to each other. After centuries of computations (which, by the way, steadily improved during this era), these stargazers became masters of time. They perfected their skills. They observed the motion of the stars, which is a purely technical skill, and they used the heavens for exactly what God designed them for:

> Then God said, "Let there be lights in the firmament of the heavens to divide the day from the night; and let them be for signs and seasons, and for days and years; and let them be for lights in the firmament of the heavens to give light on the earth"; and it was so. (Genesis 1:14–15)

What's important to recognize about the magi who showed up in Jerusalem is that they were believers who were well-versed in Scripture. They were not astrologers and magicians; they were astronomers and mathematicians. Brennan says, "One of the more widespread appellations for astrologers [in the ancient world] was 'mathematicians.'"[244]

In fact, if I'm right, we could say that the magi were more committed to Daniel's prophecies than any of the Jewish leaders whom they encountered in Jerusalem. The Pharisees were dumbfounded that the Messiah had been born. They had no idea. Why? Because they had become lost in the political games of the ruling elites of their day, and gauging from their shock, they had not been paying attention to Daniel's prophecies at all. They should have been happy when they heard the news that the Messiah had come. Instead, they were skeptical, distressed, and even antagonistic.

We face the same danger today, though. Have we, too, forgotten the grace and mercy of God in Christ? Are we so caught up in the responsibilities of life and the complexities of society that we have forgotten the reason we gather together and celebrate communion? "For as often as you eat this bread and drink this cup, you proclaim the Lord's death *till He comes*" (1 Corinthians 11:26). The magi were 500 years removed from Daniel's prophecies; we are 2,500 years removed. They were looking for the coming Messiah, but have we, like the Pharisees, become lost and begun to wander aimlessly?

The Pharisees were committed to following the letter of the law, but they began to use the law as an excuse to sin by hiding behind a superficial adherence to the law. God's law was meant to produce righteousness, not self-righteousness. Similarly, are we distorting God's love in the same way the Pharisees distorted God's law? Many people today use love as an excuse to sin by hiding behind a superficial commitment to the spirit of love. But the manger should remind us that God's love is selfless, not self-indulgent. Christ, the King of righteousness, humbled himself to become one of us. He came to serve and sacrifice himself. Are we more like him or less like him?

This brings us back to an important point: Many people feel like figuring out the date of Christ's birth doesn't really matter. Why would it matter whether he was born on December 25 of AD 1, June of 2 BC, or September of 7 BC? Does it make a difference? As long as we know he is the Son of God come to save us from our sins, isn't that all that matters?

In one sense that is true. The Incarnation is the means of our salvation, not the date. But I believe there is a lesson in the date nevertheless, and it is as important as all the other lessons, if not the very foundation of them all. God told us in Leviticus 23 the month and day Jesus would be born *for a reason*; he told us in the book of Daniel the year the Messiah would come *for a reason*. And it had to be more than for just a bit of trivia. The magi didn't go on their arduous, five-hundred-year journey in vain. They succeeded. They arrived and then they rejoiced! Our journey has not been in vain either, but to see it—to feel it to the depths of our soul—we have to crawl a few more yards. You may be feeling like you can't take another step or crawl another inch, but don't give up. We are almost there. The most magnificent vista is just beyond the next rise.

532 Years

In all honesty, at one point I struggled with the title of this book, *500 Year Journey.* I liked the sound of it, but I also knew it wasn't precisely true. As we will see in a minute, the precise truth is that the magi went on a 532-year journey, and it is amazing.

To prove this, I would like to draw your attention to another mathematical piece of evidence that helps establish the year Jesus was born. Like some of my other observations, I didn't see this until the numbers presented themselves. We already looked at Daniel's prophetic 70 weeks and the life of King Herod, but there is a feature of lunar/solar calendars that we haven't paid attention to yet: a 532-year cycle.

A fifth century Alexandrian mathematician named Victorius of Aquitaine, a man with whom Dionysius was familiar, knew that every 532 years the "lunar phases return after the completion of the period not only on the same days of the month, but also on the same days of the week as they did 532 years before."[245] The principle is that the lunar and solar cycles recalibrate every nineteen years and are approximately in the same positions as they were nineteen years previously. Then after twenty-eight of those nineteen-year cycles (19 x 28 = 532), the month, the day, and *the day of the week* synchronize. The accuracy of the cycle may be overstated since it would be difficult to prove the day of the week, and yet it is still amazingly close to the truth, most of the time being off by only a day or two. For example, there was a new moon on April 13, 1 AD, and a new moon on April 11, 533 AD. The celestial clock fine tunes itself every 532 years.

And yet this cycle wasn't a new discovery by an Alexandrian mathematician hundreds of years after Christ was born; it was a known calculation in ancient Babylon in the sixth century BC,[246] and it is known today as the Metonic Cycle, named after an Athenian astronomer who lived in the fifth century BC.

So what does all of this have to do with Daniel's prophecy? Since the ancient Babylonians knew about this mathematical cycle, then, of course, so did the magi. If you'll recall, Daniel had his second vision in the third year of Belshazzar, which was the last year of his reign (Daniel 8:1). Belshazzar's reign ended when Cyrus conquered Babylon on October 29, 539 BC.

Even though the Bible doesn't tell us what month and day Daniel had his vision, I would like to suggest that Daniel may have had his vision at the new moon of the seventh month one month before Cyrus conquered Babylon. On our calendar that would be reckoned as September 26, 539 BC.

And guess what happened exactly 532 years later?

The Messiah was born on September 25, 7 BC.[247]

12

The Heavens Declare Thy Glory

Praise the LORD!
Praise the LORD from the heavens;
Praise Him in the heights!
Praise Him, all His angels;
Praise Him, all His hosts!
Praise Him, sun and moon;
Praise Him, all you stars of light!
Praise Him, you heavens of heavens,
And you waters above the heavens!
Let them praise the name of the LORD,
For He commanded and they were created.
He also established them forever and ever;
He made a decree which shall not pass away.
—Psalm 148:1–6

The magi were from Babylon where they saw a sign in the heavens that convinced them that the Messiah had been born. But what did they see? As I mentioned at the beginning of *500 Year Journey,* I used to think that if I could find the beckoning star, I could find the right date. That seemed to be the popular approach. To my dismay, however, what I discovered was that there seemed to be as many theories as there were stars, and it slowly dawned on me that none of the theories could be verified. They all depended on what people *thought* would have been interesting enough to have caught the attention of the magi. While many were interesting, all of them relied a bit too much on astrological methods to find meaning. As we will see, that is a foundationally flawed approach.

Heavenly Writing

God made the heavens. He made the stars and planetary motions, and they are indeed magnificent. They proclaim God's glory, and when he made them, he said, "let them be for signs and seasons, and for days and years; and let them be for lights in the firmament of the heavens to give light on the earth" (Genesis 1:14).

The heavens help us keep track of time, demarcate the seasons, and give us signs. God made their motions regular and predictable, and by them we can identify the transitions between seasons with the solstices, equinoxes, and constellations. They also draw our attention upward to events like eclipses, planetary conjunctions, meteors, supernovae, and comets. But as magnificent as the heavens are, they should never be worshiped as if they had influence over our lives or over events on earth.

One form of astrology assumes that the stars directly influence us. It is an age-old practice to believe that constellations have an impact on one's personality as shown through horoscopes or natal astrology. Natal astrology isn't used to predict when someone is born. Instead it claims to take into account when someone was born and then to identify the influence the stars have had on one's personality.

St. Augustine (354–430), the most influential church father of the first five centuries, recognized the inherent danger in using this kind of astrology to identify the star of Bethlehem:

> *We, too, deny the influence of the stars upon the birth of any man; for we maintain that, by the just law of God, the free-will of man, which chooses good or evil, is under no constraint of necessity. How much less do we subject to any constellation the incarnation of the eternal Creator and Lord of all! When Christ was born after the flesh, the star which the Magi saw had no power as governing, but attended as a witness.*[248]

Augustine makes a point that the star attended as a witness, but there is a different form of astrology that the ancients used wherein specially trained individuals could read the arrangements of the constellations and planets to determine the will of the gods. This arrangement was called heavenly writing. This type of astrological "reading" is in the same class of astrology as dream interpretation and finding meaning in the way birds fly (augury), the lines on the palm of someone's hand, or other natural phenomena. Some magi were trained in the skills of translating dreams for kings, as we saw in the book of Daniel, but others were trained in translating the celestial motions into messages from the gods so that kings could make wise decisions.

Tamsyn Barton says in his book *Ancient Astrology* that a "conjunction, where the planets seem to occupy the same space in the sky, means that the influence of each planet is strongly affected by the ethereal character and particular characteristics of the other."[249] In other words, to ancient man, not only did individual planets say something about the will of the gods, but that message was magnified and influenced by a conjunction of those heavenly bodies. Barton also says, "In the earliest forms of astrology, predictions were made for different countries, and for kings as representatives of those countries."[250] This approach to interpreting the heavens required a complex methodology that took years of special training to master. If the magi used this approach to astrology to recognize the star of Bethlehem, then are we to believe that God spoke to the magi through forbidden practices? This kind of astrology is expressly prohibited in Scripture (Deuteronomy 17:2–7), and this is one of the reasons why, after years of believing that a conjunction was Jesus's star, I steered away from that way of determining what the magi may have seen. Instead I began to see that magi used the stars as a mathematical clock to track the prophecies God had given.

And yet even so, what I am about to say will at first glance appear to contradict what I've just said. The Bible does use the heavens to illustrate truths about God. Stars can represent angels (1 Kings 22:19), and they can represent false gods (Deuteronomy 4:19). They can also represent the Messiah: "the Bright and Morning star" (Revelation 22:16), and "A Star shall come out of Jacob" (Numbers 24:17). God uses them to illustrate truth or to point to it. The difference is that astrology elevates man's wisdom above God's revelation. It worships creation, not the Creator. It's an issue of supremacy. As C. S. Lewis explains:

> *Nature does not teach. A true philosophy may sometimes validate an experience of nature; an experience of nature cannot validate a philosophy. . . . She will help to show what it means. . . . [But] we must make a detour—leave the hills and woods and go back to our studies, to church, to our Bibles, to our knees. Otherwise the love of nature is beginning to turn into a nature religion. And then, even if it does not lead us to the Dark Gods, it will lead us to a great deal of nonsense.*[251]

Nature can validate God's truth but not teach it. That is why we need to start with God's Word and not with nature. And especially we should not elevate our own understanding above God's revelation. What one foundationally believes (our worldview) has an influence on what we think nature is saying to us, but that is why our source of knowledge—the spring where the water wells up—should be the Word of God.

For example, at the time of Joseph, God gave Pharaoh a dream about the future, but the Egyptian priests were unable to interpret it properly because they relied too much on their own flawed worldview. They trusted their own wisdom.

Likewise, at the time of Daniel, God gave Nebuchadnezzar a dream about the future, but he required the Chaldean priests to do something that no amount of education could ever accomplish: he wanted them to tell him first what happened in his dream and then interpret it or else he would kill them. Since they couldn't figure out what he had dreamed, God intervened by revealing the dream to Daniel, thus saving the lives of the wise men of Babylon. As Daniel explained: "The secret which the king has demanded, the wise men, the astrologers, the magicians, and the soothsayers cannot declare to the king. But there is a God in heaven who reveals secrets, and He has made known to King Nebuchadnezzar what will be in the latter days" (Daniel 2:27–28).

What this means is that no amount of education or human powers of reasoning could have deciphered the will of God based upon observations of natural phenomenon. Daniel intentionally gives credit to God for revealing the interpretation, and deflects any praise for himself. However, this does not mean that God doesn't speak to humanity through dreams, visions, and even the stars. He does. He not only spoke to Joseph, Pharaoh, and Nebuchadnezzar through visions, he also spoke to the apostle John.

In this next section, we are going to set aside the magi for a moment and explore the meaning of a vision that God gave the apostle John over seventy years after Jesus was born. It was a vision that used the stars to tell us exactly when Christ was born.

Nativity in the Sky

To prove that God will reveal to us his plans through dreams and visions, there is one final confirmation of the date of Christ's birth I need to show you, but it isn't necessarily anything that the magi would have been aware of. It wasn't revealed to Daniel but to the apostle John decades after Christ was born.

Several constellations are mentioned in Scripture (the Bear, Orion, and the Pleiades),[252] but only one of the signs of the zodiac: Virgo. Virgo is an autumnal constellation which moves along the path of the sun during September/October of every year, and in the book of Revelation God shows John a vision that involves Virgo: "Now a great sign appeared in heaven: a woman clothed with the sun, with the moon under her feet, and on her head a garland of twelve stars. Then being with child, she cried out in labor and in pain to give birth" (Revelation 12:1–2).

There has been a lot of speculation regarding what this vision means, but I have come to believe it can only mean one thing: Jesus was born on Ethanim 1. God showed John the zodiacal sign of a woman in the heavens, which was known to the ancients as the Virgin—the Maiden—and to us as Virgo. John's vision says she was clothed with the sun, which in astronomical terms means that, as the sun rises in the east, the constellation Virgo rises as well and travels with the sun all day. (See the image on the next page.) The sun and Virgo move together in sync for about a month—which makes Virgo unviewable—with every day the sun being in a slightly different position within the constellation. This happens every year, and each month is associated with a different zodiac sign. So this vision isn't telling us what year that the Messiah would be born. Rather, it is telling us the month: September/October, or the Jewish month of Ethanim.

The vision also tells us that the moon was under Virgo's feet, which happens on the first day of the month as the sun is setting. Imagine the sliver of the new moon being at the feet of Virgo in the western sky just before sunset, which is Ethanim 1, the Feast of Trumpets. This is when Christ was born.

John's vision also tells us that the Maiden is wearing a garland of twelve stars. Some people have spent a lot of time counting how many stars are in the constellation of Virgo or are above her head, but such interpretations miss the whole point of the vision. What matters is what the stars represent and why the number twelve is used. In thinking about this, I remembered that in Genesis 37:9–11, Joseph had a dream that involved eleven stars, plus the sun and the moon. The eleven stars (his brothers) bowed down to him, as did the sun and the moon (his parents, Jacob and Rachel).[253] So, if we were to add in Joseph, we would have twelve stars—the twelve tribes of Israel. So, in John's vision the woman with a garland of twelve stars must be Israel, and Israel (more specifically Mary) is giving birth to the Messiah on the new moon of the seventh month.

Star Map 1: Ethanim 1: Virgo and the New Moon

But there's another constellation that enters into John's vision:

And another sign appeared in heaven: behold, a great, fiery red dragon having seven heads and ten horns, and seven diadems on his heads. His tail drew a third of the stars of heaven and threw them to the earth. And the dragon stood before the woman who was ready to give birth, to devour her Child as soon as it was born. She bore a male Child who was to rule all nations with a rod of iron. And her Child was caught up to God and His throne. (Revelation 12:3–5)

John sees another constellation—a dragon with seven heads—which is likely the constellation Hydra.[254] Hydra was a dragon with seven heads in Babylonian mythology, and since Rome stood on seven hills, I believe Hydra represents Rome/Babylon which in another level of meaning points to the fallen world system led by Satan. In John's vision, the dragon also has ten horns, and horns typically symbolized world leaders. Daniel 7:7 says:

After this I saw in the night visions, and behold, a fourth beast, dreadful and terrible, exceedingly strong. It had huge iron teeth; it was devouring, breaking in pieces, and trampling the residue with its feet. It was different from all the beasts that were before it, and it had ten horns.

And Daniel 7:24 explains, "The ten horns are ten kings who shall arise from this kingdom," then later in Revelation 17:3 John tells us, "So he carried me away in the Spirit into the wilderness. And I saw a woman sitting on a scarlet beast which was full of names of blasphemy, having seven heads and ten horns." This scarlet beast turns out to be "MYSTERY, BABYLON THE GREAT, THE MOTHER OF HARLOTS AND OF THE ABOMINATIONS OF THE EARTH" (v. 5). This is why I believe Babylon and Rome are interchangeable names of the fallen world system. It isn't that Babylon or Rome were completely evil, but they came to symbolize the world system which is at war with God. This makes sense because Babylon had wiped out God's temple in 587 BC, and Rome wiped out the Second Temple in 70 AD. John's vision closes with the story of Satan's fall who took a third of the stars (angels) with him as revealed in Ezekiel 28:11–19 and Isaiah 14:12–15.

To put it all together, after the birth of Christ, the fallen world system tried to destroy the Messiah as soon as he was born, this being fulfilled when Herod (a tool of Rome and a symbol of evil himself) commanded the murder of all the boys under two years old in Bethlehem and surrounding districts (Matthew 2:16–18). This child, says John's vision, will someday rule the nations, although first he must be caught up to heaven "to God and His throne" (Revelation 12:5), which must be a reference to the ascension of Jesus as recorded in Luke 24:51 and Acts 1:9.

Therefore, the vision given to John in Revelation 12:1–5 is God's portrayal of the Nativity story. Just because pagans have appropriated the stars for their own stories doesn't mean that we have to shy away from seeing that God is, without a doubt, the ultimate writer, producer, and director of the greatest movie ever played on the biggest screen ever made.

Conjunction Junction, What's Your Function?

So now let's get back to our magi and to figuring out what they called "his star." Since they didn't know about John's vision and so could not have been taking that into consideration in their calculations, what did they see in the heavens? Now that we know the month, day, and year of the birth of Christ as historically and prophetically announced, here's the night sky right after sunset as viewed from Babylon on the night Christ was born. (I have removed the horizon so that you can still see the sun).[255]

Star Map 2: Ethanim 1, 7 BC (no labels)

Pretty impressive, right? Although for most of us this looks like any other night sky, is there anything up there that could be considered "his star"? Here's the same view with the planets labeled and the ecliptic (the path of the sun) drawn:

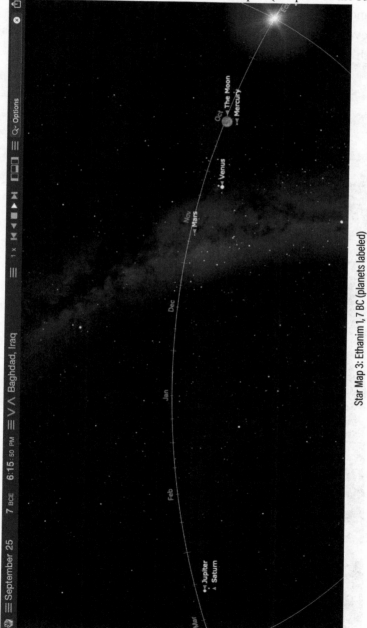

Star Map 3: Ethanim 1, 7 BC (planets labeled)

Moving from right to left, we can see the new moon, Mercury, Venus, Mars, Jupiter, and Saturn.[256] The planets are lined up in what is today called a "Parade of Planets." It is also the Autumnal Equinox. All of these planets follow the ecliptic, and they are lined up *in order* on the night Christ was born.[257]

However, there is something else we need to add: the zodiac. Here is a new photo with the zodiac labeled:

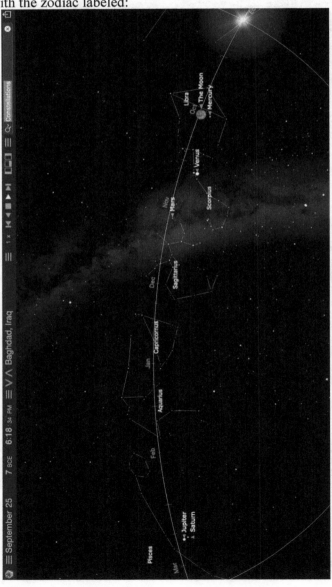

Star Map 4: Ethanim 1, 7 BC (zodiac labeled)

Now, please don't be concerned about the use of the zodiac. I am not including it because of any astrological symbolism, but because it is first and foremost a mathematical structure. Think of the zodiac as the numbers on the face of a clock. There are twelve numbers on a clock just as there are twelve signs in the zodiac. Each of the zodiac signs are associated with one month. As we talked about earlier, when Virgo is rising with the sun in the east, it can't be seen, but that means it is the sign associated with that month.

But on Ethanim 1 in the photo above, notice that Jupiter and Saturn are standing on the constellation of Pisces in the east. That may seem meaningless to us, but for the ancient Babylonian astronomers Pisces was considered the mathematical celestial meridian.[258] On earth we have a zero-degree meridian which goes through Greenwich, England from pole to pole. You may have heard it called "Greenwich mean time." It is purely a man-made choice, chosen because an Englishman developed a watch that would work at sea, making navigation much more reliable.[259] As a result of his invention, the meridian (0° longitude) now passes through Greenwich, England. If a Frenchman had won the contest, the meridian may have passed through Paris because it doesn't matter where the line is drawn as long as there is one and everyone agrees to use it. Anyway, Pisces was the ancient celestial meridian and may have been chosen because Babylon was the "capital" of stargazing, and the twin cords of Pisces were associated with the Tigris and Euphrates rivers.[260] Interestingly, our modern celestial meridian also passes through Pisces.

So why does the celestial meridian matter? It provides a mathematical marker in the night sky and functions as a common reference point. Let's take the planet Saturn, for example, also known as Kronos, which means Time. It is the furthest from the sun of the visible planets (the ones visible to the naked eye), and it orbits the sun every thirty years. How did the ancients know that? Because every thirty years Saturn crosses the celestial meridian: Pisces. In fact, this is how they knew the length of the orbits of all the planets.[261] Jupiter crosses Pisces every twelve years (approximately), and Venus crosses it once a year or so. One must say "or so" because of the imperfections of planetary orbits and the slight wobble in the earth's axis. This is one of the reasons why orbits are so difficult to calculate with pure math. The ancients had to use math combined with observation.

Anyway, to continue the comparison, the face of a clock is divided into twelve equal stations called hours and sixty smaller segments called minutes. A circle is 360 degrees, so the way we measure time is synced up with the movement of the planets through the zodiacal constellations—the signs mentioned in Genesis 1:14. On our vast celestial clock, Jupiter becomes the hour hand because it passes each constellation in a twelve-year cycle, and Venus is the minute hand which passes each constellation every year. Of course, there are 365.25 days in a year, not 360, and the ancients knew this too and made mathematical adjustments accordingly. The point is that the motions of the stars and planets through the signs of the zodiac are first and foremost a celestial clock face. The complex Orloj astronomical clock in Prague, Czechoslovakia is a great example of a clock that keeps track of all these celestial movements, and the goal is to keep all the seasons lined up with the cycles of the moon, the sun, and the planets.

So what we see on Ethanim 1, 7 BC is something that had not happened on the celestial clock face since Ethanim 1, 861 BC.[262] In purely mathematical terms, Saturn and Jupiter aligned with each other for nearly a year on both occasions. It's called a triple conjunction. That is in itself a very rare occurrence. But in addition to that, in 861 BC Jupiter and Saturn were not only aligned on Pisces but *all the planets lined up in order*. In other words, on both occasions the two heavenly events are practically identical in spite of being 856 years apart! This would be the celestial equivalent of a grandfather clock chiming at midnight.

However, as amazing as this is, there is nothing that I could find in Scripture or in Babylonian star lore that would imply that this has anything to do with announcing the Jewish Messiah. It is fantastic, but it couldn't have been what the magi called his star. To be clear: I do *not* believe the Jupiter/Saturn conjunction in 7 BC is the star of Bethlehem, nor do I believe the parade of planets is the star of Bethlehem. And yet, in spite of that, I believe these events are nevertheless mathematically significant.

For example, in December of 2020 there was a Jupiter/Saturn conjunction that was widely touted as the "Christmas Star."[263] Some mistakenly implied that Johannes Kepler, the famous sixteenth-century mathematician/astronomer, claimed that such a conjunction was the star of Bethlehem,[264] but that is inaccurate. In reality, he believed that a supernova was the star of Bethlehem, one that also appeared during the same year as the Jupiter/Saturn conjunction in AD 1603.[265] What he surmised is that a similarly bright, unpredictable supernova had appeared in 7 BC which the magi called "his star."

I confess that the Jupiter/Saturn conjunction I observed in 2020 was awe-inspiring to watch as the two planets slowly drew closer to each other over the course of several months. But when they finally met, it wasn't anything visually exciting at all. They were close, but nothing became "brighter" (as all the movies suggest),[266] and such conjunctions aren't all that rare since Jupiter and Saturn align every twenty years. The last time they converged was in May of 2000, and before that in 1980, and on backwards every twenty years.[267] Some have also suggested that a conjunction of Jupiter and Venus was rare enough and bright enough to have been the star of Bethlehem, but Jupiter and Venus align even more frequently than Jupiter and Saturn do—a rather common occurrence, actually, within the context of astronomical timeframes.

Nevertheless, Kepler's theory is mathematically important. Kepler is the genius who developed the math that astronomers use today to calculate the precise movements of all the stars and planets, and since the *Starry Night* software uses his math, I looked at all of the Jupiter/Saturn conjunctions that preceded the one on 7 BC. Yes, all of them. That is how I ended up discovering the exact same arrangement in 861 BC. But don't get me wrong. I never found any historical or biblical meaning that connected the conjunctions in 861 and 7 BC, but from my notes an unforeseen association presented itself: I discovered that there had been a seven-month-long conjunction about halfway between those two dates, from August of 444 to April of 443 BC. Do those dates sound familiar?

In chapter 9, we learned about Daniel's 70 sevens. The wall of Nehemiah was dedicated in the fall of 450 BC, which initiated the celebration of the Sabbath Year. Sabbath Years and Years of Jubilee start on Ethanim 10, the Day of

Atonement, and are completed on the next occurrence of Ethanim 1, which is the Jewish Feast of Trumpets announcing the new year and, in some traditions, the creation of the world. If you remember, I surmised that a new countdown had begun then in the fall of 449 BC.

What the following timeline shows is that the first Sabbath Year of the 62 weeks occurred right after the Jupiter/Saturn conjunction. If we play this out on a chart, the conjunction of 444–443 BC *is at the end of* the first week of Daniel's 62 weeks, and the conjunction in 7 BC *is at the end of* the 62nd week. This mathematically fits the timeline of Daniel's prophecy perfectly.

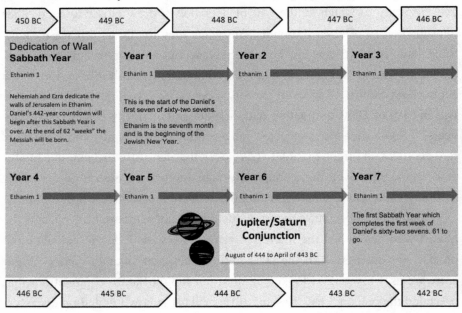

Timeline 12: Dedication of Wall – Jupiter/Saturn Conjunction

Once again, it isn't the conjunction that matters but the math, and I believe that these calculations helped our magi to know approximately when to expect the Messiah would be born. They must have had some debate among themselves as to the precise way to interpret Daniel's prophecies, but they still would have noted the mathematical significance of another triple conjunction in 7 BC, especially one that landed on Pisces, the celestial meridian. That was truly rare.

And yet, as incredible as all of this is, it does not mean that the magi called the Jupiter/Saturn conjunction or the lineup of planets "his star." Jesus's star had to be something different and separate from a regularly patterned inter-action of the planets, which was Kepler's point. He believed the unexpected supernova he saw must have been something like what the magi had seen. This is possible, but for reasons we will look at in the next section, I do not believe our magi saw a supernova. It had to be something else, and since the magi told us exactly what they did see, we should listen to them most of all.

His Star

Now that we have eliminated an entire class of contenders for the identi-fication of Jesus's star, we will now be able to see clearly what the magi called "his star." And what's fascinating is that we don't even need to be astrologers to understand what they meant. In spite of all the grand images, amazing theories, and eloquent theological musings we have looked at so far (and there are far more still), all we actually need is to understand a few literary terms and a little bit of history. To do that we must first make sure we get the story straight.

Contrary to popular opinion, the magi could not have seen one continuous star event. Matthew's account says that the magi saw the star while they were in Babylon, and then they saw it again when they were approaching Bethlehem (Matthew 2:2, 9). The Gospel account never says that the magi followed the star from the east to Jerusalem, so it couldn't have been a continuous, year-long presentation like a supernova would have been. Rather, it had to be two short-term appearances that were visible for a little while and then were gone. If it had been one continuously visible event, then after they had arrived in Jerusalem, they could have taken Herod outside, pointed to the sky, and said, "See? That's what we're talking about. His star."

But that is not what happened. Matthew's account makes it clear that the magi saw "his star" while they were in Babylon, and the sighting compelled them to make the journey to Jerusalem. Their reception, though, was odd. Nobody seemed to know what they were talking about, which must have been shocking to the magi. If my theory is correct, this particular guild of magi had been anticipating this moment for over 500 years, and they must have been flabbergasted that none of the Jewish leadership had a clue.

What could this mean? At this point self-doubt may have hit the magi hard. Could they have been wrong and miscalculated or misunderstood the prophecies? The Bible says, "When Herod the king heard this, he was troubled, and all Jerusalem with him" (Matthew 2:3). The Jews didn't seem to know what the magi were talking about at all, and their news had thrown the palace into a frenzied tumult. They had to take a moment and figure out what Scripture told them about the Messiah, and the Pharisees confirmed that he had to be born in Bethlehem, but that was all they knew for sure (vv. 5–6).

Far from appeased, Herod called a private meeting with the magi, and what did he ask? He wanted to know *when* they had seen the star (v. 7). He didn't wonder about *what* they had seen, but about *when* they had seen it. That's a revealing question that we will soon return to. However, before we get to that, let's finish the narrative.

After Herod met with the magi, he must have believed them and that the prophecies about the Messiah being born in Bethlehem had really happened. That is why he encouraged them to make the five-mile journey to Bethlehem on his behalf, albeit with an evil plot in his heart. They gladly obeyed, duped by his external demeanor, and on their way they saw "his star" again! "And behold, the star which they had seen in the East went before them, till it came and stood over where the young Child was" (v. 9). Now, if the first appearance had been enough to convince them that the Messiah had been born, this second appearance must have been like a shot of adrenaline, especially after all they had gone through in Jerusalem. They realized beyond a shadow of a doubt that all their calculations had been correct after all.

And so, what kind of star could have appeared once over Babylon and then again above Bethlehem, apparently hovering like a bright light guiding the magi to the exact location where Jesus was living? This passage does create the impression that some sort of glowing orb or roving light guided them to the manger, and this seems like it was a miracle. Perhaps it was the glory of God guiding them or an angel as some have suggested. Those solutions do make more sense than believing that a celestial object did such unnatural things.

But what if the traditional reading of this passage is wrong? What if the image that a glowing orb that hovered and guided the magi is a false image?

Literary Terms

To recap: The first appearance of the star sounds like a straightforward, realistic, celestial event. The magi told Herod they had seen "his star" while they were back east, and we can believe them. But the second sighting sounds fanciful and unrealistic. It sounds like a child's fairy-tale. That is, if we take it literally.

What we need to realize is that when the magi said that "the star . . . went on before them until it came and stood over," they were employing figurative astronomical terms that are used throughout their omen literature. We might call them idioms, and they were commonly used by Babylonian stargazers in their star diaries. As flawed as my original approach was to study Babylonian omen literature, it wasn't entirely fruitless, and I discovered that stargazers used figures of speech to describe the motions of the planets in relationship to other cosmic phenomena. Here's a list of examples I pulled from Babylonian star charts:

- "If Venus *stands inside* the Lion . . ."
- "If the star of the Old Man comes to *stand close to* the top of the moon . . ."
- "The gods Šullat and Haniš [which are stars] *were going before him* . . ."
- "If Venus keeps a stable position . . ."

Planets don't stand (as in standing up as if they had feet), and stars are not "going before" anyone or anything as if they are guiding them. The Babylonians used metaphors to describe heavenly motions.

Think about the absurd images conjured up by our own idioms: "It's raining cats and dogs" or "It cost an arm and a leg." Does the sun really "rise" or "set," and do sailors really "follow" the stars? You see, if we take these phrases literally, they're scientifically absurd, and that is the mistake we make when reading what the magi said. We're trying to visualize their terminology as if they meant it literally, but to them they were metaphorically describing their observations.

So, when Matthew says that the star "went before them," he doesn't mean that the star hovered like a glowing orb and the magi followed it. Rather, he means that "his star" was present in the heavens and guided the magi in the same sense in which we mean that the North Star guides us. And when Matthew says the star "stood over," it doesn't mean that it stopped right above the house where Jesus was. Instead it refers to how celestial phenomena appear in relationship to each other, to places on the earth, and to the human observer. The magi were traveling to Bethlehem, and they saw something in the sky standing above Bethlehem where the Child was (not his specific house).

History

So what did the magi see that "went before them" and "stood over" Bethlehem? The magi have told us all along what they saw. They saw "his star." They weren't referring to a "bright" star or a "king" star or a conjunction of planets. They called it "his" star, which is a figurative phrase that connects the appearance of a comet to the life of a famous person. That really is all it means. Some people have dismissed the possibility of the star being a comet, but that is because they are laboring under a literal phrasing of Matthew 2:9. They can't believe a comet would hover and lead the magi as described (and they're right, one couldn't do that). But as we have just learned, that isn't what those figures of speech mean.

Other people have dismissed a comet as a possibility because they say that comets were always an evil portent in the mind of the ancients.[268] But that simply isn't true. History once again comes to our rescue. While a comet would sometimes be associated with disaster, it didn't always mean that to observers. A case in point is that soon after the death of Julius Caesar, perhaps within just a few months, a comet appeared which then became associated with Caesar. Plutarch (ca. 46–119), a Greek philosopher, historian, and priest, says, "The most signal preternatural [out of the ordinary] appearances were the great comet, which shone very bright for seven nights after Caesar's death, and then disappeared."[269] Suetonius (ca. 69–130), a Roman historian, gives more details of this event:

> He [Julius Caesar] was fifty-five years old when he died, and his
> immediate deification, formally decreed in the Senate, convinced

the city as a whole, if only because, on the first day of the games given by his successor Augustus in honour of this apotheosis, a comet appeared about an hour before sunset and shone for seven days running. This was held to be Caesar's soul, elevated to heaven; hence the star now placed above the forehead of his divine image.[270]

Photograph 2: Augustus Image (left) and the Star of Caesar Image (right)

This comet—the star—became associated with Caesar because of its proximity to his death. Augustus put it on coins to honor Julius Caesar, but also, subtly, to amplify his own glory. Remember how good Augustus was at marketing himself? Also, this association with a heavenly event did not occur because of anything significant about the comet itself, except that it appeared soon after Caesar died. Therefore it became "his star."

In a similar manner, I believe the magi associated the birth of Christ with the appearance of the comet they saw. Indeed, that is what Herod must have understood the report of the magi to mean, for when they told him "We have seen his star," Herod called a secret meeting with the magi and asked them to explain *when* they had seen his star. At no point did he wonder *what* they had seen. He didn't ask, "What do you mean by 'You saw his star'?" Herod had no question about what they had seen because he realized that they were referring to the appearance of a short-term comet that they claimed confirmed the Messiah had been born.

Instead, he wanted to know *when* that comet had appeared. He's wondering if there had been any significant births that had transpired at the same time as the comet they had seen. His question could be paraphrased: "Now, when did you see that? I'm trying to remember if anyone important was born at that time who could be considered the Messiah."

Maybe the magi's answer triggered some memory for Herod. Maybe he made an association to events that had been occurring at the time they mentioned. But whether their answer did or not, it convinced him of the truth, which then led him to command the infamous slaughter of all the baby boys in the region who were under two years old. He made such a broad command because he wanted to end the Messiah. "Devour her child," as John's vision portrays (Revelation 12:4). And since the magi may have arrived in the summer of 6 BC, about ten months after Jesus was born, Herod must have made such a broadly applicable massacre in order to make sure the usurper to his throne wouldn't escape.

But to strengthen the idea that the magi had seen a comet and to understand what kind of comet they had seen, the early church father Origen (second century AD) also believed that Jesus's star was a comet. As he said:

> The star that was seen in the east we consider to have been a new star, unlike any of the other well-known planetary bodies, either those in the firmament above or those among the lower orbs, but partaking of the nature of those celestial bodies which appear at times, such as comets, or those meteors which resemble beams of wood, or beards, or wine jars, or any of those other names by which the Greeks are accustomed to describe their varying appearances.[271]

Notice that Origen is speaking in astronomical, not astrological, terms, and that comets are not as rare as one might think. We think of comets as only having long, bright tails, but he points out that there is a whole class of celestial bodies which are unpredictable ("varying appearances") and which take on unusual shapes.

A case in point is a comet I observed in December of 2021, *Leonard C/2021 A1*. I was excited when I first heard about it because I had never seen a comet before. This was my chance to finally see that long, silvery tail! When I first saw it through my telescope, though, I thought my telescope was out of focus. It was the comet alright, but all I saw was a fuzzy cotton ball of diffused light. No long tail at all. I was disappointed, but I kept hoping that a tail would eventually form.

On December 13, 2021, I went out about an hour before sunrise and there was the comet, visible to the naked eye. But once again, no tail. It merely looked like another bright planet, about as bright as Jupiter (-2 magnitude), although a little more twinkly and out of place. However, I had come this far so I figured I'd take a closer look through my telescope. I'm glad I did. It was one of the most beautiful things I have ever seen! It shimmered with the colors of red, green, yellow, and white,[272] and it danced in the eyepiece like a sparkler on the fourth of July. I couldn't look at it long enough. I was able to get a picture of it with my camera through the scope, but it doesn't do justice to what I saw. Seeing it alive with motion is seared into my mind; I will never forget it.

I believe the magi saw such a comet in Babylon before dawn on Ethanim 1, and another one almost a year later. Intriguingly, as I was finalizing this book, another comet (c/2022 E3) was visible with the naked eye for about a week in late January and early February of 2023. I was able to observe it multiple times over several nights in the northeastern sky before dawn, and it was easier to see than the one on December of 2021 because it was higher above the horizon. I never did see a tail, though, even through my telescope, and its magnitude was also about the same as Jupiter, like the previous comet. In other words, only a little over a year after the 2021 comet, I saw another one that also looked like a twinkling star.

For me, personally, the appearances of these two comets have confirmed what I have come to believe about what the magi saw. They saw two different comets that became significant to the magi *because of their timing*. The first one appeared when they already expected the Christ to be born based on Daniel's prophecies, and the second one because it appeared as they were coming toward Bethlehem. The first comet compelled them to make the trip to Jerusalem, but it was the appearance of the second comet that caused them to raise their hands in praise: they "rejoiced with exceedingly great joy" (Matthew 2:10). Their journey was about complete.

However, since neither of these comets were dramatically bright with tails as long as a kite, neither of them would have made it into any astronomical record books, nor may we ever see them again. They served their purpose. And yet one could say about them, and not be wrong, that they were humble comets, like the Savior they were announcing.

The Celestial Dance

So now let's put all of these details together. What has become truly stunning to me as I studied the stars is the miracle of the stars themselves. I studied them like I never had before, and what I learned has forever changed my perspective on what I see every night. But as I looked more closely at them on my computer, tracking their movements year after year (especially watching every minute of every day of 7 and 6 BC), trying to sort out what I was seeking to learn, I pieced together something that I have never heard anybody else mention. As far as I have been able to tell, the only other time a similar event happened was in 861 to 860 BC. I have been reluctant to bring it up because, well, it sounds rather unbelievable. But the planets did do this.

The stars above us are miracles. The rotation of the planets, the earth orbiting the sun, the moon orbiting the earth. All of nature is a miracle. The bird's wing, the owl's hoot, the birth of a child, a crane flying overhead, ducks landing on water, and the roll of thunder. It's all miraculous but so common that we don't see it or appreciate it as often as we should. So God gets our attention every now and then with something dramatic, unexpected, and so spectacular that even the most hardened heart might soften, at least for a moment.

As already noted, at dusk on Ethanim 1, 7 BC, all the planets were lined up across the night sky like a necklace draped on the neck of the universe. But now we must add a comet to the arrangement, which floated like a sparkling diamond somewhere in the night sky confirming all their dreams. But time didn't stop after that happened. The comet disappeared from view, and the planets continued on their paths. They kept rotating, spinning, revolving, and orbiting. They also kept aligning with one another over the next ten months in nothing less than what could be described as a heavenly waltz that—dare I say it—strikes me as one filled with joy. Calling it a waltz seems too formal. It seems to me that it was more like a square dance, and the planets did something similar to a do-si-do and an allemande left.[273]

Essentially what I saw was that, over the course of the next ten months, every planet aligned with each other at least once *and then lined up again on the other side of the sun. In order!* It was literally one nonstop conjunction after another as they rearranged themselves. It was amazing!

This square dance lasted from September of 7 BC to July of 6 BC. I have posted a video on my website (www.500yearjourney.com) so you can get an idea of how amazing it is, but here are some pictures from the *Starry Night* software with the planets exaggerated in size.

Star Map 5: September 25, 7 BC (five visible planets—Mercury, Venus, Mars, Jupiter, and Saturn—arrayed in order from the sun, right to left, after sunset and a new moon on the night Christ was born)

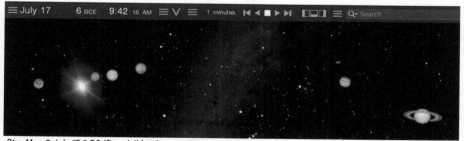

Star Map 6: July 17, 6 BC (five visible planets—Mercury, Venus, Mars, Jupiter, and Saturn—arrayed in order, left to right, before sunrise with a new moon to the left of the sun, potentially when the magi journeyed to Bethlehem)

God did something extraordinary between the time of Christ's birth and the time that the magi likely arrived on the scene the following year. His power and foresight were on display. Who else could do what he did? As God asked Job:

Can you bind the cluster of the Pleiades,
Or loose the belt of Orion?
Can you bring out Mazzaroth [the zodiac] in its season?
Or can you guide the Great Bear with its cubs?
Do you know the ordinances of the heavens?
Can you set their dominion over the earth? (Job 38:31–33)

God commands the stars and they obey, and nothing demonstrates his power over the universe of motion more than the birth of Christ. Think of the timing of it all! The stars lined up to worship him—twice!—and both times a comet confirmed God's carefully synchronized plan.

Augustus did not have that kind of power. Nor did Herod. Nor does any other world ruler, corporate president, church leader, or any other human being.

But God does.

And the final miracle of the entire sequence of events is that the planets bowed down to the King of kings on the night he was born, and then almost a year later they bowed again along with the faithful magi at the end of their 500-year journey.

Sept. 24, 7 BC	*Feast of Trumpets - Ethanim 1* *Birth of Christ*	*All the visible planets line up* *before sunset at the new moon.*
Oct. 23, 7 BC	Total Solar Eclipse (8 AM)	
Oct. 24, 7 BC	New Moon near Venus (6 PM)	
Nov 15, 7 BC	Mercury-Venus	
Feb 19, 6 BC	Saturn-Mars	
Feb 20, 6 BC	Saturn-Mars-Jupiter-(New Moon)	
Mar 5, 6 BC	Mars-Jupiter	
Mar 30, 6 BC	Saturn-Mercury	
Apr 4, 6 BC	Mercury-Jupiter	
Apr 15, 6 BC	Mercury-Mars	April 15 - 20: The moon aligns
Apr 18, 6 BC	Annular Solar Eclipse	with each planet
Apr 24, 6 BC	Saturn-Venus	
May 8, 6 BC	Jupiter-Venus	
Jul 1, 6 BC	Mars-Venus	
Jul 8, 6 BC	Mars-Venus-Mercury (at dawn)	
Jul 11, 6 BC	Mercury-Venus	
Jul 16-19, 6 BC	**All the planets visible before sunrise in order at the new moon.**	Heliacal rising of Sirius. Egyptian New Year.

Table 5: 10 Months of Planetary Conjunctions (the hyphens between planets indicate those conjunctions)

13

Day of Grace

Sing aloud to God our strength;
Make a joyful shout to the God of Jacob.
Raise a song and strike the timbrel,
The pleasant harp with the lute.
Blow the trumpet at the time of the New Moon,
At the full moon, on our solemn feast day.
—*Psalm 81:1–3*

We strut about this earth seeking to do our will, implementing our plans, manipulating markets, and coercing people, all in order to force compliance to a version of a world community that aligns with the image of man we conceive of for ourselves. Money, power, fame, indulgence, and pride lure us to think we have the answers to cure all the problems of humanity. But here's the reality: all of this striving, posturing, and scheming can end in a moment. Gone.

But Jesus is, was, and forever will be the true King of kings. He is eternal because he wasn't created. He is the Creator of the universe. And he isn't the ultimate ruler because he forces us to worship him, but because he is the One who made all things and preserves all things. All that is, is his. What he has made, he can unmake simply by removing his sustaining power. But some of what he can do he has chosen not to. Because, as we see in Jesus, God's own Son, the Lord of all is humble, selfless, empathetic, and understanding. He stands up for truth (he is the Truth) but not self-righteously. He cares for us, but he also allows us to make our own choices. He judges sin but is willing to forgive those who do sin. Jesus is the Son of God, the Messiah, and heir to the throne of David. He is our Creator and our Lord. As the apostle John wrote many centuries ago:

> That which was from the beginning, which we have heard, which we have seen with our eyes, which we have looked upon, and our hands have handled, concerning the Word of life—the life was manifested, and we have seen, and bear witness, and declare to you that eternal life which was with the Father and was manifested to us—that which we have seen and heard we declare to you, that you also may have fellowship with us; and truly our fellowship is with the Father and with His Son Jesus Christ. And these things we write to you that your joy may be full. (1 John 1:1–4)

God is empirical too. He has revealed himself to us through what he has made and what he has inspired to be written. The historically verified birth of Christ proves God is not a figment of our imagination nor a fictional archetype. He is God in the flesh come to save us from our sins.

Julius Caesar fought his way to the top of people's affections by warfare, political maneuvering, and prideful, stubborn ambition.

Augustus tried to be all that an ideal emperor was supposed to be, but he died only hoping that he had acted his part well enough.

King Herod manipulated, fought, murdered, and bribed his way to what he thought was the pinnacle of power, but no matter how much he pretended, he knew he had never won the people's hearts, and he had only succeeded at inspiring fear and animosity. Herod knew he had usurped the throne and wasn't really the king of the Jews, and yet he was willing to murder babies to keep the stolen title.

But for the past two thousand years, look at for whom people have been willing to lay down their lives: Jesus Christ. Born in a manger, crucified by mankind, and yet never did he harm anyone nor say anything other than the absolute truth. He correctly framed reality, and humanity hated him for it. He revealed our pride and self-destructive behaviors, and we killed him. The God of the universe, the Creator of heaven and earth, the all-powerful and most merciful Lord God Almighty who with a whisper could wipe us all out of existence, chose instead to humble himself and to become quietly, gently, one of us. Why? To buy us back from the indignity and shame of our own sin.

People accuse God of being a despotic tyrant, but if that were the case, why would he come humbly in a manger, and why wouldn't he crush anyone who stood against him? God must be either pathetic or truly good. If he were an all-powerful being who knew all, was everywhere present, *and* who demanded mindless obedience, why would he allow anyone to defy him? How *could* anyone defy him? If he were truly a tyrant, everyone would be absorbed into the very essence of his will, Big Brother-style, and would know nothing else other than what he allowed them to know. And yet look at how many people on earth rebel against him. What a pathetically weak God if he could stop us from rebelling, and yet he doesn't. We stray, we doubt, we malign, and we despise him. No tyrant worth his salt would allow that to go on if he could stop it.

Or it could mean that he has chosen not to use his power tyrannically because he is infinitely good. He is all-powerful, but patient; he wants us to follow him because we have been convinced, not coerced; he invites us, he doesn't threaten us; he is gracious and accessible, not egotistical and vindictive.

Freedom of choice to God meant choosing to humble himself and to give his life for the sake of the weak, the innocent, and the downtrodden of this world. He came to seek and to save that which was lost. Freedom of choice means to us that if we had ultimate power, then we would have the right to crush anyone who stands in our way. That's what we think power is for. But the all-powerful God who actually does have all the power instead wants intelligent, informed men and women who will follow him with a willing heart *because he is good* (Matthew 11:28; Psalm 23; John 3:16–17; Romans 2:4).

God is all-powerful, but he isn't a tyrant. God humbled himself and, through his Son, willingly sacrificed himself to deal with our sin and rebellion. That isn't weakness; that's true strength. He used his ultimate power to humbly serve us. His holiness demands that he will judge sin—evil will be held accountable—but his holiness also demands that he provide the path to forgiveness: himself. Just because he doesn't instantly punish us doesn't mean he is weak; it means he is patient.

And that is why he wrapped his goodness in swaddling cloths in a manger more than two thousand years ago. And that is why he proved through every means necessary that he had come to serve, not to be served. Hope came at the right time, the predicted time, the time of God's own choosing. Our Savior came into the world for us, and he wants to come to you, now.

May we not miss the advent of God's Son into our hearts, and may we be attentive, like the magi, and rejoice with great joy just as they did so long ago.

A Final Word

I know that the Christmas season is firmly rooted in our cultural psyche and expectations. So many good things come from it economically and, yes, even spiritually. Even though I do not believe Christ was born on December 25th, I imagine that the cultural traditions will continue as they stand, and that's fine. This book was not about the Christmas holiday anyway. It was about the birth of Christ. There's a big difference. You see, at the time Jesus emerged from Mary's womb, only a few people knew about it. There were no stockings or toys. There was no bright star. There were no kings from the orient. It was a simple, quiet, and yet sacrosanct night when Jesus was born. Only the shepherds showed up, and the magi wouldn't arrive for another ten months.

But that is why on the first appearance of the new moon at sunset in the western sky on Ethanim 1 every year, I will now stand outside and take a moment to quietly remember the birth of Christ. Traditions can be changed, but the truth cannot. In fact, I am sitting here as I am writing this, looking at the heavenly fingernail of God one year before this book will be published.

I want to honor him, and I want to get away from the glitz and glamor and clamor of the way Christmas is celebrated. This is a peaceful moment for me, and a profound one. Nobody else is doing this. People are driving home, and the weather is calm, warm, and beautiful, at least where I live. It's perfect, really. Still, people behave just as they did centuries ago. My wife is out with friends; my daughter is getting ready for a spiritual retreat at her school; my son is about to go to bed. I had to buy milk and eggs today. The family dinner was fabulous as always.

It would be fun to throw a big birthday bash for Christ as the new moon appears on the night he was born, but perhaps we should instead worship him quietly. Maybe a typical birthday party celebration is a bit too gawdy for what took place, and it would be more meaningful to open God's humble gift to us in the quiet peace he brings to our hearts. As Mary sang while still pregnant with Jesus:

My soul magnifies the Lord,
And my spirit has rejoiced in God my Savior. . . .
For He who is mighty has done great things for me,
And holy is His name.
And His mercy is on those who fear Him
From generation to generation.
He has shown strength with His arm;
He has scattered the proud in the imagination of their hearts.
He has put down the mighty from their thrones,
And exalted the lowly.
He has filled the hungry with good things,
And the rich He has sent away empty.
He has helped His servant Israel,
In remembrance of His mercy,
As He spoke to our fathers,
To Abraham and to his seed forever. (Luke 1:46–55)

Amen.

Acknowledgments

Thank you to my wife, Beth, and my children for putting up with me "hiding" in my office for so many evenings while I researched and wrote. Sometimes they would just have to barge in and remind me that there were other realities in this world. I am thankful for their persistence and their patience.

I would also like to thank those who took the time to read my manuscript early. It definitely was a rough draft, and yet your kind insights helped guide the development of this book. And a special thank you to those who gave an early endorsement. There are many controversial issues in this book, and whether you agreed with all my conclusions or not, you took the step to support me. I will appreciate that for eternity.

Also, my deepest gratitude is reserved for our Lord, who guided me to the man who has in so many ways made this book publishable. My raw data was difficult to convert into readable prose, and so thank you, William D. Watkins, for your patience and wisdom. Who knew all those long conversations in the hallway of the school where we met would lead us to here.

About the Author

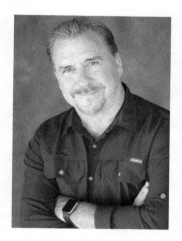

Since becoming a teacher in 1997, Corey Piper has taught for private Christian schools and currently teaches history, literature, and theology (Omnibus) for Veritas Scholars Academy. His writing appeared in *Christian Parenting Today* with his first article, "A Tear and a Laugh," in 1996—which won the Whitworth University writing award. He published his first book, *To Conquer Death: Seeing Beyond the Darkness,* in 2015.

Corey has previously lived in Arizona, California, Oregon, Washington, and Colorado, but he currently resides in Wichita, Kansas with his wife and children where he has learned to love the flowing beauty of the prairie. His favorite places on earth are the Grand Canyon, Colorado, and the Oregon Coast, where his family heritage is rooted in fishing and dairy farming in the Tillamook Valley.

Bibliography

Anderson, Steven David. "Darius the Mede: A Reappraisal." PhD diss., Dallas Theological Seminary, 2014.

Andrews, Samuel J. *The Life of Our Lord upon the Earth: Considered in Its Historical, Chronological, and Geographical Relations.* 1867. Reprint, Miami, FL: Hardpress, 2013.

Augustus, Imperator Caesar. Translated with commentary by Alison E. Cooley. *Res Gestae Divi Augusti.* New York: Cambridge University Press, 2010.

Bagnall, Roger S., and Bruce W. Frier. *The Demography of Roman Egypt.* 1994. Reprint, Wiltshire, Great Britain: Cambridge University Press, 1995. https://archive.org/details/demographyofroma0000bagn/page/n11/mode/2up?view=theater.

Barclay, Joseph, trans. *The Talmud.* By Evinity Publishing, 1878. Reprint, London: J. Murray, 2009. Kindle. Also online at https://www.sacred-texts.com/jud/bar/index.htm#contents. The temple plan is at https://www.sacred-texts.com/jud/bar/img/tempplan.jpg.

Barnstone, Willis, and Marvin W. Meyer. *The Gnostic Bible.* Boston, MA: Shambhala, 2009.

Beard, Mary. *SPQR: A History of Ancient Rome.* New York: Liveright, 2015.

Bede. *The Ecclesiastical History of the English People.* Translated by A. M. Sellar. Reprint, New York: Dover Publications, 2011. Kindle.

Beyond Today, "The Feast of Trumpets: A Turning Point in History." United Church of God. Posted May 31, 2013. https://www.ucg.org/bible-study-tools/booklets/gods-holy-day-plan-the-promise-of-hope-for-all-man-kind/the-feast-of-trumpets-a-turning-point-in-history.

Brennan, Christopher W. *Hellenistic Astrology: The Study of Fate and Fortune*. Denver, CO: Amor Fati, 2017.

Brindle, Wayne. "The Census and Quirinius: Luke 2:2" (1984). *SOR Faculty Publications and Presentations*. Paper 73. http://digitalcommons.liberty.edu/sor_fac_pubs/73. First published in the *Journal of the Evangelical Society* 27, no. 1 (March 1984): 43–52.

Butler, Eliza Marian. *The Myths of the Magus*. 1948. Reprint, Cambridge, England: Cambridge University Press, 1993.

Cassius Dio. *The Complete Works of Cassius Dio*. Hastings, East Sussex, United Kingdom: Delphi Classics, 2014.

Censorinus. *De Die Natale*. Translated by William Maude. New York: The Cambridge Encyclopedia Co., 1900. https://babel.hathitrust.org/cgi/pt?id=uc1.31175006887700&view=1up&seq=21&skin=2021.

Chrysostom, John. *Homily on the Birthday of Christ, sections a & b*. Translation by Andrew Maguire. Early Church Texts. https://www.earlychurchtexts.com/mainsub/johnchrysostom/in_diem_natalem_domini_nostri_jesu_christi.shtml. In Diem Natalem Domini Nostri Jesu Christi (sections 1 and 2), Greek text from Migne PG, vol. 49, col. 351. Translation by Andrew Maguire (Early Church Texts Webmaster).

Clement of Alexandria. *The Complete Works of Clement of Alexandria*. Hastings, East Sussex, United Kingdom: Delphi Classics, 2016. Kindle.

Dawson, W. F. *Christmas: Its Origin and Associations, Together with Its Historical Events and Festive Celebrations during Nineteen Centuries*. London: Elliot Stock, 1902.

Declercq, Georges. *Anno Domini: The Origins of the Christian Era*. Turnhout, Belgium: Brepols, 2000.

Declercq, Georges. "Dionysius Exiguus and the Introduction of the Christian Era." *Sacris Erudiri* 41 (2002): 165–246.

Dionysius Exiguus. *On Easter, or, the Paschal Cycle (2003)*. Translated by Roger Pearse and Michael Deckers. tertullian.org, 2006. https://tertullian.org/fathers/dionysius_exiguus_easter_01.htm.

Early, Justin Whitmel. *The Common Rule*. Downers Grove, IL: InterVarsity Press, 2019.

Eight Days That Made Rome. Smithsonian Channel. "Rome's First Emperor." Episode 4. Aired 2019. https://www.smithsonianchannel.com/shows/eight-days-that-made-rome.

Eratosthenes. *Eratosthenes' Geography*. Translated by Duane W. Roller. Princeton, NJ: Princeton University Press, 2010.

Eusebius. *The Church History of Eusebius*. Grand Rapids, MI: Aeterna Press, 2016. Kindle.

Gaius Suetonius Tranquillus. *The Twelve Caesars*. Translated by Robert Graves. 1985. Reprint, London: Penguin Books, 2007.

Gertoux, Gérard. *Absolute Egyptian Chronology: From Narmer (2838–2808) to Nakhtnebef II (360–342)*. Published by Gérard Gertoux, Lulu.com, February 23, 2022. Kindle.

Gertoux, Gérard. *Queen Esther Wife of Xerxes: Chronological, Historical and Archaeological Evidence*. Published by Gérard Gertoux, Lulu.com, 2016 edition.

Harper, Kyle. *From Shame to Sin: The Christian Transformation of Sexual Morality in Late Antiquity*. Cambridge, MA: Harvard University Press, 2016.

Harriman, K. R. "Why Is Christmas on December 25?" Academia.edu., 2018. https://www.academia.edu/40525319/Why_Is_Christmas_on_December_25.

Heiser, Michael S. *Angels: What the Bible Really Says about God's Heavenly Host*. Bellingham, WA: Lexham Press, 2018.

Liddell, Henry George, and Robert Scott. *A Greek-English Lexicon*. Oxford, England: Clarendon Press, 1951.

Hesemann, Michael, and Michael J. Miller. *Mary of Nazareth: History, Archaeology, Legends*. San Francisco, CA: Ignatius Press, 2016.

Hijmans, Steven. "Sol Invictus, the Winter Solstice, and the Origins of Christmas." *Mouseion: Journal of the Classical Association of Canada* XLVII, series III, vol. 3 (2003): 377–99.

Hoehner, Harold W. *Chronological Aspects of the Life of Christ*. Grand Rapids, MI: Zondervan, 1977.

Hoehner, Harold W. *Herod Antipas*. 1972. Reprint, Grand Rapids, MI.: Zondervan, 1980.

Hutchison, Dwight. "Matthew's Magi Never Visually Followed a Star Anywhere, But . . . ." *Perspectives on Science and Christian Faith* 71, no. 3 (September 2019): 160–73. https://www.asa3.org/ASA/PSCF/2019/PSCF9-19dyn.html.

Irenaeus. *The Writings of Irenaeus*. Translated by Alexander Roberts and W. H. Rambaut. 1883. Reprint, Edinburgh, Scotland: T. & T. Clark, 2015. Kindle.

Ironside, H. A. *Lectures on Daniel the Prophet*. Neptune, NJ: Loizeaux Brothers, 1920.

Jacobson, David. "The Jerusalem Temple of Herod the Great." In *The World of the Herods and the Nabataeans*, edited by Nikos Kokkinos, vol. 1 of the International Conference held at the British Museum, 145–76. Stuttgart, Germany: Franz Steiner Verlag, 2007.

Jewish Virtual Library. https://www.jewishvirtuallibrary.org.

Jones, Alexander Raymond. "Ptolemy." In *Encyclopedia Britannica*. Article last modified January 13, 2023. https://www.britannica.com/biography/Ptolemy.

Josephus, Flavius. *The New Complete Works of Josephus*. Translated by William Whiston. Rev. ed. Grand Rapids, MI: Kregel, 1999.

Justin Martyr. *Dialogue with Trypho*. Reprint, The Fig Classic Series. 2012. Kindle.

Landau, Brent. *Revelation of the Magi: The Lost Tale of the Wise Men's Journey to Bethlehem*. New York: Harperone, 2010. EPub.

Lewis, C. S. *Out of the Silent Planet*. 1938. Reprint, New York: Scribner, 2003.

Livy. *The Early History of Rome*. Translated by Aubrey de Sélincourt. 1960. Reprint, London: The Folio Society, 2006.

Longenecker, Dwight. *Mystery of the Magi: The Quest to Identify the Three Wise Men*. Washington, DC: Regnery, 2017.

Lowery, R. H. *Sabbath and Jubilee*. St. Louis, MO: Chalice Press, 2000.

Lucius' Romans. n.d. "Why Were Newborn Children Left to Die in Ancient Rome?" University of Kent. https://blogs.kent.ac.uk/lucius-romans/2016/06/15/why-were-new-born-children-left-to-die-in-ancient-rome.

Macarthur, John. *The MacArthur Bible Handbook*. Nashville, TN: Thomas Nelson, 2003.

Martin, James C., John A. Beck, and David G. Hansen. *A Visual Guide to Bible Events: Fascinating Insights into Where They Happened and Why*. Grand Rapids, MI: Baker Books, 2015.

Maximus the Confessor. *The Life of the Virgin*. Translated by Stephen J. Shoemaker. Reprint, New Haven, NJ: Yale University Press, 2012.

Meldau, Fred John. *The Prophets Still Speak: Messiah in Both Testaments*. Bellmawr, NJ: Friends of Israel Gospel Ministry, 1988.

Melito of Sardis. *On Pascha: With the Fragments of Melito and Other Material Related to the Quartodecimans*. Translated by Alistair C. Stewart. Yonkers, NY: St. Vladimir's Seminary Press, 2016.

Milton, John. *The Poetical Works of John Milton*. Edited by Henry Charles Beeching. London: Humphrey Milford, 1914.

Nicolet, Claude. *The World of the Citizen in Republican Rome*. Translated by P. S. Falla. London: Batsford Academic and Education Ltd., 1980. https://archive.org/details/worldofcitizenin0000nico/page/n7/mode/2up.

Norten, Michael. *Unlocking the Secrets of the Feasts: The Prophecies in the Feasts of Leviticus*. Nashville, TN: Westbow Press, 2015.

Phlegon. *Phlegon of Tralles' Book of Marvels*. Translated by William Hansen. Reprint, Exeter, England: University of Exeter Press, 1996.

Plutarch. *Plutarch's Lives*, Volumes I & II. Translated by John Dryden. New York: Modern Library, 2001.

Qumran Calendar. PDF of Solar Calendar based upon Calendrical Documents 4Q320 and 4Q321. https://grace5.webs.com›YHWH-Qumran-Calendar.pdf.

Ruark, Michael. "Feast of Trumpets—The 'Day of Blasting' " (blog). August 27, 2017. https://michaelruark.blog/2017/08/20/feast-of-trumpets-the-day-of-blasting.

Ruark, Michael. "Was Jesus Born on the Feast of Trumpets (911)" (blog). August 20, 2017. https://michaelruark.blog/2017/08/20/jesus-born-on-the-day-of-trumpets-911.

Sampson, Robin, and Linda Pierce. *A Family Guide to the Biblical Holidays: With Activities for All Ages*. Woodbridge, VA: Heart of Wisdom Publishing, 1997.

Simmons, Kurt. n.d. "Loosing the Riddle of Clement Alexandria's Dates for the Nativity, Baptism, Passion, and Epiphany of Christ." Dec 25th. info. http://www.dec25th.info/Loosing%20the%20Riddle%20of%20Clement%20Alexandria%27s%20Dates%20for%20the%20Nativity,%20Baptism,%20Passion,%20and%20Epiphany%20of%20Christ.html.

Smith, Steven D. *Pagans and Christians in the City: Culture Wars from the Tiber to the Potomac*. Grand Rapids, MI: William B. Eerdmans, 2021.

Sobel, Dava. *Longitude: The True Story of a Lone Genius Who Solved the Greatest Scientific Problem of His Time*. New York: Walker & Co., 1995.

Sobel, Jason. *Aligning with God's Appointed Times: Discover the Prophetic and Spiritual Meaning of the Biblical Holidays*. North Hollywood, CA: RJS Publishing, 2020.

Sperber, Daniel. n.d. "Mishmarot & Ma'amadot." Jewish Virtual Library. https://www.jewishvirtuallibrary.org/mishmarot-ma-amadot.

Spier, Jeffrey, editor. *Picturing the Bible: The Earliest Christian Art*. New Haven, CT: Yale University Press, 2009.

Stern, David H., and Barry Rubin. *The Complete Jewish Study Bible*. Updated ed. Peabody, MA: Hendrickson Publishers, 2016.

Stetzer, Ed. "Church Attendance during Christmastime: Stats on Christmas Outreach." Church Leaders. December 16, 2021. https://churchleaders.com/voices/411818-church-attendance-during-christmastime-stats-on-christmas-outreach.html.

Strabo. *The Geography of Strabo*. Edited by Duane W. Roller. Cambridge, England: Cambridge University Press, 2014.

Sullivan, Charles A. "Dionysius Exiguus and the AD Calendar System." April 4, 2021. https://charlesasullivan.com/1842/dionysius-exiguus-and-the-ad-calendar-system/.

Tertullian. *The Works of Tertullian*. Edited by Alexander Roberts, Sir James Donaldson, and Arthur Cleveland Coxe. 1885. Reprint, Hastings, England: Delphi Classics, 2018. Kindle.

Vidano, Stephen, dir. *The Star of Bethlehem*. 2007. Presentation by Frederick A. Larson. Los Angeles, CA: MPower Pictures, 2007. DVD.

Torah Times Messianic Ministry. n.d. "The Qumran Calendar." https://www.torahtimes.org/writings/qumran-calendar/article.html.

Tuland, Carl G. "Josephus, Antiquities, Book XI: Correction or Confirmation of Biblical Post-Exilic Records?" *Andrews University Seminary Studies (AUSS)* 4, no. 2 (1966). https://digitalcommons.andrews.edu/auss/vol4/iss2/5.

Van Dorn, Doug, and Matt Foreman. *The Angel of the Lord: A Biblical, Historical, and Theological Study*. Dacono, CO: Waters of Creation, 2020. Kindle.

White, Gavin. *Babylonian Star-Lore: An Illustrated Guide to the Stars and Constellations of Ancient Babylonia*. London: Solaria Publications, 2014.

William Mitchell Ramsay. *Was Christ Born at Bethlehem? A Study on the Credibility of St. Luke*. London: Hodder and Stoughton, 1898.

Xenophon. *Xenophon's Cyrus the Great: The Arts of Leadership and War*. New York: St. Martin's Press, 2013. Kindle.

Endnotes

1   Merrill F. Unger, *The New Unger's Bible Dictionary*, ed. R. K. Harrison (Chicago, IL: Moody Press, 1988), s.v. "Calendar."

2   Harold W. Hoehner, *Chronological Aspects of the Life of Christ* (Grand Rapids, MI: Zondervan, 1977), 27.

3   "Prague Astronomical Clock (Orloj): Facts, Legends, Location & Video," PragueGo, accessed November 11, 2022, https://www.praguego.com/attractions/astronomical-clock-orloj.

4   Jason Sobel, *Aligning with God's Appointed Times: Discover the Prophetic and Spiritual Meaning of the Biblical Holidays* (North Hollywood, CA: RJS Publishing, 2020), 127.

5   John MacArthur, "Luke: Author and Date," *The MacArthur Bible Handbook* (Nashville, TN: Thomas Nelson, 2003).

6   MacArthur, "Luke: Author and Date."

7   John was in Jerusalem at the council of Jerusalem, which took place around AD 50.

8   William Mitchell Ramsay, *Was Christ Born at Bethlehem? A Study on the Credibility of St. Luke*, reprint ed. (1898; repr., Sagwan Press, 2018), chap. 4, 74.

9   See my first book, *To Conquer Death: Seeing beyond the Darkness* (Hygiene, CO: Horatio Press, 2015).

10   To read a fuller account, please go to my website, http://www.to conquerdeath, and look for my blog, "The Moment I Almost Gave Up."

11   Daniel Sperber, n.d., "Mishmarot & Ma'amadot," Jewish Virtual Library, accessed August 10, 2022, https://www.jewishvirtuallibrary. org/mishmarot-ma-amadot.

12   Joseph Barclay, trans., *The Talmud . . . with Illustrations and Plan of the Temple*, reprint ed. (1878; repr., London: J. Murray, 2009), 13.5.4. Kindle. Also at https://www.sacred-texts.com/jud/bar/bar099.htm.

13   *The Talmud*, 13.6.3.

14   *The Talmud*, 13.7.4.

15   See the diagram of Herod's temple at https://www.sacred-texts.com/ jud/bar/img/tempplan.jpg. The altar of incense is found at #43 in the diagram.

16   I do not mean fallen angels will be redeemed but that the spiritual war with them will eventually end.

17   *Strong's Concordance*, 4397, s.v. "malak," Bible Hub, https://biblehub. com/hebrew/4397.htm.

18   In Genesis 18, one of the "messengers" is the Lord himself, but the other two who were with him were angels as shown in Genesis 19 and how they were treated by the Sodomites. For a full treatment, see Doug Van Dorn and Matt Foreman, *The Angel of the Lord: A Biblical, Historical, and Theological Study* (Dacono, CO: Waters of Creation, 2020), esp. chap. 2, 42–46.

19   Michael S. Heiser, *Angels: What the Bible Really Says about God's Heavenly Host* (Bellingham, WA: Lexham Press, 2018), 24.

20   In Exodus 32:19, Moses broke the first set of tablets God wrote because Israel, led by Aaron, had made a golden calf to worship while Moses was in the presence of God on Mt. Sinai.

21   Seraphim have six wings, but I will not be talking about them here.

22   C. S. Lewis, *Out of the Silent Planet* (New York: Scribner, 2003), chap. 15, 100.

23   This is a story not found in the Old Testament but in some extra-biblical Jewish writings. This does not mean the story did not occur in history;

it's just not recorded in the books that comprise the canon of Scripture. The fact that Jude mentions it, though, elevates its authenticity.

24 The exact quote: "No one upholds me against these, except Michael your prince." The phrase "your prince" seems at first to be a reference to Daniel, but in the context it must mean "Israel's prince."

25 Heiser, *Angels*, 73–75.

26 John Milton, *Paradise Lost*, bk. I, lines 157–61.

27 The first six chapters of the book of Daniel are chronological and historical. Chapters 7–12 contain his visions, and they are keyed to the times in his life recorded in chapters 1–6.

28 The one who commands Gabriel is the preincarnate Jesus who is frequently referred to as "the Angel of the Lord." Jerome in his commentary on Daniel specifically interprets Daniel 8:15 this way. See Dorn and Foreman, *The Angel of the Lord*, 256.

29 H. A. Ironside, *Lectures on Daniel the Prophet* (Neptune, NJ: Loizeaux Brothers, 1920), 35: "Darius is generally supposed to be Cyaxares II, the last king of Media." See also Steven D. Anderson, *Darius the Mede: A Reappraisal* (Grand Rapids, MI: Steven D. Anderson, 2014), 53.

30 Xenophon, *Xenophon's Cyrus the Great: The Arts of Leadership and War* (New York: St. Martin's Press, 2013), 275.

31 *Strong's Concordance*, 7620, s.v. "shabua," Bible Hub, https://biblehub.com/hebrew/7620.htm.

32 The Day of Atonement is also known as Yom Kippur and is celebrated with a week-long fast.

33 Josephus, *Antiquities,* 3.12.3, emphasis added.

34 To see why there needs to be ten additional years, please refer to the timeline on my website and look for the year 450 BC and track the correct column to 7 BC. www.500yearjourney.com.

35 Ironside, *Lectures on Daniel the Prophet*, 165–66.

36 Some have interpreted this to refer to Jesus's crucifixion and others to his baptism. In the following sections, I will try to demonstrate why it refers to his birth, but just from a plain reading it seems obvious: "Until Messiah the Prince" *arrives*.

37 Artaxerxes's decree (Nehemiah 2:7–8) permitted Nehemiah to complete the city's wall, which happened many years later after the temple was completed. Ezra puts the three decrees together here (even though he and Nehemiah arrived in Jerusalem after the temple had been completed) because rebuilding the walls of Jerusalem completed the entirety of the decree made by Cyrus.

38 *Strong's Concordance*, 7339, s.v. "rechob," Blue Letter Bible, https://www.blueletterbible.org/lexicon/h7339/kjv/wlc/0-1.

39 Gérard Gertoux, *Absolute Egyptian Chronology: From Narmer (2838–2808) To Nakhtnebef II (360–342).* Published by Gérard Gertoux, February 2022, pp. 236–37.

40 Some of the dates I use might be different than what are listed in textbooks or traditional sources, but there has been a lot of great scholarship done in the last twenty years or so that calls into question some "established" dates. One of the best books I've read is by Gerard Gertoux, *Absolute Egyptian Chronology.* He does a masterful job syncing up multiple calendar systems and linking them to astronomical events. He also takes into account corulerships (overlapping reigns), which some older chronologies do not take into account.

41 There is a specific time mentioned in Nehemiah 6:15: "So the wall was finished on the twenty-fifth day of Elul, in fifty-two days." But this is not referring to the entirety of the work on the wall but rather to how long it took between when Nehemiah thwarted the plans of the wicked men mentioned in v. 14 and when he oversaw the hanging of the final gate in the wall.

42 It isn't likely that it normally would take that long, but Ezra was leading thousands of Jews back to Jerusalem, hence the longer travel time.

43 I have put on my website a chart of the data I've gleaned from multiple sources, and I have gone over the numbers for years, looking for incongruencies and impossibilities. The challenge is that when one scholar disagrees with another one, who do you trust? I have put a lot of effort into the background information I include here, and if you would like to see my work on this, please visit my website.

44 My hypothesis shall be tested in subsequent chapters. My dates slightly differ from some accepted chronologies, but I did derive them from scholars who challenged those chronologies. As noted before, this is a heavily debated timeframe.

45 "Studying Nehemiah's account, Dr. Mazar noted that the construction of the Northern Tower and associated wall, which she had scientifically dated to circa 450 b.c.e., matched precisely with the biblical account. Not only did the dates match, so did the quality of construction. *The tower and wall were not masterpieces of engineering. Their construction quality showed that they had been built hastily*—just as Nehemiah recorded" (Christopher Eames, "Discovered: Nehemiah's Wall," Armstrong Institute of Biblical Archaeology, October 31, 2019, emphasis added, https://armstronginstitute.org/204-discovered-nehemiahs-wall). What's interesting is that Dr. Eilat Mazar dates the construction of the tower to 450 BC but continues to use the traditional date of Nehemiah's arrival in 445 BC. How could the tower be built five years before Nehemiah even arrived? The date Dr. Mazar gives actually defends the dates of my theory, which teaches that the wall was dedicated in 450 BC.

46 The Sabbath Year is different than the Year of Jubilee.

47 One other detail I should explain is that the traditionally accepted 490-year interpretation of Daniel's 70 weeks only fits if the first 483 years (49 + 434) are consecutive and start at Artaxerxes's decree after Nehemiah returns to Jerusalem and then ends at Christ's crucifixion, 483 years later. The problem I see with this, and what caused me to look deeper, is that Ezra and the Babylonian Jews considered Cyrus's decree to be the fulfillment of Daniel's prophecies. Hence the development of my theory, which, again, I hope to substantiate by definitively proving the date of Christ's birth.

48 Adoption Center, http://adopt.org/adoption-laws.

49 Leah Ward, "What Is the Difference between Adoption and Fostering?," Gladney Center for Adoption, March 22, 2020, emphasis added, https://adoption.org/difference-adoption-fostering.

50 *Jewish Encyclopedia* online, s.v. "Marriage Laws," by Solomon Schechter and Julius H. Greenstone, accessed October 5, 2022, https://www.jewishencyclopedia.com/articles/10435-marriage-laws.

51 There are apocryphal accounts that claim Mary's mother's name was Anne and her father's name was Joachim, but evaluating such accounts goes way beyond the scope of this book.

52 To see what I mean, one must read Matthew 1:18–24 and then read Luke 1:26–45. Matthew talks about Joseph's response, and Luke focuses on Mary's response. Combining the two we can see a timeline unfold where Joseph is wavering about putting Mary away (Matthew), she goes to live with Elizabeth (Luke), and when she returns he welcomes her back because during that time Gabriel had spoken to him too.

53 Paul lists James, Jesus's brother, as one of those who saw Jesus alive from the dead (1 Corinthians 15:7). James eventually became one of the leaders of the early church (Galatians 1:19; 2:9; Acts 15:13–21; 21:19), and he even wrote the epistle of James found in the New Testament.

54 The abbreviation AUC stands for *anno urbis conditae*, which is Latin for "in the year since the city's founding." The Roman historian Livy wrote his monumental history of Rome entitled *Ab urbe Condita* from 27–9 BC. In the same way we use BC/AD, first century Roman and early Christian historians used AUC. In these next two chapters about Augustus and Herod, I will periodically use the AUC date while primarily using BC/AD dates because we are more familiar with that nomenclature.

55 Cassius Dio records that they were consuls in AUC 691 (63 BC). Cassius Dio, *The Complete Works of Cassius Dio* (United Kingdom: Delphi Classics, 2014), bk. 37, 278.

56 Suetonius, *The Twelve Caesars*, trans. Robert Graves (New York: Penguin Classics, 2007), "Divus Augustus," para. 5, p. 45.

57 Suetonius, *The Twelve Caesars*, "Divus Augustus," para. 6, p. 45.

58 Censorinus, *De Die Natale*, trans. William Maude (New York: Cambridge Encyclopedia Co., 1900), chap. X (XXI) "The Historical Period," p. 32, https://babel.hathitrust.org/cgi/pt?id=uc1.31175006887700&view=1up&seq=21&skin=2021.

59 *Eight Days That Made Rome*, Smithsonian Channel, episode 4, "Rome's First Emperor."

60 Cassius Dio, *The Complete Works of Cassius Dio*, 52.2.

61 Cassius Dio, *The Complete Works of Cassius Dio*, 52.40.

62 Plutarch, "Numa Pompilius," *Plutarch's Lives,* Volume I, The Modern Library series (New York: Random House, 2001), 89.

63 Censorinus, *De Die Natale*, 32. Cassius Dio confirms that 27 BC is Augustus's seventh consulship and Agrippa's third (Cassius Dio, *The Complete Works of Cassius Dio*, 53.734).

64 Cassius Dio, *The Complete Works of Cassius Dio*, 52.715.

65 Steven D. Smith, *Pagans and Christians in the City: Culture Wars from the Tiber to the Potomac* (Grand Rapids, MI: William B. Eerdmans, 2018), 75.

66 Suetonius, *The Twelve Caesars*, "Divus Augustus," para. 34, p. 63.

67 JV99, n.d., "Why Were Born Children Left to Die in Ancient Rome," University of Kent, https://blogs.kent.ac.uk/lucius-romans/2016/06/15/why-were-new-born-children-left-to-die-in-ancient-rome. Also see Shelia Cook, n.d., "Roman Women and Children, Part 3—Newborns," Vindolanda Charitable Trust, https://www.vindolanda.com/Blog/roman-women-and-children-part-3. Juvenal, a Roman satirist during the first and early second centuries AD, said, "So great is the skill, so powerful the drugs, of the abortionist, paid to murder mankind within the womb." And "I say nothing of supposititious children, of the hopes and prayers so often cheated at those filthy pools from which are supplied Priests and Salii, with bodies that will falsely bear the name of Scauri. There Fortune shamelessly takes her stand by night, smiling on the naked babes; she fondles them all and folds them in her bosom, and then, to provide herself with a secret comedy, she sends them forth to the houses of the great" (Juvenal, *The Complete Works of Juvenal*, Delphi Classics [Hastings, England: Delphi, 2014], loc. 809 of 7604, Kindle).

68 Suetonius, *The Twelve Caesars*, "Divus Augustus," para. 99, p. 100.

69 Suetonius, *The Twelve Caesars*, "Divus Augustus," para. 97, p. 98.

70 Augustus, *Res Gestae*, which is roughly translated "Some stuff I did." It is also a great example of how Augustus loved to spin his reign.

71 Augustus, *Res Gestae*, para. 8. Augustus gives the names of the consuls of the respective years, which the Roman historian Cassius Dio identifies as ruling in AUC 725, 746, and 767. https://www.livius.org/sources/content/augustus-res-gestae.

72 Suetonius, *The Twelve Caesars*, "Divus Augustus," para. 97, p. 99.

73 The non-italicized portion of the quoted passage is my translation. See also Wayne Brindle, "The Census and Quirinius: Luke 2:2," SOR Faculty Publications and Presentations, paper 73, (1984), http://digitalcommons.liberty.edu/sor_fac_pubs/73. This essay was initially published in the *Journal of the Evangelical Theological Society* 27, no. 1 (March 1984), 43–52.

74 Samuel J. Andrews, *The Life of Our Lord upon the Earth; Considered in Its Historical, Chronological, and Geographical Relations* (1867; repr., Miami, FL: Hardpress Publishing, 2013). He believes that Quirinius first governed Syria from 4 to 1 BC. Loc. 284 of 10296, Kindle.

75 Josephus, *Antiquities*, 18.1.1 (1).

76 Josephus, *Antiquities*, 17.13.2 (342).

77 And oath of loyalty is implicit in the act of a census. A census was a survey of the property of the people, and Julius Caesar had excused the Jews from being subjected to taxation, recognizing their demeanor that worshiping God above the state was of upmost importance to them.

78 Josephus, *Antiquities*, 18.1.4.

79 Here is the actual Greek of Luke 2:2: "αὕτη ἀπογραφὴ πρώτη ἐγένετο ἡγεμονεύοντος τῆς Συρίας Κυρηνίου."

80 Hoehner gives a detailed history of the debate about this census confusion and its proposed solutions in chapter 1 of his book *Chronological Aspects of the Life of Christ*.

81 Flavius Josephus, *The Complete Works of Flavius Josephus*, trans. William Whiston, 14.1.3 (9).

82 Josephus, *Anitquities*, 16.4.1. Not a direct quote, but a summary of Herod's complaint before Caesar Augustus.

83 Josephus, *Antiquities*, 16.4.4. A summary of Augustus's judgment.

84 The Hasmonean dynasty were descendants of Aaron, and their reign goes back over a hundred years to Judas Maccabees, of Hanukkah fame. The Hasmoneans were not from the line of David.

85 Josephus, *Antiquities*, 14.1.2 (4).

86 Erastothenes, *Geography*, 16.34.

87 Harold Hoehner, *Herod Antipas*, reprint ed. (Grand Rapids, MI: Zondervan, 1980), fn. 1.

88 Josephus, *Antiquities*, 14.4 (66–71). "The city was taken on the third month, on the day of the fast, upon the hundred and seventy-ninth Olympiad, when Caius Antonius and Marcus Tullius Cicero were consuls." According to Cassius Dio, Antonius and Cicero were consuls in AUC 691 (63 BC).

89 Aristobulus was eventually released by Julius Caesar and sent with an army back to Judea to set things right, but Aristobulus was poisoned by loyalists to Pompey, Julius Caesar's enemy at that time. Josephus, *Antiquities*, 14.7.4 (124).

90 Josephus, *Antiquities*, 14.7.3 (121).

91 Josephus, *Antiquities*, 14.8.3 (137); 8.5 (143).

92 Josephus, *Antiquities*, 14.9.4 (174–75).

93 Josephus, *Antiquities*, 14.13.4 (339).

94 Leviticus 21:16–23.

95 Josephus, *Antiquities*, 14.14.5 (388–89).

96 Hyrcanus was still alive in Parthia but completely powerless.

97 Josephus, *Antiquities*, 15.2.2 (14).

98 Josephus, *Antiquities*, 15.3.3 (55).

99 Josephus, *Antiquities*, 15.6.2 (173); 6.3 (174–76).

100 Josephus, *Antiquities*, 15.7.8 (251).

101 Herod had one child with her, named Herod Philip, but after he divorced her, he took them both out of his will.

102 David Jacobson, "The Jerusalem Temple of Herod the Great," in *The World of the Herods and the Nabataeans*, ed. Nikos Kokkinos, vol. 1 of the International Conference held at the British Museum. (Stuttgart, Germany: Franz Steiner Verlag, 2007), 145–76.

103 Josephus, *Antiquities*, 15.11.1 (380); 6 (421).

104 Josephus, *Antiquities*, 16.7.2 (190).

105 Josephus, *Antiquities*, 16.7.3 (200).

106 Sylleus never did repay his debt nor was he executed.

107 Josephus, *Antiquities*, 16.11.1 (359).

108 These women were Pheroras's wife, her mother and her aunt, and Antipater's mother, Doris. See Josephus, *Antiquities*, 17.2.4 (34).

109 Josephus, *Antiquities*, 17.2.4, emphasis added.

110 Phlegon, *Phlegon of Tralles' Book of Marvels*, trans. William Hansen (repr., Exeter, England: University of Exeter Press, 1996), translator's commentary, 177.

111 Claude Nicolet, *The World of the Citizen in Republican Rome*, trans. P. S. Falla (London: Batsford Academic and Education Ltd., 1980). On p. 61, Nicolet cites the quote as from Dionysius of Halicarnassus, *The Roman Antiquities* 4.15.6. I borrowed Claude Nicolet's book from "The Internet Archive," https://archive.org/details/worldofcitizenin0000nico. I also borrowed Dionysius's book to confirm the quote. See https://archive.org/details/romanantiquities0002dion_c5a8/page/320/mode/2up?view=theater.

112 Ramsay, *Was Christ Born at Bethlehem?*, chap. 7.

113 Tertullian, *Against Marcion*, 4.19, emphasis added.

114 Ramsay, *Was Christ Born at Bethlehem?*, chap. 7.

115 My defense for the idea that Jesus was born in the fall will come in later chapters.

116 James C. Martin et al, *A Visual Guide to Bible Events* (Grand Rapids, MI: Baker Books, 2009), 346, emphasis added.

117 *Strong's Concordance*, 2646, s.v. "kataluma," Bible Hub, https://biblehub.com/greek/2646.htm.

118 *Strong's Concordance*, 3829, s.v. "pandocheion," Bible Hub, https://biblehub.com/greek/3829.htm.

119 John Chrysostom, "Homily on the Birthday of Christ (b)," presented sometime between AD 386 and 388. Trans. Andrew Maguire, Early Church Texts, https://www.earlychurchtexts.com/mainsub/johnchrysostom/in_diem_natalem.shtml.

120 Justin Whitmel Earley, *The Common Rule: Habits of Purpose for an Age of Distraction* (Downers Grove, IL: InterVarsity Press, 2019), 12, loc. 233 of 3106, Kindle.

121 Chrysostom, "Homily on the Birthday of Christ (a)."

122 Chrysostom, "Homily on the Birthday of Christ (a)."

123 Chrysostom, "Homily on the Birthday of Christ (a)."

124 Acts 5:17–42.

125 See Ed Stetzer, "Church Attendance during Christmastime: Stats on Christmas Outreach," Church Leaders, December 16, 2021, https://churchleaders.com/voices/411818-church-attendance-during-christmas-time-stats-on-christmas-outreach.html.

126 See O. G. Oliver Jr., "Christmas," *Evangelical Dictionary of Theology*, ed. Walter A. Elwell (Grand Rapids, MI: Baker Book House, 1984), 220.

127 James Taylor, "Christmas," *The New International Dictionary of the Christian Church*, gen. ed. J. D. Douglas (Grand Rapids, MI: Zondervan, 1978), 223.

128 John Chrysostom, "Homily on the Birthday of Christ (b)," presented sometime between AD 386 and 388, trans. Andrew Maguire, Early Church Texts, https://www.earlychurchtexts.com/mainsub/johnchrysostom/in_diem_natalem.shtml.

129 Roger S. Bagnall and Bruce W. Frier, *The Demography of Roman Egypt* (Wiltshire, England: Cambridge University Press, 1995), 14.

130 "The only place in which we have actual evidence that census records were stored in the first century BC is the temple of the Nymphs." Nicolet, *The World of the Citizen in Republican Rome*, 64.

131 C. P. E. Nothaft, "The Origins of the Christmas Date," *Church History* 81, no. 4 (December 2012), 905.

132 Today it is about December 21 or 22.

133 K. R. Harriman, "Why Is Christmas on December 25?," Academia.edu, 2018, 6. https://www.academia.edu/40525319/Why_Is_Christmas_on_December_25.

134 *The Chronography of 354*, https://www.tertullian.org/fathers/index. htm#Chronography_of_354. See Part 12. In Part 6, scroll down to December 25.

135 Steven Hijmans, "Sol Invictus, the Winter Solstice, and the Origins of Christmas," *Mouseion: Journal of the Classical Association of Canada*, XLVII, series III, vol. 3 (2003): 384.

136 Harriman, "Why Is Christmas on December 25?," 3.

137 If you are interested in this topic, one of the best resources I've found is a book by William Francis Dawson, *Christmas: Its Origin and Associations, Together with Its Historical Events and Festive Celebrations during Nineteen Centuries* (1902), public domain. Dawson provides a fairly thorough account that's quite illuminating.

138 Alistair C. Stewart, in his "Introduction" to the work he translated by Melito of Sardis, *On Pascha* (Yonkers, NY: St. Vladimir's Seminary Press, 2016), 42.

139 Harriman, "Why Is Christmas on December 25?," 10.

140 Harriman, "Why Is Christmas on December 25?," 12–15.

141 Harriman, "Why Is Christmas on December 25?," 11. The date he gives for the baptism of Jesus is Tubi the 15th, which equates to our January and is the origin of choosing January 6th as the date of Christ's baptism.

142 Clement of Alexandria, *Stromata*, chap. 21, loc. 7395 of 42814, Kindle.

143 Clement of Alexandria, *Stromata*, chap. 21, loc. 7395 of 42814, Kindle.

144 Clement expressly teaches that he believes Jesus ministered for only one year: "It was necessary for Him to preach only a year." *Stromata*, chap. 21. Many among the early church fathers believed this.

145 Kurt Simmons, "Loosing the Riddle of Clement Alexandria's Dates for the Nativity, Baptism, Passion, and Epiphany of Christ," Dec25th. info, http://www.dec25th.info/Loosing%20the%20Riddle%20of%20 Clement%20Alexandria%27s%20Dates%20for%20the%20Nativity,%20 Baptism,%20Passion,%20and%20Epiphany%20of%20Christ.html.

146 Bagnall and Frier, *The Demography of Roman Egypt*, "Preface," p. xv: "During the early Roman Empire, the provincial government of Egypt conducted a periodic census of all residents. Among tens of thousands

of documentary papyri from Roman Egypt, there survive just over three hundred census returns filed by ordinary Egyptian declarants. Extant returns run from AD 11/12 down to the last known census in 257/258, but the vast majority date to the second and early third centuries." https://archive.org/details/demographyofroma0000bagn/page/n19/mode/2up?view=theater.

147 Alexander Raymond Jones, "Ptolemy," in *Encyclopedia Britannica*, article last modified January 13, 2023, https://www.britannica.com/biography/Ptolemy.

148 Gavin White, *Babylonian Star-Lore: An Illustrated Guide to the Stars and Constellations of Ancient Babylonia* (London: Solaria Publications, 2014), 45–46.

149 White, *Babylonian Star-Lore*, 54.

150 There are also a little over 50 weeks in a normal lunar year of 354 days, and almost 55 weeks in a 13-month lunar year. Seven just doesn't divide evenly into a lunar or solar year.

151 There are 52 weeks in a solar year.

152 Qumran Calendar, PDF of Solar Calendar based upon Calendrical Documents 4Q320 and 4Q321, https://grace5.webs.com/YHWH-Qumran-Calendar.pdf.

153 For more on the Dead Sea Scrolls and the Essenes, see Merrill F. Unger, *The New Unger's Bible Dictionary*, ed. R. K. Harrison (Chicago, IL: Moody Press, 1988), s.vv. "Dead Sea Scrolls, The" and "Essenes."

154 Torahtimes Messianic Ministry, n.d., "The Qumran Calendar," accessed August 10, 2022, https://www.torahtimes.org/writings/qumran-calendar/article.html.

155 John C. Lefgren and John P. Pratt, "Dead Sea Scrolls May Solve Mystery," *Meridian Magazine*, March 12, 2003, https://latterdaysaintmag.com/article-1-5435.

156 Fred John Meldau, *The Prophets Still Speak* (Bellmawr, NJ: Friends of Israel Gospel Ministry, 1988), 21, emphasis added.

157 John's Gospel puts this conversation during the first Passover after Jesus's baptism. Since Jesus was baptized sometime in AD 28 (the

15th year of Tiberius), and because Herod rebuilt the temple from 20 to 19 BC in a year and a half (Josephus, *Antiquities*, 15.11.1 & 6), these dates sync up. Continual renovations were being done to the temple, which explains why the Pharisees phrase their question the way they do, although the temple was functionally complete in 19/18 BC, 46 years earlier (remember, there is no 0 BC).

158 Matthew Newsome, n.d., "John the Baptist, Priest & Prophet," WCU Catholic Campus Ministry, accessed September 21, 2022, http://wcucatholic.org/john-baptist-priest-prophet.

159 If you are interested in learning more about these, I have found the Jewish Virtual Library to be extremely helpful: https://www.jewishvirtuallibrary.org.

160 For a great article on the Jewish months, please read Chabad.org, n.d., "The Jewish Month," https://www.chabad.org/library/article_cdo/aid/3921740/jewish/The-Jewish-Month.htm.

161 Michael Norten, *Unlocking the Secrets of the Feasts: The Prophecies in the Feasts of Leviticus* (Nashville, TN: Westbow Press, 2015), loc. 90 of 1110, Kindle.

162 *Babylonian Talmud*, 7.4.

163 M. Liddell, *Sinai Lexicon*, emphasis added, https://www.perseus.tufts.edu/hopper/text?doc=Perseus:text:1999.04.0057:entry=w(/ra2.

164 Abib is considered the first month, but Ethanim, the seventh month, is when Rosh Hashanah, the New Year festival, is to be celebrated. Abib is considered a new year for the kings, what we might call a civil year; and Ethanim is considered the new year for the years, meaning the cycle of a year.

165 Josephus, *Antiquities*, 7.6.6.

166 Mishnah Zevachim 14, https://www.sefaria.org/Mishnah_Zevachim.14.10?ven=William_Davidson_Edition_-_English&lang=bi.

167 The Hebrew word *Ethanim* means "the month of perennial streams." See Gesenius' *Hebrew-Chaldee Lexicon*, n.d., https://www.blueletterbible.org/lexicon/h388/kjv/wlc/0-1.

168 Leviticus 25:8–17.

169 Jewish Virtual Library, n.d., "Circumcision," https://www.jewish virtuallibrary.org/circumcision. Admittedly this comment about Abraham is not found in the Bible, though it is a long-standing Jewish tradition.

170 "Circumcision," Jewish Virtual Library, emphasis added.

171 Cyrus conquered Babylon on October 29, 539 BC, got to know the Jews over several months, then made his decree.

172 The year of the crucifixion is also highly contested, but I am not going to try to resolve that here.

173 Diane Severance, "Irenaeus: John's Spiritual Grandson," Christianity. com, May 3, 2010, https://www.christianity.com/church/church-history/ timeline/1-300/irenaeus-johns-spiritual-grandson-11629607.html.

174 Irenaeus, *Against Heresies,* 2.22.5.

175 Irenaeus, *Against Heresies*, 2.22.6.

176 Georges Declercq, "Dionysius Exiguus and the Introduction of the Christian Era," *Sacris Erudiri* 41 (2002): 222. In a footnote on that page: "On the discrepancy with regard to the length of Jesus's public ministry (one year at the most according to the three synoptic gospels, at least three years according to the Gospel of John), see Finegan, *Handbook of Biblical Chronology,* 349–53. In the second and third centuries, the synoptic chronology was without question the dominant tradition. Early in the fourth century, however, the influential bishop Eusebius of Caesarea pronounced repeatedly in favour of the long chronology of John's Gospel. . . . In the West, the short chronology showed a much greater resistance for it would take till the time of Bede before the version following the fourth gospel could ultimately impose itself throughout Latin Christendom."

177 Evan Andrews, "What Was the Gordian Knot?," History, August 29, 2018, https://www.history.com/news/what-was-the-gordian-knot.

178 Declercq, "Dionysius Exiguus and the Introduction of the Christian Era," 246.

179 Hoehner, *Chronological Aspects of the Life of Christ*, 6.

180 https://www.starrynight.com/starry-night-8-professional-astrono-my-telescope-control-software.html.

181 Josephus, *Antiquities,* 17.4.1.

182 Josephus, *Antiquities,* 17.5.2 (89).

183 Joseph Jacobs and Schulim Ochser, n.d., "Varus, Quintilius," *Jewish Encyclopedia*, https://www.jewishencyclopedia.com/articles/14647-varus-quintilius.

184 Josephus, *Antiquities*, 17.5.5 (110).

185 Josephus, *Antiquities*, 14.9.2 (158).

186 Josephus, *Antiquities*, 14.8.5 (148).

187 Josephus, *Antiquities*, 14.1.2 (4).

188 Josephus, *Antiquities*, 17.6.2 (150).

189 Josephus, *Antiquities*, 17.6.2 (151).

190 Petrus Cunaeus, *The Hebrew Republic*, trans. Peter Wyetzner (New York: Shalem Press, 2006), bk. 2, chap. 1, 79–80.

191 Josephus, *Antiquities,* 17.6.4 (166), emphasis added.

192 Josephus, Antiquities, 3.12.2 (278).

193 Paul Maier, translator and commentator, *The New Complete Works of Josephus* (Grand Rapids, MI: Kregel, 1999), 566, fn. 2.

194 White, *Babylonian Star-Lore*, 293.

195 On my website I have posted some pictures that my daughter took through my telescope. They need to be seen in color. There was another full lunar eclipse on November 8, 2022, but I could not view it because of clouds in my area.

196 Normally, Purim is on Adar 14 (in February), but 4 BC was a leap year so Purim would have been celebrated in Adar II (March).

197 Josephus, *Antiquities*, 17.6.5 (168–69).

198 Josephus, *Antiquities*, 17.6.5 (173); *The Jewish War*, 1.33.6 (659).

199 "King Herod the Great also built at Jericho, including a hippodrome theatre, aqueducts, and a palace, remnants of which can still be seen." All about Archaeology, n.d., "Jericho," https://www.allaboutarchaeology.org/jericho-archaeology.htm.

200 Josephus, *Antiquities*, 17.6.5 (175).

201 Converting between solar and lunar calendars can be confusing, but the fast of the tenth month always occurs on the tenth of the tenth month:

Tebeth 10. The dates on our calendar change, so January 6, 1 BC is Tebeth 10 (the eclipse is a few days later, on January 10), and December 25, 1 BC is Tebeth 10 (the eclipse happens a few days later, on December 29).

202 Dionysius Exiguus, *On Easter, or, the Paschal Cycle (2003)*, trans. Roger Pearse and Michael Deckers, tertullian.org, 2006, https://tertullian.org/fathers/dionysius_exiguus_easter_01.htm. See the beginning of the table.

203 The Venerable Bede, *The Ecclesiastical History of the English People*, ed. and trans. A. M. Sellar, (repr., New York: Dover Publications, 2011), loc. 684 of 9033, Kindle.

204 Clement of Alexandria, *The Stromata, or Miscellanies*, loc. 7386 of 42814, Kindle.

205 Clement gives other theories for how long Augustus reigned, but the one he personally accepted was forty-three years as reckoned from the death of Cleopatra. *The Stromata*, loc. 7369 of 42814, Kindle.

206 Tertullian, "Against the Jews," *The Complete Works of Tertullian*, ed. Alexander Roberts et al (Hastings, England: Delphi Classics, 2018), 8.

207 Eusebius, *The Church History of Eusebius* (Grand Rapids, MI: Aeterna Press, 2016), loc. 263 of 7408, Kindle.

208 The 42nd year from the assassination of Julius Caesar.

209 Quoted from Declercq, "Dionysius Exiguus and the Introduction of the Christian Era," 211.

210 Bede, *The Ecclesiastical History of the English People*, bk. I, chap. 3.

211 Josephus, *Antiquities*, 15.5.2.

212 Josephus, *Antiquities*, 7.8.1.

213 Andrews, *The Life of Our Lord upon the Earth*, loc. 792 of 10296, Kindle.

214 Wade Cox, "Christ's Age at Baptism and the Duration of His Ministry," Christian Churches of God, 2022, http://www.ccg.org/weblibs/study-papers/p019.html.

215 This endnote is here for those individuals who believe that since the early church fathers unanimously agreed that Jesus was born 28 years after the death of Cleopatra—which we now identify as 3 BC—there-

252 | 500 YEAR JOURNEY

fore Christ was born in 3 BC. This is also why the eclipse in January of 1 BC is so important. I understand and respect those who hold this point of view, but here's the odd dilemma that it produces and which must be accounted for: Why is that year not 1 BC? If the early church fathers all considered it 1 BC, why do we call it 3 BC? Who changed it and why? When did that happen? I will present my theory (which is actually Declercq's theory) at the end of chapter 11, but it is rooted in the idea that the church was more committed to calculations than to actual history. Therefore, I think it is unfair to make Josephus a scapegoat for why the calendar is off. It is easy to blame him, but he never used the phrase "4 BC." His history is sound and confirmable within the context of how the ancients calculated history, and it is only later calculations that have confused the issue.

216 Realistically, the date could either be September 24 or 25, 7 BC because the Israelites determine the new moon by its first visibility. However, the moon was only 10 degrees away from the sun on September 24, so it wasn't likely to be visible. Our modern Gregorian calendar date is not what is important, though. What matters is that Ethanim 1 was chosen by the first visibility of the moon.

217 Declercq, "Dionysius Exiguus and the Introduction of the Christian Era," 237–38.

218 Josephus, *Antiquities*, 17.2.

219 "Astrology and astronomy were intertwined at this time, and astrologers assumed both the duties of observers as well as interpreters of the stars." Chris Brennan, *Hellenistic Astrology: The Study of Fate and Fortune* (Denver, CO: Amor Fati Publications, 2017), 2.

220 Brent Landau, *Revelation of the Magi* (New York: HarperCollins, 2010), loc. 52 of 1959, Kindle.

221 Landau, *Revelation of the Magi*, loc. 258 of 1959, Kindle.

222 Landau, *Revelation of the Magi*, loc. 371 of 1959, Kindle.

223 Dwight Longenecker, *Mystery of the Magi: The Quest to Identify the Three Wise Men* (Washington, DC: Regnery, 2017), loc. 811 of 2493, Kindle.

224 Strabo, *The Geography of Strabo*, trans. Duane W. Roller (New York: Cambridge University Press, 2014), 15.15.

225 Herodotus, *The Histories*, 1.101, 120.

226 Herodotus, *The Histories*, 1.128.

227 Herodotus, *The Histories*, 7.37.

228 Strabo, *The Geography of Strabo*, 1.2.15.

229 Strabo, *The Geography of Strabo*, 16.3.1.

230 https://www.davidrumsey.com/luna/servlet/detail/RUMSEY~8~1~ 35244~1180869:Map-of-the-World-According-to-Strab?sort=pub_list_ no_initialsort%2Cpub_date%2Cpub_list_no%2Cseries_no&qvq=q: strabo%20playfair;sort:pub_list_no_initialsort%2Cpub_date%2 Cpub_list_no%2Cseries_no;lc:RUMSEY~8~1&mi=0&trs=1. Used by permission.

231 I also want to give credit to Dwight Longenecker for drawing my attention to Justin Martyr's dialogue.

232 Justin Martyr, *Dialogue with Trypho*, chap. 78, loc. 1637 of 2978 to 1641 of 2978, Kindle.

233 *Ellicott's Commentary for English Readers*, Judges 6:3, https://biblehub. com/commentaries/ellicott/judges/6.htm

234 *Pulpit Commentary*, Judges 6:3, https://biblehub.com/commentaries/ pulpit/judges/6.htm

235 Justin Martyr, *Dialogue with Trypho*, chap. 77, loc. 1631 of 2978, Kindle.

236 ESV Study Bible Notes, Psalm 72:5–15 (Olive Tree Bible Software, 1998–2022, version 6.12.2 [2685]).

237 Eratosthenes, *Geographika*, 3.93.

238 Darius the Mede coruled with Cyrus and was, I believe, Cyrus's uncle Syazarees. A fantastic dissertation on this is by Steven David Anderson, "Darius the Mede: A Reappraisal," PhD diss., Dallas Theological Seminary, 2014.

239 *Tehran Times*, "Susa and the Tomb of Daniel," April 22, 2012, https:// www.tehrantimes.com/news/399019/Susa-and-the-tomb-of-Daniel.

240 Brennan, *Hellenistic Astrology*, 24, emphasis added.

241 Brennan, *Hellenistic Astrology*, 25.

242 Brennan, *Hellenistic Astrology*, 46.

243 Strabo, *The Geography of Strabo*, 16.1.6.

244 Brennan, *Hellenistic Astrology*, 61.

245 Declercq, "Dionysius Exiguus and the Introduction of the Christian Era," 181.

246 R. H. van Gent, "The Babylonian Calendar," July 2021, https://webspace.science.uu.nl/~gent0113/babylon/babycal.htm.

247 The way the Bible calculates a new moon is by first visibility. According to the *Starry Night* software, Ethanim 1 is on September 26, 539 BC and then 532 years later on September 25, 7 BC. Our calendar configuration appears to be a day or two off, but if we go with Ethanim 1 (the first appearance of the new moon), the new moons are exactly 532 years apart. Using the Hebrew method of first visibility confirms the 532-year cycle. A helpful resource can be found at https://keisan.casio.com/exec/system/1227780009. My technique is to find the Julian Number in Starry Night for a particular date, then go to the Keisan website to find the Julian Date and the Gregorian date. Technically, the September 25, 7 BC date is a Julian date, and so the Gregorian date is September 23, 7 BC. For your reference, the Julian number is 1719134.12555.

248 Augustine, *St. Augustine's Writings against the Manichaeans and against the Donatists* (Altenmünster, Germany: Jazzybee Verlag, 2012), *Reply to Faustus the Manichean*, 2.5.318.

249 Tamysn Barton, *Ancient Astrology* (London: Routledge, 1994), 99.

250 Barton, *Ancient Astrology*, 180.

251 C. S. Lewis, *The Four Loves*, 1st ed. (1960; repr., San Francisco: Harperone, 1960), 26–27.

252 Job 9:9.

253 Rachel had died giving birth to Benjamin, Joseph's younger brother, and so maybe this verse is referring to Leah.

254 Gavin White, *Babylonian Star-Lore*. "Listed among the monsters which Ninurta defeated is a seven-headed dragon, which is an obvious prototype for the Greek *Hydra*" (p. 105).

255 The following photos are screenshots of *Starry Night Pro 8*.

256 The planets visible to the naked eye are Mercury, Venus, Mars, Jupiter, and Saturn. The ancients never mentioned Neptune, Uranus, or Pluto.

257 I am considering that Jupiter and Saturn are in alignment.

258 White, *Babylonian Star-Lore*, 384.

259 Dava Sobel, *Longitude: The True Story of a Lone Genius Who Solved the Greatest Scientific Problem of His Time* (New York: Walker & Co., 1995).

260 White, *Babylonian Star-Lore*, 139.

261 Please note that nothing about this is "astrological." It is all purely mathematical and paying attention to the motions of the celestial bodies.

262 Ethanim 1 was September 16 in 861 BC.

263 Graham Jones and Konstantin Bikos, n.d., "The December 2020 Great Conjunction," *TimeandDate*, accessed December 14, 2022, https://www.timeanddate.com/astronomy/planets/great-conjunction.

264 Charles Q. Choi, "Jupiter and Saturn's Great Conjunction Is the Best in 800 Years—Here's How to See It," *Scientific American,* December 17, 2020, https://www.scientificamerican.com/article/jupiter-and-saturns-great-conjunction-is-the-best-in-800-years-heres-how-to-see-it.

265 William Eamon, "Kepler and the Star of Bethlehem," blog, December 24, 2011, https://williameamon.com/kepler-and-the-star-of-bethlehem.

266 And anyone who suggests that a conjunction of two or more planets would produce a beam of light is dealing with pure fantasy.

267 Here's a link to a Jupiter/Saturn conjunction chart if you are interested: https://www.astropro.com/features/tables/geo/ju-sa/ju000sa.html.

268 Frederick Larson, presenter, *The Star of Bethlehem*, dir. Stephen Vidano (Los Angeles, CA: MPower Pictures, 2007), DVD.

269 Plutarch, "Caesar," *Plutarch's Lives*, Volume 2, The Modern Library series (New York: Random House, 2001), 244.

270 Suetonius, *The Twelve Caesars*, "Divus Julius," para. 88, p. 42.

271 Origen, *Against Celsus*, bk. I, chap. LVIII.

272 The coloration may have been due to the lens that I was looking through.

273 For square dancing terms, see "How to Square Dance – 12 Basic Calls for Square Dancing," Hallmark Channel, n.d., accessed February 10, 2023, https://www.hallmarkchannel.com/home-and-family/how-to/12-basic-calls-for-square-dancing.

274 The icon images used in the chart are from www.flaticon.com. Some of the chart designs are from www.slidemodel.com.

A free ebook edition is available with the purchase of this book.

To claim your free ebook edition:

1. Visit MorganJamesBOGO.com
2. Sign your name CLEARLY in the space
3. Complete the form and submit a photo of the entire copyright page
4. You or your friend can download the ebook to your preferred device

A **FREE** ebook edition is available for you or a friend with the purchase of this print book.

CLEARLY SIGN YOUR NAME ABOVE

Instructions to claim your free ebook edition:
1. Visit MorganJamesBOGO.com
2. Sign your name CLEARLY in the space above
3. Complete the form and submit a photo of this entire page
4. You or your friend can download the ebook to your preferred device

Print & Digital Together Forever.

Snap a photo

Free ebook

Read anywhere